THE EDWARDIAN HOUSE

Studies in design and material culture

GENERAL EDITOR'S FOREWORD

Between 1880 and 1914 there was a house building boom in
Britain. A substantial number of us live now in houses which
were erected then, and still enjoy the opulence and craftsmanship
of their fittings and fixtures. In retrospect, the Edwardian house
appears clearly to have been the high-water mark of British
achievement in mass, speculative housing. Helen Long explains
to us how exactly these houses were built, how they were used,
and what they meant at the time.

PAUL GREENHALGH

HELEN C. LONG

studied at University College London, University of East Anglia
and the University of Brighton. She is a lecturer in design history
in the Faculty of Art and Design, Cardiff Institute of Higher
Education and has written articles on aspects of the Victorian
and Edwardian house and on design and architectural history,
also contributing to TV and film productions.

THE EDWARDIAN HOUSE

THE MIDDLE-CLASS HOME IN BRITAIN 1880-1914

Helen C. Long

MANCHESTER UNIVERSITY PRESS

MANCHESTER AND NEW YORK

distributed exclusively in the USA and Canada by St. Martin's Press

Published by Manchester University Press
Oxford Road, Manchester M13 9PL, UK
and Room 400, 175 Fifth Avenue, New York, NY 10010, USA
Dis*tributed exclusively in the USA and Canada*
by St. Martin's Press, Inc., 175 Fifth Avenue, New York, NY 10010, USA

British Library Cataloguing-in-Publication Data
A catalogue record for this book is available from the British Library

Library of Congress Cataloging-in-Publication Data
Long, Helen C., 1958–
        The Edwardian house : the middle-class home in Britain 1880–1914 / Helen C. Long.
            p.   c.m. — (Studies in design and material culture)
        Includes bibliographical references and index.
        ISBN 0-7190-3728-x (cloth). — ISBN 0-7190-3729-8 (paper)
            1. Architecture, Domestic—Great Britain. 2 Architecture, Edwardian—Great Britain.
    3. Interior decoration—Great Britain—History—19th century. 4. Interior decoration—
    Great Britain—History—20th century. 5.Great Britain—Social life and customs.
        I. Title. II Series.
        NA7328.L66   1993
        728'.0942'09034—dc20   93-14634

ISBN 0 7190 3728 x *hardback*
ISBN 0 7190 3729 8 *paperback*

Typeset in Monotype Baskerville with Castellar
by Koinonia Limited, Manchester

Printed in Great Britain
by Bell & Bain Limited, Glasgow

TO MY PARENTS

AND MY BROTHER,
DAVID

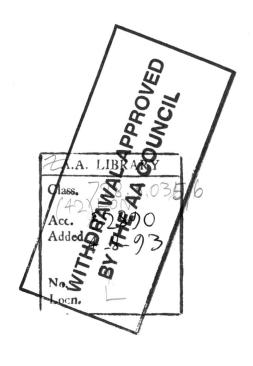

CONTENTS

FIGURES

PLATES

FOREWORD

In the past ten years we have witnessed a major revolution in taste, or, more precisely speaking, we actually helped to bring it about ourselves, at least those of us who like to live in the older suburban areas. The estate agent knows how to whet our appetite when he or she tells us about a 'fine set of original Edwardian fittings preserved in situ'. Those less fortunate will want to go out and buy a couple of reconstituted Edwardian tiled fireplaces, which might set them back a thousand pounds or two. The change in taste can, in its magnitude, be compared only with the revitalisation of the rural cottage, which, as we know, had been reviled for a long time, but during the nineteenth century became the most desirable style of residence. We use taste here in the simplest sense of the word, as acquiring a liking for, and shedding a dislike of, a certain style or type of artefact. The revival of the late-Victorian and Edwardian 'town house' also forms part of the revaluation of Victorian and Edwardian architecture as a whole. Of course, those houses do not show the inventiveness of church architecture of that period, or the splendours of the town halls; nevertheless they constitute our greatest treasure because of their sheer quantity. For once, we might use the word heritage in a more precise sense, because the history and art embodied in these houses is ours, it is the art that we, the more ordinary kind of citizen, or the likes of us in the past, could afford. We were the patrons; these fittings mean more to us than the ordinary antique object.

Do the houses belong to high art or low art? In any case, we now see them as treasure houses of design and craftsmanship. The varieties of technique which this book reveals is astonishing and many of them went back a long way, fully deserving the chief Arts and Crafts epithet: traditional. On the other hand, the new patterns of industrialisation and especially of countrywide distribution of manufactured decoration, contributed to a greater likeness of houses throughout the country. That, however, does not change the way the decorations appear to us as styles of the past and works of the past with all the values of authenticity attached. In addition, today's mostly plastic imitations lend special value to the 'real thing'. Largely because of the enormous rise in the cost of skilled labour, those objects of the past have become very much more valuable than they ever were before.

The chief value of this book lies in the in-depth analysis of this vast range of decorations and how they were made. Interior decoration is a classic field of design and design history because the overall aim was, and is, completeness. This book first of all does justice to the processes of designing for unity, from floor to ceiling, from the front to the back of the house, exercising great control over a variety of crafts and manufactures. It was in the later nineteenth century, when there was a new interest on the part of the top architects and artists in interior design and craftsmanship, that Britain acquired a world reputation in these matters. This book traces the way these higher concepts filtered down to the mass market.

The evidence was gathered, on the one hand, through the investigation of many houses in many English cities. This in itself is an astonishing feat, a public revelation of all these intensely private treasures in their private surroundings, and it makes this book a document of the present state of the inside of our houses. The second source is the considerable literature of the trade, that is, books and journals on how to decorate houses, addressed to the owners as well as the trade; in addition, there were sale catalogues of stores and firms. Both kinds of evidence are then combined and the result must surely be one of the most authoritative books on the history of any kind of decoration in Britain.

In order to understand how and when these particular kinds of decoration originated or gained popularity, a closer analysis of the patrons as well as the world of craft and manufacture is necessary. We need to map precisely the position of the owners and makers within the social and economic hierarchy. While today we are inclined to stress the art and individual craftsmanship element in all these products and thus take them as one-off and free kinds of artefacts, at the time of their origin they were usually subject to the most stringent calculation involving transport costs, credit facilities, timing of manufacture, and sale and profit margins within an intensely competitive set-up as a whole. In that sense this book tells the story, not just of a world of craftsmanship of the past, but about the development of the kinds of businesses which still dominate house-building. In many ways, the years around 1900 with rapidly increasing output of houses, especially in the medium and lower price-ranges, mark the beginning of the 'building industry' as we know it today.

The craftsperson and the Do-it-Yourselfer will thus find much in this book that he or she is familiar with. It might help them to find the right way of handling restorations. Others would do well to immerse themselves at least into some of the technical aspects of decoration. Once comprehended, this kind of understanding adds infinitely to our sense of value, especially for those objects which we own ourselves.

Stefan Muthesius

ACKNOWLEDGEMENTS

First and foremost, I owe a very great debt to the residents of the houses I studied at first hand in the course of researching the material for this book, who are too numerous to mention individually, but without whose extraordinary co-operation and generosity, this research would have not been possible. Initial thanks also to my editors, Paul Greenhalgh and Katharine Reeve, who have been enormously helpful and patient. My grateful thanks go also to Tom Piper, Chris Lloyd and Jenny Godfrey for their help with the illustrations, and to David Long, Celia Crowther, Elisabeth Bogdan and Carol McKay for proof-reading, and for their patience and care in undertaking these tasks. This book is based on PhD research undertaken between 1982 and 1989, and so I have also to thank my PhD supervisors, Suzette Worden and Pat Kirkham, from whom I learnt so much.

Numerous libraries, archives, museums, societies and firms greatly assisted my task; Bridewell Museum Archives, Norwich (J. Renton and D. Jones); The British Library, Brixton Local Library; Bruce Castle Museum Archives (R. Reed); The Business Archives Council (Lesley Richmond); Cardiff Central Reference Library; The Geffrye Museum; The Greater London Record Office; The Guildhall Library; John Harvard Library; Hornsey Building Control and Planning Departments; Hornsey Public Library; Ironbridge Gorge Museum; Lambeth Archives; The Milne Museum (Mr Norris); The National Monuments Records Office; The National Register of Archives; Norwich Record Office; The RIBA Library; South Glamorgan rates office (Mr. Westcomb) and planning department (Jill Taylor); The South Glamorgan Record Office; The Victoria & Albert Museum Library and Picture Department (Edwin Wallace); The Welsh Folk Museum and Library (Alun Davies); Anjex Ltd; Bond and White Ltd (M. Pares); Doulton Ltd; H. Gibbon and Sons, Green and Veronese Ltd; House of Fraser Archives (Alison Turton); Paintmakers Association; Tidmarsh and Sons; Herne Hill Society (Patricia Jenkyns, Monica Wood, Jane Fenwick); Hornsey Historical Society (Joan Schwitzer, Ken Gay, Peter Barber); Muswell Hill and Fortis Green Residents Association; The Decorative Arts Society; The Victorian Society; Burnet, Ware and Graves, Nicholas Shepherd, and Warmans estate agents of London.

Many other people helped in different ways – Jackie Alkema, Bronwen Bell, John Beynon, Elizabeth Bogdan, Mick and Tony Casson, Barry Cook, Mike and Celia Crowther, Tricia Cusack, Geoff Davies, Sian Evans, Flow Farmer, Liz Farrelly, Peter Feltham, Martin Gaughan, David and Maria Gould, Belinda Greenhalgh, Howard Harris, Jack Ingram, Don Jackson, Alan Lane, Carol Mckay, Stefan Muthesius, Gillian Naylor, Francis Power, Sarah Richards, Terry Setch, Jean Shell, Mafalda Spencer, Peter Starkey and Noel Upfold. Finally, I would like to thank my parents, my brother David, and Tom and Ben Piper for their unfailing support throughout this project.

INTRODUCTION

EDWARDIAN
SOCIETY

0.1
From Mrs Stuart Macrae, *Cassell's Household Guide*, 1911, V. The caption to the illustration reads 'Exaggerated stories of your own heroic actions are not, and never can be, interesting to the ordinary listener.'

HOUSES IN THE HIGH ROAD, NORTH FINCHLEY.
(Corner of Woodside Lane).

Rents from £52. Price £625. Low Ground Rent.

SINGLE FRONTS – Containing Two Reception Rooms and Five good Bedrooms, large kitchen and scullery, good pantry and wine cellar; good bathroom, well fitted with hot and cold water, two separate w.c's; extra large coal cellar. Tiled halls and forecourts, fitted with gas, speaking tubes, electric bells, and could easily be fitted with electric light, if required. Good gardens all laid out. These houses are well fitted with every modern improvement. The roads are made up and paid for, and included in the price stated.

Apply for further particulars to

CHARLES ROOK

BUILDER AND CONTRACTOR, "CHARLEVILLE", CECIL ROAD, MUSWELL HILL.

This advertisement in the *Hornsey Journal*, 24 February 1905, highlights many of the features typical of the houses with which this book will be concerned and with which the millions of people who live in such houses today will be familiar. By 1911 only three per cent of all dwellings in England and Wales were flats, ten per cent were detached or semi-detached and the rest were largely terraced.[1] Nineteenth- and early-twentieth-century housing makes up the vast bulk of the housing stock of this country and, along with Edwardian public architecture, has a huge presence in our towns and cities. This is not only because of its sheer amount, but also because no other period before or since has witnessed such variety of detailing and material usage on the inside and outside of ordinary homes.

Late-Victorian and Edwardian speculatively built houses have been largely neglected as a topic for serious study until quite recently. Because it is such a ubiquitous type of housing, we take it for granted and so much in this book may seem self-evident. But such an important type of architecture as ordinary housing, which plays a key role in our lives, needs researching and recording. Edwardian housing went out of favour as new ideas about house form dominated the avant-garde scene in the period from the 1940s to the 1970s, and such houses were often condemned for using ugly and needless decoration. Since then its value has been generally reassessed, and in the last decade or so these houses have become vastly popular. House advertisements now stress original features, and a wealth of firms selling antique and reproduction fittings for these houses, and magazines on the period home, have emerged to cater for the new interest in preserving one's house or restoring it to its original condition. In many houses now, a visitor might be struck by an elaborate tiled hallway, a cast-iron fireplace with art nouveau tiles, a small conservatory with coloured leaded lights, an ornate foliage ceiling rose or a carved newel post, all painstakingly restored or collected. It is not only the features, but also the unique shape and proportions, creating a sense of light and space, which give the Edwardian house its unique character and charm and distinguish it from its Georgian or mid-Victorian counterpart, which have an altogether different flavour.

For those who are curious about why the Edwardian house looks as it does, and how it might have originally been decorated and used, one needs to ask who built these houses, for whom were they built, when were they built, and how were they built. Some answers to these questions are sought in this book by examining the social, technical and economic forces which shaped these houses. The book explains the trends in the form and decoration of the middle-class house between 1880 and 1914, drawing distinctions between houses within the middle-class bracket, and investigates how houses provided by builders compared with the 'ideal home' promoted through books and journals of the time. The text begins by looking at the growth of middle-class suburbia in the late nineteenth and early twentieth centuries, and goes on to discuss the layout, exterior details and interior fittings and furnishings. The main focus of the book is the interior of the house. The speculative and suburban nature of much middle-class housing raises questions about the nature of building and tenure which are peculiar to this type of housing and different from those questions suggested by other categories of housing, such as flats and architect-designed housing, and the book focuses on the middle to upper end of the speculative market, those houses identifiably 'middle-class', where external and internal design and decoration were richest in variety and detail. As well as considering the social determinants of design, the book stresses the vital role which other factors, such as land economics and the manufacture and retail of building materials and components, played in the creation of the Edwardian house. The study of the 'typical' rather than the 'rare' and the consideration of the Edwardian house as a social and historical phenomenon[2] involve a pluralist approach, using a range of different historical disciplines, for example, architectural, urban, social and business history. Written and other sources on the 'ideal home' are compared with actual interiors, studied 'in the flesh', so to speak to establish how far the 'ideal' and 'real' home correlated. A consideration of regional variations as well as similarities is important when studying the Edwardian house, and three in-depth case studies in London and Cardiff undertake to demonstrate some of the local influences on design.

If you wish to find out about the history of a particular house, maybe your own, there are several sources from which you can glean information. House deeds are a good starting point. Thereafter, depending on where you are in Britain, the types of documents described below may be held at the county record office, the public library, the local reference library, or local museums and archive collections. Old local maps (e.g. twenty-five inches to one mile Ordnance Survey maps, some reprinted and available commercially) are useful for seeing the general development of an area and roughly dating your house. The Census records, taken every ten years from 1841, will give information about the names and occupations of those registered at your address. Rate books also give very useful information on inhabitants' names and occupations, figures for rentals and rates, the owner's and builder's names, and the original cost of building the house. Particulars from the sales of large estates on which your house might be built may contain details such as the builder's name, building dates and block plans, and written descriptions of the housing development. Surviving individual house plans, sometimes kept on microfiche, might also be located at one of the above sources. Local newspapers from the time provide a fascinating insight into the lives of the people who lived in the area in the Edwardian period and you may find your house listed in the house advertisements or those requesting servant help.

It is well worth having a look at some of these items as the visual and tactile qualities of using primary sources such as these really brings the period, the people and the houses alive. In doing the research for this book I relied heavily on primary sources, and I have tried to convey the atmosphere of the period by frequently quoting contemporary sources directly and showing original catalogue and other visual material.

The recent interest in the Victorian and Edwardian house has helped preserve decorative features, although an interior can never be reconstructed in its entirety as colour schemes and furnishings will have inevitably changed and some fittings may have been removed or altered. Furthermore, today such houses are viewed through eyes of a generation with a different system of values from those of the original inhabitants.[3] Nevertheless, it is important to examine buildings at first hand, for, even if photographs exist – not usually the case in this type of house – 'hands on' experience can contribute so much valuable understanding about scale, texture and manufacture and the way decorative details and materials relate to one another.

Design reflects social priorities. The revolutions and tensions, concerns and values, of the late nineteenth and early twentieth centuries are clearly reflected in the form and decoration of the Edwardian house. So it is necessary to begin by looking briefly at the society which produced these houses.

THE EDWARDIAN ERA

> We are on the eve of great electrification movements. The automobile has come to stay, and there are even some people who predict that in another generation our traffic will be horseless.... Women are coming into more and more competition with men in business, and even well-to-do girls are devoting themselves to callings other than nursing. (R. D. Blumenfield, 1901)[4]

Strickly speaking, the Edwardian era began when Queen Victoria died in 1901 and ended when King George V took over in 1910. But to call

4

the years 1901 to 1910 the Edwardian era is misleading, as the whole social and political scene was in a process of transformation, beginning in the 1880s and not completed until after the First World War.[5] This period has a flavour of its own; there is a sense in which it is a time of transition between the Victorian age and our own. This period was not simply a continuation of the Victorian era, which had its heyday between 1840 and 1880.[6] By the 1880s and 1890s the Victorian era was losing its distinctive character. Certainly, things did not change overnight; many Victorian views and habits persisted. Nor was the period 1880-1914 consistent; it did not remain static – the Britain approaching the First World War was very different from turn-of-the-century Britain, for example, which was different again from Britain in the 1880s and 1890s. But there is a certain coherence to this period of time, a certain set of tensions and upheavals which bind this period together, which was reflected in its domestic architecture.

One's lasting impression of the Edwardian period might perhaps be that of a golden era. When Victoria died, while there was genuine grief on the part of the public, there was also an air of relief and anticipation for the future. Edward VII, who was popular with the public, transformed the image of monarchy, spearheading England's lead in the extravaganza of status, wealth and glamour in Europe's capital cities which was further enriched by the American 'dollar princesses'.[7] The idle rich worked hard at occupying their time with weekend trips and parties. The motor car was an important new fashion accessory; 338,000 cars were bought in 1913 at an average price of £340 each.[8]

Leisure time was on the increase generally, although hours of work were still long. Bank holidays were instituted in 1871 and people made the most of the new forms of transport to take them on day trips to their local seaside resort; for example, Mancunians headed for Blackpool, which responded with entertainments and sea-front boarding houses. The rich, in their desire to escape the proximity of the lower classes, began to take holidays abroad. At home, new forms of leisure opened up: 'New expenses have come into the category of necessities ... the cheap but better-class music hall and the picture palace, the cheap periodicals and books'.[9] The *Daily Mail*, *Daily Mirror* and *Daily Express* all began around the turn of the century, for example. The number of daily newspaper readers doubled between 1896 and 1906 and doubled again by 1914. One traditional working-class leisure was Drink, 'the shortest way out of Manchester', as it was known,[10] but the boom of pub building in the 1890s languished somewhat in the Edwardian period under the impact of the coffee-house movement and Temperance.

Edwardian society was an ageing society. The population of the United Kingdom rose from 41,500,000 in 1901 to 45,200,000 in 1911. Despite the overall rise, the birth rate had been declining from the 1870s, and by the Edwardian period the upper and middle classes in particular were raising smaller families than their Victorian counter-parts. Improvements in medicine, hygiene and housing cut the infant mortality rate and raised life-expectancy. The demographic condition of the country was further changed by emigration, especially of young people, to the Empire.[11]

The gap between rich and poor remained huge, as it had been the century before. A high court judge earned £5000 a year, and a char-woman £30.[12] Compared to the years 1880-96 when wages had risen by forty per cent, working people were worse off, as prices had risen a little while wages stayed the same.[13] Industrial disturbances hit the coalmining and railway industries and the unskilled and low-paid workers generally. Rowntree's and Booth's findings had shown that one third of the urban working classes were living below the poverty line (thus undermining the Victorian assumption that poverty was connected with personal character flaws).[14] In response, as Victorian philanthropy gave way to Edwardian ideas about social reform, a 'social service state' began to emerge by 1914.

With the continued redistribution of employment from the countryside to the town, important new industries, such as metal working and machine making, joined the list of traditional trades in this period. Urbanisation spawned the five main conurbations (a word coined at this time) – greater London, south east Lancashire, west Midlands, west Yorkshire, and Merseyside. Their total population figures doubled compared to those of 1871; London grew from 3,890,000 to 7,256,000.[15] Between 1881 and 1891, the largest population increases occurred in Middlesex, Surrey and Essex; the largest growth areas between 1891 and 1901 included East Ham, Walthamstow, Willesden, Hornsey, Tottenham and Croydon around London, King's Norton, Handsworth and Smethwick around Birmingham, and Wallasey near Liverpool.[16] About half the population lived in smaller towns, concentrated on a single industry (for example, the textile towns of the north, and the boot, hat and hosiery towns of the Midlands); market and seaside towns, inland spas, ports, and steel and coal towns, each had their own distinct and very different social make-up.[17]

The numbers of houses being built more than doubled from about three and a half million in the middle of the nineteenth century to just over seven and a half million by 1911.

> East, west, north and south our cities and towns are extending themselves
> into the country…. Houses spring up everywhere…. Streets, squares,
> crescents, terraces, Albert villas, Victoria villas and things of the same
> inviting character stand up everywhere against the horizon, and invite us
> to take them.[18]

In 1901 60.1 per cent of the population of England and Wales lived in houses with five rooms or more, the great majority living in five-roomed houses,[19] comprising two rooms on the ground floor and a scullery, and

6

two or three rooms upstairs, with either a small hall, a 'half-entranced' hall or no hall at all. Many of these new houses were built in the emerging suburbs on the outskirts of towns and cities. Clapham summed up the essence of suburbia for the author of *The Suburbans*, writing in 1905, with its

> penny buses, gramophones, bamboo furniture, pleasant Sunday afternoons, Glory Songs, modern language teas, golf, tennis, high school education, dubious fiction, shilling's worth of comic writing, picture postcards, miraculous hair restorers.[20]

There was a falling away by two-thirds of the numbers of houses under construction by 1912-13, compared to the average of 150,000 built per annum between 1898 and 1903.[21] The cycle of building did not depend only on the demand for houses in any one area, but also on whether creditors sought other types of investment in preference. In particular, the numbers of working-class homes had declined significantly as builders found themselves threatened by the 1909 Budget.[22] Solutions to housing problems were sought in garden city schemes, such as Letchworth (1905), but 1914 still witnessed a worrying housing shortage which prompted the 'homes fit for heroes' campaign after the First World War.

The idea of the Edwardian golden age was to some extent a myth, viewed in the light of the human tragedy of the First World War.[23] The period was one of massive and fundamental social and political upheaval – women's suffrage, debates about the state and the individual, and about Free Trade, Home Rule for Ireland and the rise of organised labour, the growth of the popular press and the growing influence of America, together with new, far-reaching inventions, such as the motor car and the telephone, Bleriot's airflight across the Channel in 1909, challenging new European art and design movements such as Cubism and Futurism, the challenge to Victorian conformity from writers like Wells and Shaw, and new leisure activities, such as bridge and the tango, coinciding as they did with the beginning of a new century and the death of Queen Victoria after sixty years on the throne.

These upheavals, and the challenge generally to Victorian certainties, values and habits, were both exciting and disconcerting for many, and provoked an atmosphere of nervous insecurity in the midst of expectation and pride, as C. F. G. Masterman commented in 1908, 'We are uncertain whether civilisation is about to blossom into flower or wither in ruined tangle of dead leaves and faded gold.'[24] Behind this, most importantly, lay the blow to Edwardian confidence struck by developments concerning Britain's Empire. Dramatic Imperial gains in Africa and Asia in the 1880s had caused an explosion of national pride and jingoism which – fuelled by Social Darwinism, the popular press and the music hall – reached its peak in 1897, the year of Victoria's Diamond Jubilee. Thereafter, the costly and hard-won Boer War, which ended in 1902, succeeded in fundamentally shaking defiant Victorian certainty and complacency about the invincibility of the British Empire. Nostalgia for the past, the search for national identity and fading Empire, and fear for the future, were reflected in the clinging to national styles, such as Jacobean or Georgian, in architecture and design. At the 1900 Exhibition in Paris, for example, the Rue des Nations displayed several hundred metres of national pavilions, each projecting its own distinct national image; the British pavilion was an English country house designed by Lutyens. At the Franco-British Exhibition eight years later, the Arts-and-Crafts-based vernacular style was dominant in domestic architecture and artefacts; the converse style representing Britain for public architecture was Edwardian baroque, also based on an English tradition, that of Wren, Hawksmoor and Vanbrugh.[25]

More than any other section of society, it was the middle classes which embodied these tensions and extremes,[26] representing the new spirit of the Edwardian era and yet, the nostalgia for the Victorian world, producing and debating the new ideas and developments, yet at the same time fearing a decline in manners and morals, Empire and nation.

THE MIDDLE CLASSES

Two crucial factors in considering the people for whom the Edwardian house was built, are, first, the nature of speculative development whereby houses were built without a particular purchaser in mind, and, second, the system of tenure, where unfavourable rates for mortgages meant that ninety per cent[27] of all houses in Britain were rented on leases of anything up to three years. In a period without the present-day ideology of home ownership, renting was socially acceptable, and indeed was more common among the middle classes than the working classes. A saleable or lettable house thus had to allow for variables such as whether the unknown purchaser might want the house as a personal home or as an investment to let out, and the builder's interpretation of such market needs was crucial to his success.

The middle class was hard to define. Rather than being a cohesive group, it was a tier or hierarchy of groups, but with, nevertheless, a collective identity apparent to contemporaries which was distinguishable from the classes above and below it in society. Its members rose to three million, or one-sixth of the population of England and Wales by 1851, and included the professions, public administration, trade (wholesale and retail), commerce, farming and people with modest independent means.[28] These occupations accounted for seventeen per cent of the population by 1881 and rose to twenty per cent by the Edwardian period.[29] A definition of 'middle class' in terms of income alone is problematic: in 1909, L. C. Money set the middle-class income bracket at anything between £160 (the point where income tax began) and £700 a year, which accounted for 4,100,000 people out of a total of the forty-four and half million population in this country.[30] Membership was never simply a question of income or occupation, but was also a question of collective values, attitudes, habits and lifestyle. Many clerks who earned only £60 to £80 a year would have regarded themselves as middle class. In 1891, 2.7 per cent of the total population of south London were commercial clerks. *The South London Chronicle*, 1870, explained the appeal of this field of work: 'clerical work has always been the major channel of upward social mobility from the working class to the middle class'.[31] The struggle of the lower middle class was immortalised in *The Diary of a Nobody*, first published in 1892, which tells the story of Mr Pooter, a clerk, who worked in the city and lived in a six-roomed house, called 'The Laurels' in Brickfield Terrace, Holloway, which had a front breakfast parlour, and a garden backing on to the railway line. The frustrations of keeping up appearances for the Pooters is a constant theme in this book; 'the parlour bell is broken, and the front door rings up in the servant's room, which is ridiculous'.[32]

Stefan Muthesius subdivides the middle-class range of life-styles thus; at the top and overlapping with the upper classes were two hundred thousand families of lawyers, merchants and top civil servants, earning about £1000 to £3000 a year, living in fifteen-roomed houses which cost about £1000 to £3000 to build and £100 a year to rent, and employing a butler, two maids, a cook and governess. Below this category were other professionals, such as lawyers, doctors, top clerks, earning £500 to £700 and living in houses costing £1000 to build or up to £100 a year to rent. Lower-paid professionals, for example, higher clerks, earned £350 and rented seven- to eight-roomed £500 houses at £40 to £60 a year and kept one or two servants. Lower clerks and shopkeepers on £200 a year, who could afford a house costing £200 to £300 or rented at £25 to £45, generally kept a young maid. At the bottom of the middle classes were the lower clerks on £100 to £150, whose houses had five or six rooms and cost £120 to £200 to buy or £12 to £30 rent, and who did not have a live-in servant but probably had help of some kind.[33]

What were the beliefs which united such a wide range of experiences? In 1909, C. F. G. Masterman isolated 'security' and 'respectability' as key middle-class values, but these terms did not refer to a truely urban, distinct middle-class identity, for this did not exist in Britain, but were instead characteristics which were the outcome of a preoccupation with 'class'. Anxious to maintain their newly acquired status, the middle classes sought to gain confidence and respectability by distinguishing themselves from those below them in society, through physically separating themselves from 'bothersome families', and by the 'upward emulation'[34] of the habits and lifestyle of the upper classes. George Orwell illustrates the subtleties of class; his family lived on £400 a year but he regarded his background as 'lower-upper-middle-class':

People in this class owned no land, but they felt that they were landowners in the sight of God and kept up a semi-aristocratic outlook by going into the professions and the fighting services rather than into trade.... To belong to this class when you were at the £400 a year level was a queer business, for it meant that your gentility was almost purely theoretical.... Theoretically you knew how to wear your clothes and how to order a dinner, although in practice you could never afford to go to a decent tailor or a decent restaurant. Theoretically you knew how to shoot and ride, although in practice you had no horses to ride and not an inch of ground to shoot over.[35]

Etiquette was central to a middle-class lifestyle. The newness of this class meant that many needed clear guidelines on how to behave, as offered in the wealth of cheap texts on the subject, such as *Society Small Talk; What to Say and When to Say it*, written by 'a member of the aristocracy'; G. R. M. Devereux, *Etiquette For Men*, 1911; and *Speeches For All Occasions* by 'An Oxford M.A.' *Manners and Tone of Good Society*, 1899, by 'a member of the aristocracy' demonstrates the rigid nature of access to different social circles, stressing the vital role of card-leaving: 'Leaving cards, or card-leaving, is one of the most important of social observances, as it is the groundwork or nucleus in general society of all acquaintanceships.'[36] *Etiquette For Men*, 1911, however, admitted that 'There are few things in life a man dreads more wholeheartedly or shirks more consistently than the paying of calls. It has been asserted gravely that many a man marries in order that he may have someone to relieve him of these duties.' The same book gave detailed instructions to young men on all aspects of life, including personal habits such as 'Don't caress your moustache incessantly, however delicate or robust its growth', along with guidelines for proper behaviour, for example concerning the latest craze for bicycling: 'Avoid shooting past at high speed; it is rude and dangerous, and is apt to give both persons and horses a nasty start.... Be merciful too and tactful in ringing your bell; never sound it violently just as you are close to a person or an animal.'[37] The wealth of books with titles such as *Appearances. How to Keep Them Up on a Limited Income*, by Mrs A. Praga, 1899, suggest how hard many found it to conform to the rigours of etiquette.

Crucial to the maintenance of etiquette and thus one of the most important outward symbols of having acquired middle-class status was, as suggested earlier, the employment of domestic help of some kind; indeed, Seebohm Rowntree defined middle-classness in these very terms in 1901.[38] Examples of ways of budgeting household expenses in Mrs Peel's *How to Keep House*, 1902, a book aimed at a middle-class reader-ship, all include domestic help of some kind, for example, a 'lady' living on £200 a year was advised to budget for a 'woman' to help every morning, while a family with four small daughters on £1200 a year could have afforded a cook, a parlourmaid, a housemaid, a nurse, a useful-maid and a governess.[39] The importance of domestic servants is

0.2
Front cover of Madge of *Truth's Manners for Men*, about 1897

shown by the Census records of England and Wales which reveal that in 1891 there were 2,329,000 people, or 16.1 per cent of the working population, employed in domestic service of some kind.[40] The 'conspicuous consumption' of material goods was a further means of expressing one's social standing and aspirations; it is significant that the phrase 'keeping up with the Joneses' was coined in America in 1913. Such reliance on a code of conduct and good taste endorsed by the upper classes suggests that conservatism was a strong force behind the development of the suburban middle-class house, which promised a scaled-down version of the life-style of the country gentry on their rural estates at a price the middle classes could afford.

Class was a strong motivating force in the formation of suburbia. It also drew subtle distinctions between localities and signified varying shades of respectability. The most desireable areas of London in the last decade of the nineteenth century, for instance, were in the south and west, although they existed side by side with less favoured districts. Mrs Panton, in *From Kitchen to Garret*, 1887, considered that

> Penge and Dulwich are dreary and damp, they are evidently well supported and much lived in, but the higher parts of Sydenham, are to be preferred; while Forest Hill, the higher parts of Lordship Lane, Elmers End – where there are some extremely pretty and convenient villas – and the best parts of Bromley, Kent, are all they should be. Still, to those who do not mind the north side of London, Finchley, Bush Hill Park – where the houses are nice to look at and excellently arranged – and Enfield are all worthy of consideration.[41]

Camberwell, which had the greatest percentage of clerks in south London, was often referred to in novels by Matthew Arnold, George Gissing and C. F. G. Masterman as the epitome of middle-class uniformity, with houses which 'make some pretence – with coloured glass in the panels of the doors, brass knockers, and electric bells – to comeliness'.[42] In the production of areas of socially homogeneous populations, H. J. Dyos has pinpointed ways in which subtle demarcations were drawn between localities which gave clues as to the standing of the locality (and thus of its residents) in society, using, for example, street names, the width of the road, and whether it was planted with planes and horse-chestnuts, limes, laburnums and acacias, or simply tarmacadamed, and provision for, and access to, parks and shops.[43]

The growth of suburbia, a word coined in the 1890s, signalled the increased actual distance between, and growing contrast in, the meaning of home and workplace. The home was seen as a haven, a refuge affording privacy and comfort from the stresses of life in the world outside. The emphasis on the single family unit and the domestic ideal of protection and privacy was reflected in the preference for the detached or semi-detached house, screened off from neighbours and passers-by with gardens, hedges, walls and gates, blinds and lace curtains. The nineteenth-century middle-class home was the physical setting for, and embodiment of, Victorian values of moral virtue, industry, thrift and sobriety, male superiority and the obedience of wives and children. It was not acceptable for the woman of the house to work; her *raison d'être* was to be a good wife and mother. She was entrusted with upholding the principles of the household and with the home's public image and its running. A woman's appearance and her taste in furnishings were seen as a mirror of character, as 'curling pins have done as much to hinder the social advancement of the women who leave them in their hair until after breakfast',[44] and her husband's deportment on leaving and returning home each day was seen as an indication of how well she was looking after him.

Central to the middle-class identity also was the increasing obsession with health as a reaction to the dirt and disease of the inner cities. The expansion of the transportation system provided the opportunity for those who could afford it to move out of the centres of towns and cities into the newly created suburbs where the houses had small gardens and conservatories and yet were cheaper than town dwellings. Health became fashionable and, along with class, underlay the suburban ideal. Indeed, by the Edwardian period, health in the home dominated and replaced the strict moral and spiritual emphasis of the Victorian home. House advertisements in middle-class districts emphasised height of land above sea level and low death rates. *Where to Live Round London; Southern Side,* 1909, stress the healthy benefits of areas such as Croydon, which was recorded as the healthiest large town in the country with a death rate of 12.3 per thousand, Telford Park on Streatham Hill, which rose 180 feet above sea level and Sydenham and Forest Hill, which were 120 feet to 345 feet above sea level.

Many have suggested that there was a crisis at the end of the Edwardian period which heralded the end of an era. Virginia Woolf noted that, 'All human relations have shifted – those between masters and servants, husbands and wives, parents and children. And when human relations change there is at the same time a change in religion, conduct, politics, and literature. Let us agree to place one of these changes about the year 1910.'[45] Seeds of change had been sown, certainly. The upheavals of the time began to alter relationships in society slowly undermining some of the Victorian values held dear and effecting a subtle relaxation in etiquette and lifestyle. Some began to question, for example, the exclusivity and formality of Morning Calls and other practices, particularly when domestic servants became less easily available after 1900. *Cassell's Household Guide,* 1912, condemned the 'planning, pinching and squeezing that frequently go to the keeping up of this foolish little show':

> It is all very well for wealthy folks to give a dinner, and have a number of
> extra friends invited to drop in, later in the evening, for a dance; but

entertaining becomes absurd when the middle class woman, with one small maid of fifteen or so, receives among her callers on the fixed 'At-Home' day a special clique who are chartered to remain for 'proper tea' after the social function is over, and who will by and by be invited to clear up the remains of the afternoon feast at a nine o'clock supper, thus cramming three meals into the space of five hours.[46]

The tendency towards a more relaxed approach to manners and decorum in the new century was also fortunate for many middle-class households as less formal occasions such as luncheons, at-homes and picnics became popular. The fashion for five o'clock tea was thought to be particularly fortunate for those who could not afford to entertain lavishly.[47] With speedier communications, fashions changed quickly; 'the phrase "At-Home" is one of those elusive expressions which will bear half a dozen interpretations, either or all of which may be old fashioned within a year or two from the time of writing'.[48] Combined restaurant meal and theatre trips were all the rage by 1911 and the casual weekend break had also become stylish: 'The week-end visitor, like the diligent follower after "At-Homes", is very largely a product of the twentieth century. Fifteen years ago – ten years even – it would have been considered a sheer waste of money…. A cursory glance at our railway timetables will show to what an extent the week-end habit has already grown.'[49]

But the extent to which things changed should not be over-estimated; alongside change, as remarked previously, there was also an overwhelming sense of the continuity of Victorian values, of the paramountcy of status, patriotism and tradition, reinforced through institutions, and in many respects the uncertainty of the new century consolidated a sense of nostalgia for the past. Even the First World War did not destroy the hold which the rigours of ceremonial calls, At Homes and so on had on the middle classes; indeed, such priorities continued to be important forces in governing society until the Second World War. Such basic and enduring middle-class conservatism called for houses which would communicate the respectability and values of their inhabitants to others. For the average tenant, it was deemed necessary for a house to be 'up-to-date' in style and with all the latest amenities, yet 'safe' rather than avant-garde. These criteria applied equally if a house was destined for a landlord, for whom a house must remain appealing enough to successfully let out, and yet not become quickly dated to ensure a safe investment. These needs and beliefs were reinforced, subtly transformed and given visual form in house layout and decoration through various media, such as literature, theatre, shops and exhibitions, which were an increasingly important force in determining taste and which will be dealt with in the next chapter.

THE ORIGINS
OF THE
EDWARDIAN
HOUSE

London Transport
advertisement, 1908

PLATE I

Elevation and plan of a
house near Guildford by
C. F. A. Voysey

View of Cardiff Castle,
added to by William Burges

PLATES 2 & 3

1

THE DISSEMINATION
OF TASTE

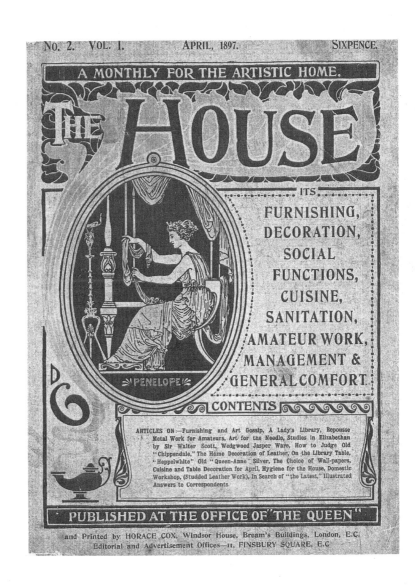

1.1
Front cover of *The House*,
April 1897

The rising economic status of the middle classes meant that a greater proportion of their income could be spent on non-essentials, such as furnishings. The purchasing power of the pound rose from 1890, reaching a peak in 1896, declining thereafter, and falling dramatically about 1914. The house became one of the key means of displaying wealth and status; as early as 1875 *The Queen* noted 'the present rage for house decoration'.[1] Indeed, contemporary photographs show middle-class houses far more cluttered with objects and furniture than wealthy homes or their mid-nineteenth-century equivalents. Many struggled to maintain expectations; the total household expenses of a lower-middle class clerk on £150 a year in 1901 would absorb a greater percentage, one third, of his wage, compared to a skilled worker on comparable pay. The wealthy could afford to employ fashionable architects to design their houses and high-class firms to decorate and furnish them; 'very rich people can place themselves unreservedly in the hands of a professional decorator'.[2] This was not an option available to the middle classes, but their insecurity in matters of taste created a demand for and practical advice and instruction on what their homes should look like.

AVANT-GARDE ARCHITECTS AND DESIGNERS

The need for a reassuring, up-to-date, but approved, solution to the problem of house style, meant that the architectural avant-garde, designing homes for the wealthy, asserted a huge influence on the style of the suburban middle-class house. Speculative builders and manufacturers of materials and building components could see for themselves the designs of these architects reproduced in building journals such as *The Builder*, and in books of plans and books on the home which were readily available.

Housing from the 1860s onwards reflected the 'Battle of the Styles', as it was known; Robert Kerr, writing in *The Gentleman's House*, 1871, described no less than eleven styles, drawn from classical or Gothic sources, which a customer could choose for a house. Greek and Roman classical had disappeared rapidly out of fashion in the early part of the century but Italian Renaissance remained popular for country houses, as seen in the work of Sir Charles Barry at Trentham Hall, Staffordshire, 1834-42, and Thomas Cubitt at Osborne House on the Isle of White, begun in 1845. Increasingly, however, houses began to be built in English styles, such as Gothic and Elizabethan. Some architects stuck firmly to their chosen style, while others were happy to design in either the Gothic or classical style. An early major exponent of the Gothic style was A. W. Pugin, who designed Scarisbrick Hall, near Southport, 1837-45 (continued by his son E. W. Pugin, 1862-8) to imitate a real medieval manor house. Pugin reintroduced the large medieval hall as a romantic element in design, and it became a feature of many later country houses.

The Elizabethan style was used by Anthony Salvin for Harlaxton Manner, near Grantham, 1831-7 (with W. Burn, 1838-44). The period 1855-75 saw the peak of country-house building.[3] High Victorian Gothic country houses used features such as multi-coloured brickwork, an irregular plan and a varied roofline. Examples of architects working in this manner include William Butterfield (Milton Ernest Hall, near Bedford, 1853-8), Sir George Gilbert Scott (Kelham Hall, Nottinghamshire, 1858-61), and Alfred Waterhouse (Eaton Hall, Cheshire, 1867-80). The castle tradition had also been revived for country houses and a late and exceptional example of this can be seen at Cardiff Castle, built by William Burges, 1866-85 (see plate 3).

Small, simple, Gothic houses and vicarages designed by G. E. Street in the mid 1850s inspired Philip Webb's Red House built for William Morris in 1859 in reaction to the ill effects of the Industrial Revolution. Solid and unpretentious, it was two-storeyed, built of red brick, asymmetrical in plan and elevation, with a red-tiled, high-pitched roof, and incorporated romantic features, such as oriel and staircase windows, gables and a turret. In a miniaturised and adapted form, it remained the dominant influence on the form of large and small houses through to the Tudor semi-detached houses of the inter-war years.[4]

Following the lead of Pugin, Street and Webb, from the 1870s onwards architects looked for inspiration towards simpler, less grandiose, vernacular sources. The 'vernacular revival', or 'Old English' style as it became known (see p. 33), returned to more modest styles of the sixteenth, seventeenth and early eighteenth centuries, expounded by, among others, George Devey (Betteshanger, Kent, 1856-82) and Norman Shaw (Leyswood, Sussex, 1866, built in the Sussex Wealden style which he also used elsewhere, for example, at Cragside, Northumberland, 1869-84). The same group of architects developed another style, the Queen Anne revival style, an early example being Eden Nesfield's Kimnel Park, Denbighshire, of 1868. Shaw was the main populariser of the Queen Anne style, as seen at Bedford Park, London, (1875-81). Here, spacious, light, wide-fronted, semi-detached and detached houses were built in a variety of designs, with features such as semi-elliptical pediments and scrolls to window areas, first-floor balconies, non-basement kitchens and internal toilets. This new style had a huge impact on speculative builders, particularly in London, who used the same formula, adding details such as porches to suit. Parker and Unwin, architects of Hampstead Garden Suburb, also drew inspiration from Bedford Park. Running in tandem with 'Queen Anne' was the Aesthetic Movement, which applied notably to interiors and furnishings, exemplified by the work of Edward Godwin, who designed 44 Tite Street, Chelsea, London in 1878, and in its most popularised form epitomised by the fashion for Japanese fans and blue-and-white-china.

The vernacular revival was further developed by later architects, such as C. F. A. Voysey (Perrycroft, Herefordshire, 1893-4) and Edwin

Lutyens (Tigbourne Court, Surrey, 1899), with ideas based on fitness as the basis of beauty, simplicity of design and the use of local materials and good craftsmanship. Voysey's houses typically had green slate roofs and roughcast cement on brick walls, long low rooms and windows. Ernest Gimson used indigenous stone for Stoneywell Cottage, Leicestershire, 1898-9, and contructed it on different levels so that it appears as if it has grown over the course of centuries rather than having been built at one time. The designs of M. H. Baillie Scott (White Lodge, Berkshire, 1898-9), Edward Prior (The Barn, Exmouth, 1896-7), William Lethaby (Avon Tyrell, Hampshire, 1891-2) were also popularised and appeared in scaled-down versions in speculative builders' middle-class houses after 1900. The influence of all these styles mentioned here survived in some form in speculatively built housing well into the Edwardian period.

BOOKS

One important means of conveying advice on home decoration and life-style to the middle classes was through books and journals, which became cheaper and more widely available by the late nineteenth century. The growth in literacy with compulsory education for all created for the publishing industry new markets, hitherto not catered for, from the 1870s. Publishers responded to this growth in literacy, which was accom-panied by an overall increase in leisure time and a purchasing power among a wider section of the population, set against a background of Liberalism with its philosophy of self-help and self-improvement, with

1.2
Folly Farm, Berks,
by Sir Edwin Lutyens,
1906 and 1912

increased output of cheap fiction and non-fiction books.

One of the earliest and most influential books on home decoration was Charles Eastlake's *Hints on Household Taste*, 1867, compiled from his articles in the *Cornhill Magazine*. Books on the subject followed in increasing numbers. For example, between 1876 and 1878, Macmillan brought out their 'Art at Home' series, which included W. J. Loftie,[5] *A Plea for Art in the Home*, 1877, Lady Barker, *The Bedroom and the Boudoir*, 1878, and Lucy Orrinsmith, *The Drawing Room*, 1878. Around the same time, Chatto and Windus published *The Art of Beauty*, 1878, and *The Art of Decoration*, 1881, by the well-known writer, Mrs Haweis. One of the most popular authors in this field was Mrs Panton, whose book, *From Kitchen to Garrett*, 1887, was in its eleventh edition ten years later.

Many of the earlier books were aimed at the better-off middle classes or at the very consciously artistic. The first decade of the twentieth century, however, saw a rise in the numbers of books on the subject of house decoration and a widening of the market aimed at. Some of the books for the top end of the market made use of recent technical developments, and were quite lavish, particularly those supported by furnishing firms, for instance, H. J. Jennings, *Our Homes and How to Beautify Them*, 1902, whose images were supplied by Waring and Gillow.

Books on other aspects of the home appeared, including legal and related aspects of the home, for example, Tarbuck's *Handbook of House Property*, 1892, and C. Emanuel and E. M. Joseph, *How to Choose a House*, 1910, (see fig. 1.4), and, as we have already seen, books on etiquette, for example, 'Madge' of *Truth*'s guides, which included *Manners for Girls*, 1901. Overlapping in terms of content with all these books were those on domestic economy,[6] although the emphasis was more practical with a bias towards economy, repairing and making do, and full of useful recipes for medicines, cooking, cleaning and other household tasks. The first book of this kind to be aimed at the middle classes with servants was Mrs Beeton's *Book of Household Management*, 1861, costing 7s 6d, which had first appeared in 1859 in monthly parts in her husband's magazine *The Englishwoman's Domestic Magazine*. A cheaper volume at half the price was brought out in 1865, called the *Everyday Cookery and Housekeeping Book*, to cater for a wider market, and by the 1890s there was a whole series of Mrs Beeton books on cookery and gardening costing around 1s. As the market for domestic economy books grew and widened over the latter quarter of the century, some aimed specifically at those of moderate or limited means, the respectable servantless class, or the middle classes who had fallen on hard times: for example, Mrs D. C. Peel, *How to Keep House*, 1902, and A. E. L., *How She Managed without a Servant*. The glossy multi-volume production appeared, pioneered by *Cassell's Book of the Household* (four volumes), 1869-71, a comprehensive guide to all aspects of the home, from choosing a home to its furnishing, decorating, running, the care of children, the garden, and home entertainment, and made great use of developments in colour illustration and photographic reproduction.

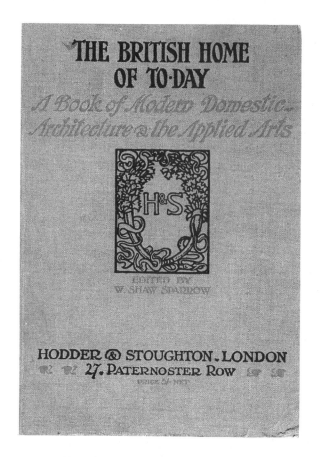

The authors of such books, where identified, were usually women, and were frequently associated in some way with a college or school; indeed, some of these books were designed as textbooks for domestic science syllabuses which had been introduced into schools. Some authors wrote columns for popular magazines and were therefore already familiar to readers; for instance, 'Isobel' of *Home Notes* wrote *Pearson's Home Management*, 1901, and produced a series of 'Isobel' Handbooks. Alfred Harmsworth's Amalgamated Press produced *The Best Way*, 1909, 'the cheapest cookery book in the world', written 'by housewives for housewives' and compiled from 1d weekly magazines – the 'Best Way' pages of *Woman's World*, the 'Help One Another' pages of *The Home Companion* and the 'Save Your Pennies' columns of the *Family Journal*. Mrs C. E. Humphry, better known as 'Madge' of *Truth*, edited six volumes of *The Book of the Home*, 1909, which boasted contributions from a hundred experts.

MAGAZINES

Magazines were another important source for women on how to improve the home in the period 1880 to 1914 (see fig. 1.1). Most of the late-eighteenth- and early-nineteenth-century general magazines had reflected the tastes of the leisured classes, the only people who could afford to buy them. The entertaining content of many of the eighteenth-century magazines was supplanted by a tone of strict high moral sobriety as domesticity became the ideal in the mid nineteenth century, as in *The Ladies' Treasury*, 1857-95, and reinforced the conservatism of readers with features on paper-flower making, needlework and other ways of occupying the hours of enforced leisure time in the home. Magazines such as these retained their high-class readership with a price of around 1s. But the rising incomes and growing social expectations of the middle classes created a demand for cheaper journals to address the needs of a wider female market. One of the earliest, set up in 1852, was Beeton's *The Englishwoman's Domestic Magazine*, costing 2d. It was the first woman's journal to deal with the subject of the management of the home, and offered practical instruction with columns on cookery and fashion. Beeton went on to publish *The Queen* in 1861, a weekly which contained topical features and novel factual articles on fine art, literature and fashion, as well as the usual items on home duties.

There still remained a large female market as yet not catered for, which was becoming increasingly literate by the end of the nineteenth century. The first magazine aimed specifically at the needs of a mass public was *Weldon's Ladies' Journal* in 1875. The number of titles for women doubled in the latter decades of the nineteenth century,[7] with major cheap weekly publications of the mid 1890s, such as Pearson's *Home Notes* and Harmsworth's *Home Chat*. *Home Chat* had a circulation of 186,000 by 1895, compared to sales of the higher-class magazine, *The Lady*, which rose from 1,683 in 1885, the year it was founded, to 27,949 in 1905.[8] *Home Notes* and *Home Chat* set the trend for women's magazines in the twentieth century, such as *Woman's World* (1903), aimed specifically at women without servants. These magazines, again, tended to be conservative and home-centred in character, mirroring and restating the fashions and values of the upper classes.[9]

More specialist journals on art and design, such as *The Art Journal*, *The Magazine of Art* and *The Studio*, were a source for more avant-garde taste and might include the work of leading designers outside Britain. These journals often acted as a mouthpiece for a particular artistic tendency, such as *The Burlington*, 1881, which supported the Aesthetic Movement, and later *The Studio*, 1893, promoting the Arts and Crafts Movement. Magazines such as these frequently wrote about home crafts, reflecting a growing trend apparent also in the emergence of home arts and industries associations. Such ideas gradually filtered into popular journalism and had a major effect on attitudes towards home decoration. Mrs Panton, who worked between 1881 and 1900 on *The Lady's Pictorial*, and wrote thirty-three books between 1887 and 1923, became known as the pioneer of home decoration and management by correspondence. In the preface of *From Kitchen to Garrett*, Mrs Panton advertised that, for a fee of one guinea, she would visit readers in their homes to give them personal advice on how to decorate their houses and where to shop for the required items. She was also willing to buy goods for 'country ladies' and to write letters of advice for a set fee.[10] Mrs Panton started a 'society' for the employment of women who would undertake to decorate an entire house, make curtains, chair covers and so on. Other women took on similar tasks; Mrs McCelland had a studio of girls specialising in hand-painted decoration who would work *in situ*. Other decorators and art furnishers of the time included Miss Frith and Lady Monckton. This new profession was considered highly respectable and suitable for women of taste to indulge in, but entry was not open to all as one had to be of 'a sufficient social status to be above the suspicion of taking commissions or bribes from trades people to advertise their wares'.[11] Readers were also encouraged by Aesthetic Movement enthusiasts and others to decorate surfaces themselves; in Hardy's *The Hand of Ethelberta*, 1876,

> The decorations tended towards the artistic gymnastics prevalent in some quarters at the present day. Upon a general flat tint of duck's egg green appeared quaint patterns of conventional foliage, and birds, done in bright auburn.... Upon the glazed tiles within the chimney-piece were the forms of owls, bats, snakes, frogs, mice, spiders in their webs, moles and other objects of aversion and darkness, shaped in black and burnt in after the approved fashion.
> 'My brothers Sol and Dan did most of the actual work', said Ethelberta.[12]

Another acceptable occupation for Society women and the socially ambitious *nouveaux riches* which involved home crafts was charity work. *Beeton's Ladies' Bazaar and Fancy Fair Book*, about 1890, describes how to make such items as a lamp mat, an embroidered foot-warmer for carriages, a key basket, a thermometer frame made from cones and acorns, a cigar stand, and a circular pen-wiper. The frivolous and marginal nature of such products subjected this sort of work to frequent male derision. Nevertheless, charity work was important for social relations among this class of women and was thus highly regarded by them.[13]

MODEL INTERIORS

Suggestions to consumers on decorating the home were also available from shops and department stores. The Victorian and Edwardian period was the age of the department store, for example, Liberty's, Selfridges, Harrods and Debenhams, which catered primarily for an expanded wealthy middle class. Besides offering a decorating service, and selling individual pieces of furniture and embellishments, large stores offered convenient, ready-made room schemes. Specialist furnishing shops such as Hampton's, Heals, Maples, and Waring and Gillow's sold stylistically coordinated furniture, furnishings and interior detailing, displayed in showrooms and illustrated in lavish catalogues to facilitate buying.

Writers acknowledged the role shops played in the formation of public taste; Florence Jack, writing in 1911, commented that 'a visit to any of these model houses is an education in itself, and nothing is calculated to be of greater assistance in giving reliable guidance to the shopper as to how her money may be spent'.[14] Liberty's furnishing department was regarded as very avant-garde in matters of taste, featuring room schemes in the Japanese, Moorish or New Art styles in the late nineteenth and early twentieth centuries. *Furniture and Decoration* also pointed in 1897 to another mode of transmitting ideas, the theatre: 'As a rule the examples exposed in the shop windows, and more especially the drawing-rooms reproduced on the stage, offer the public a fair idea of the prevailing fashion.'[15] Shops could also specialise: Selfridges, for example, aimed particularly for women, with their frilly lampshades and boudoir-style drawing-room schemes. Moreover, by the new century, these schemes were not simply owned by the richer middle class, as firms such as Oetzmann's and Hewetson's targetted cheaper markets. For this category of purchaser, the introduction of hire-purchase facilities made it possible for people to acquire the life-style aspired to; Mr Lord, described in Gissing's *In the Year of Jubilee*, 1894, was a dealer in pianofortes, and the majority of his customers were people on a very small income who bought on hire-purchase.[16] Mail order was another means of easy purchasing introduced at this time: Gamage's, for example, aimed their catalogues at the middle and artisan classes, selling everything for the house and garden.

Exhibitions provided a further platform for receiving information about good taste in home furnishing (see fig. 1.5). Visitors to the Franco-British exhibition held in London in 1908 would have seen André Delieux's display of art nouveau designs from five hundred individuals and firms

1.5
Oetzmann, bungalow cottage as exhibited at the Franco-British Exhibition of 1908 in London, containing a living-room, three bedrooms, hall, kitchen, etc., costing £200 to £230 to build and 45 guineas to furnish; lit by non-explosive air-gas (Cox's Patent)

from all over France.[17] In addition to the large-scale international exhibitions, other more specialist exhibitions were a good indicator of the latest styles and products and reflected contemporary concerns such as health and convenience, for example the Building Trades Exhibitions, the International Health Exhibition of 1884, and – in particular from our point of view – the Ideal Home Exhibitions, initiated in the Edwardian period. The Ideal Home Exhibition of 1910 held a competition to equip and furnish an 'ideal home', to include a drawing-room, dining-room, study, four bedrooms and a nursery. Photographs of the rich and famous and of the country house Season were also an important means whereby information about the homes and life-styles of the upper classes was made accessible to the middle classes.[18]

All these sources provided the consumer with information on the latest taste in every aspect of the building, planning and furnishing of the house, and operated as instruments of change in these respects also. If their recommendations were followed, a tasteful home was guaranteed: such assurance was crucial to those without previous experience in matters of taste but for whom nuances of class were all-important.

2

HOMES AND GARDENS

2.1

Cartoon about new approaches to house planning in J. G. Allen, *The Cheap Cottage and Small House*, 1913

HOUSE-PLANNING.

Sometimes internal comfort has to be sacrificed to external beauty, and this is the cause of some slight inconvenience— when the Plumber comes into your bedroom to examine the cistern at 6.30 a.m.   when the Bathroom and the Scullery are combined ; when the Dustman's only way lies through the Drawing-room ; when the roof-lines of the picturesque Study get in your way ; and when the Larder window faces South.

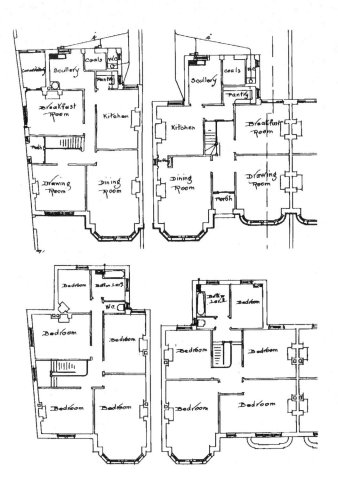

2.2, 2.3 *this page*
High-quality housing,
Ninian Road, Cardiff, 1901,
with rateable values from
left to right of £60 (costing
£110 to build) and £68 in
1909

2.4, 2.5 *facing page*
A range of medium-sized
houses, Kimberley Road,
Cardiff, 1909, with rateable
values in 1909 from left to
right of £35 10s, £24, £27
10s and £26

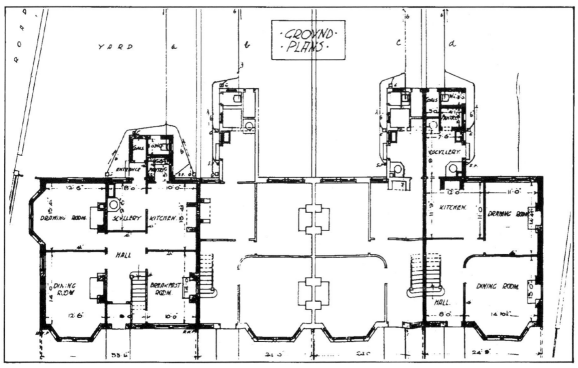

But these people know at least what a complete house is, even if it is in miniature, they have their drawing-room, their dining-room and a number of bedrooms, their bath with hot water piped from the kitchen-stove, in short, a real house, as befits those people known in England as 'respectable people'. (H. Muthesius, *Das Englische Haus*, Berlin, 1904-5, translated as *The English House*, London, 1979)[1]

While there was clearly an image of 'middle classness' which could be conjured up in the public mind, there was in fact a wide banding of house sizes designed to suit a diverse range of pockets. Combining annual house values and original building costs of houses, (London prices for building houses were twenty per cent above provincial prices[2]), with information on accommodation and occupations of residents where known (see Appendix 1) from the three case-study suburbs detailed in chapter 3, and with the work of historians such as Stefan Muthesius and John Burnett on this subject, it is possible to suggest an approximate hierarchy of middle-class housing. Thus, conclusions can be drawn about the types of interior fittings in relation to class of house, which will be discussed later in the book.

2.6 *left*
Small standard-plan house in Waldemar Road, Wimbledon, London, 1880s, with a rateable value of about £30 in 1914

2.7
Designs for a small house costing £200 to build, in *Building World*, 1896

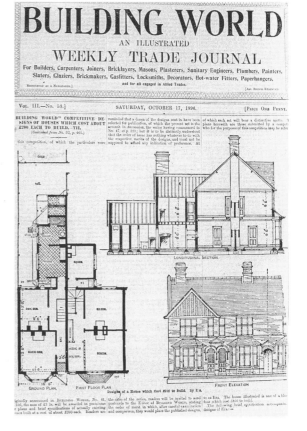

Allowing for a certain overlap between categories and some blurring at the top and bottom ends of the scale, the middle-class range of houses can be divided into the following five groups. The accommodation in a top-category house might consist of four reception rooms and seven bedrooms, a nursery, a billiard-room, dressing-rooms and *en-suite* bathroom, a large conservatory and a drive-way. This type of house would be in a prime location, on a wide, main thoroughfare or in a secluded, sought-after road, or perhaps overlooking parkland or the sea. The second group consists of houses with three or four reception rooms, about five bedrooms and some extra amenities, such as a good-sized conservatory and a dressing-room. A large number of houses fell into a third, middle group: houses in this category generally had two reception rooms, with perhaps a large living/kitchen as well, four bedrooms and maybe a small conservatory. In the band below this, houses usually had two reception rooms and three bedrooms. The smallest houses in the range had two reception rooms and two bedrooms, and were often not markedly different in terms of accommodation from the category above or from that provided for the skilled working-class bracket. The top two categories broadly represent large houses aimed at the upper middle class, the third group were medium-sized houses for the middle middle class, and the last two groups in the list represented the smaller homes of the lower middle classes (these classifications will be used later when referring to fittings in houses).

IDEAL HOMES

The notion of the 'ideal home' was a common one by the early twentieth century; but what exactly was meant by the term and how did the ideal compare with the range of housing that builders actually provided as described above? The 1910 Ideal Home Exhibition displayed a full-scale 'ideal small home', costing £600 to build and containing eight rooms, a hall, living-room, parlour or 'social room', four bedrooms, bathroom and kitchen. At the same exhibition, Arding and Hobbs furnished a real eight-roomed house, 19, Veronica Road, Balham, comprising three reception rooms, a drawing-room, dining-room and morning- or breakfast-room, four bedrooms and a servant's bedroom. Arding and Hobbs described it as 'a very ordinary house.... There is nothing extravagant about this ideal home. It is designed to show just what we can do to meet the demands of the limited income.'[3] At the following Ideal Home Exhibition in 1912, a full-scale ideal house was shown which cost £1100 to build and had eleven rooms, including a dining-room, drawing-room, five bedrooms, dressing-rooms and lounge/hall, with electric light and furnishings by Barkers 'well within moderate means'.[4] Home manuals illustrate a similar range, for example, Mrs Humphry's *Book of the Home*, 1909, which gave advice on how a ten-roomed house could be furnished for £500 or a seven-roomed house for

£100, and had chapters on the breakfast-room and the library or study in addition to the more standard rooms.[5] Some books even gave practical advice on prices and where to shop for specific goods, and offered cheaper or home-made alternatives. Where a scheme was clearly invented, it was intended as an ideal to be copied either in part or as a whole, as finances allowed.

The Edwardian 'ideal home', then, indicated a house with between eight and eleven rooms including three reception rooms and four or five bedrooms, a bathroom and electric light, which cost between £600 and £1100 to build. Comparing this with our previous breakdown of house sizes, it seems that when contemporaries used the term 'ideal home', they were referring to a house at the mid to top end of the middle-class scale, within financial reach for some and to be aspired to by others, but not way beyond reach for the middle classes as a whole. This conclusion may seem predictable, but it needs confirming when we are dealing with the important question of whether builders provided people with the houses they had been encouraged to want.

SOCIAL DIVISIONS

But whatever the size of house, allowing for such regional variations on the theme as existed, the basic plan was the same. The standard middle-class house of the 1870s and 1880s was terraced, with a tall narrow frontage and a long back addition, with two or more main rooms on the ground floor and three or more bedrooms on the floor or floors above; 'the quickness with which the individuals of the house run up and down, and perch on the different storeys, gives the idea of a cage with its sticks and birds', it was said of houses of a similar type in 1817.[6] In imitation of much larger houses, public and private, master and servant, areas were kept separate in front and back sections of the house respectively, reflecting class within the house and the contrasts between formal visiting and trade delivery functions where different entrances would be used. The nineteenth-century domestic ideal of morality and social duty encouraged segregation and privacy. This was achieved through a proliferation of passages, built into the design to avoid going through other rooms, and through an increased number of rooms, albeit of reduced size, which were carefully differentiated according to function and gender, in the manner of much grander houses. This can be seen, for example, in the number of bedrooms, designed to divide adults and children, brothers and sisters, with their doors arranged as far apart as possible and hung so as to shield the room from view.[7] This principle applied regardless of the size of the house. A large house might have three or four reception rooms which were reserved for different members of the household to be used at different times during the day. The drawing-room, 'the ladies' room', in use for morning calls and At-Homes, and the dining-room and library, which were the preserve of the men of the household, echoed the multiplicity of other rooms divided by gender, such as the ladies' boudoir and gentlemen's billiard- and smoking-rooms. Even in small houses where there was not much space, custom dictated that houses were built with a front 'parlour' which would be reserved for special occasions after the manner of wealthier homes.[8] This convention persisted into the second half of the twentieth century, despite the inconvenience of having to double up other rooms as living-bedrooms, and despite the attempts of housing reformers in the early twentieth century to persuade people to give up the 'foolish pretence of designing small houses to ape the methods of larger ones' and drop the separate parlour in favour of one large living-room.[9]

A NEW STYLE

This style of house, however, had increasingly vocal critics: 'the ordinary speculative builder surpasses himself, for, as a rule, the moment one opens the front door one falls up the staircase, or else one is confronted by a long, hopeless passage, which strikes chill into the stoutest heart';[10] another writer condemned the 'terrible, stuffy little front parlour and narrow passage, with its miserable arch and plaster brackets, and stairs going straight up opposite the front door, and a back living-room crowded in between projecting scullery and kitchen at the back of the house'.[11] In the last quarter of the nineteenth century, there emerged a new domestic ideal and notion of home, forged initially by the fashionable architects of the Queen Anne revival and the vernacular revival or 'Old English' style (the fully developed stage of the domestic revival which began with the *cottage ornée* around 1800), such as Shaw and Nesfield, and later by the architects associated with the Arts and Crafts Movement, like Voysey and Baillie Scott, mentioned earlier. Together they transformed the new domestic ideal into a physical reality using architecture of periods prior to the Industrial Revolution, based for inspiration on asymmetry and variety rather than rules, regularity and standardisation.

Influenced by architect-designed houses for the wealthy and artistic, speculative builders had evolved a new standard house-type by the Edwardian period based on these new fashions. The new ideal expressed contemporary concerns and practical needs, reflecting the growing importance attached to health and convenience, responding to the appeal of individuality, flexibility and informality in the home, and seeking an atmosphere of 'cosy homeliness' and modesty, in contrast to the gilding, pomp and show of homes a few decades previously. This new type of house had to cater for the increasing preference for one-family occupation, and for the smaller average family who operated increasingly without a live-in servant due to a shortage of '£20' servants after 1900[12] following the expansion of new and better career opportunities in shop and office work; as Rolfe in Gissing's *The Whirlpool*,

1897, comments, 'There isn't a servant to be had – unless you're a Duke.... All ordinary housekeepers are at the mercy of the filth and insolence of a draggle-tailed novelette reading feminine democracy.'[13]

This new style applied to all categories of the middle-class house, although of course the smallest in the range tended to be more restricted by site size and the need for economy. The standard house which emerged was detached, preferably, or semi-detached, or at least terraced masquarading as semi-detached, and the layout and style of the facade now focused inwards on the family rather than outwards to the street. In shape, the house was squarer and more compact in plan, with a short, wide hall, and kitchen and back bedroom squeezed in at the back, discarding the long back addition and corridors (see plate 18). The new house was generally squatter, often on two floors only. The strict Victorian spatial divisions mentioned above were cut down to allow a flexible use of space.[14]

The new type of house was lighter and airier as dark and draughty passages were eliminated. Even in small houses, while the plan was basically unchanged through needs of economy, there was more of a feeling of space and light. By the Edwardian period the mid-Victorian moral home had given way to the healthy home.[15] Words like 'comfort', 'hygiene', 'utility', 'convenience' and 'economy' recur constantly in writings about the home in the new century. Health governed aspect, plan, room use and room decoration and furnishing; as Mrs Panton explained,

> sunshine is the very first necessary of life; without it, sickness comes.... [I would] be guided by the sunshine obtaining in each [room] rather than the builder's plan, [and] utterly refuse to enter a shop until I had made up my mind how the rooms are to be appropriated.... Do not be guided in your choice of rooms by the fact that the builder has made a sunless, dark-looking room the dining room, and a cheerful, light, and pretty chamber the drawing room. The white marble mantlepiece does not matter one bit.[16]

Greater flexibility in room use was urged, mirroring and encouraging shifts in life-style in the Edwardian period. The new-style wider hall was no longer intended to be merely a passage into the house, but more of a multi-functional, separate living-room/hall, to be furnished after medieval precedents, with window-seats, an inglenook and writing desk (see fig. 13.4). 'The most striking development in the sitting-room accommodation is the provision of one large living-room or hall, in place of two or more smaller rooms.'[17] Those in older-style houses were encouraged to use all the rooms, and not leave them empty, reserved for best. Florence Jack in 1911 advised against stiff formality in the treatment of rooms, 'the drawing room of today is not a room for show but a room for use', she instructed (see plate 25).[18] The same applied to the best bedroom, conventionally used for occasions such as births, deaths and accommodating guests; 'I take it as a happy sign of the times that the "best bedroom" has been bundled out of existence along with its evil companion, the gaudy and tawdry drawing room.'[19]

Individuality, too, a key feature of the new approach to house planning, appeared in the tendency to treat the interior more as an architectural whole, with special attention to details and a preference for the unexpected and idiosyncratic.

> Some few years ago, before the introduction of the Queen Anne style into our domestic architecture, the approaches which led from the streets to our sitting rooms were seldom anything more than mere passage-ways a few feet wide.... Now-a-days, however, thanks to the efforts of modern architects, the halls of even our middle class villas are at least amenable to some degree of interesting treatment. There are occasional recesses and corners in the modern hall, the staircases are made with one or more turns.[20]

Cassell's Household Guide, 1912, spoke of 'the modern hatred of the expected and straightforward, the desire for inglenooks and quaint corners'.[21] Indeed, by the new century writers claimed such features as *de rigueur*, declaring that 'a window seat is an indispensable part of the furnishing of the hall'[22] and 'every well designed hall has its ingle-nook'.[23] The wider house-frontage meant that a dressing-room next to the main bedroom at the front of the house became feasible, at least for top-quality houses; indeed, by the end of the Edwardian period, one writer went so far as to say that 'no modern architect would design a house without a dressing-room'.[24]

INTERIOR DECORATION

Room schemes became generally simpler and furnishings less cluttered by the Edwardian period, as Vita Sackville-West describes in *The Edwardians*.

> The very rooms in which they dwelt differed from Sylvia's rooms or the rooms of her friends. There, a certain fashion for expensive simplicity was beginning to make itself felt; a certain taste was arising, which tended to eliminate unnecessary objects. Here, the overcrowded rooms preserved the unhappy confusion of an earlier day.... There were too many chairs, too many hassocks, too many small tables, too much pampas grass in crane-necked vases, too many blinds and curtains looped and festooned about the window.... the overmantel bore its load of ornaments on each bracket, the mantel-shelf itself was decked with a strip of damask heavily fringed.[25]

Magazines and books charted the trends in the decoration of the ideal home. In the context of the general search for a national style to represent the age, and the growing demand for more rapid replacement of furniture and furnishings than had hitherto been the case, the pace of stylistic change was rapid and the variety of designs available at any one point bewildering. In 1893, for instance, *Furniture and Decoration* featured schemes in 'Rococo', 'Louis Seize', 'Queen Anne', 'Classic', 'Italian Renaissance' and 'Aesthetic', and revealed that 'The fluctuations of fashion from Japanese art to Chippendale, and from Chippendale to Louis Quinze.... The Adam style, with its festoons and dropping husks, its oval pateras and dainty vases, has long since given place to the Chinese frets and rag carving of the Chippendale style.'[26] Style was a useful device for differentiating between the rooms of the house and their intended functions, and certain styles were thought appropriate for specific rooms. In 1902, H. J. Jennings recommended light styles such as 'Empire', 'Louis XV', 'Chippendale' and 'Adam', along with colour schemes in blues, or yellows and whites, for the drawing-room, traditionally regarded as the woman's domain, in contrast to 'national' styles and darker colours, like greens and reds, for the dining-room, which were felt to impart a sense of grandeur and dignity appropriate to such a male preserve (see fig 2.8): 'For the dining-room you may have it Italian Renaissance, François Premier, Elizabethan, Jacobean, eighteenth-century English or modern English Renaissance. French styles may be put to one side for an English Dining-Room, so may Gothic Anglais.'[27]

The Edwardian period saw a preference for seventeenth- and eighteenth-century classical revival styles, such as Jacobean and Adam, for reasons (already mentioned) concerning nostalgia for a more certain

2.8
Waring and Gillow, Jacobean dining-room scheme exhibited at the 1900 Exhibition, illustrated in H. J. Jennings, Our *Homes and How to Beautify Them*, 1902

past, the continuing search for national identity, and the middle-class need for security and status. Side by side with these were 'modern' styles filtering down from custom-built houses and also from new ideas about design coming from continental Europe. The Ideal Home Exhibitions are a good barometer of the public mood: Waring and Gillow Ltd's stand for an 'ideal home de luxe' in 1908 showed an Elizabethan-style billiard-room with a 'picturesque inglenook on a raised platform' and a Sheraton-style bedroom with fitted furniture 'to meet the latest conditions of modern comfort and hygiene, and to economise space'.[28] Hamptons furnished the ideal house at the 1910 Ideal Home Exhibition for a total cost of £350; the hall was Jacobean, the social room eighteenth-century, the living-room Jacobean with an oak dado and beamed ceiling.[29] Arding and Hobbs' ideal house at the same exhibition was furnished as follows: the dining-room was decorated in white and green in the Georgian style, with 'massive mahogany furniture covered with morocco leather'; the drawing-room scheme was ivory in colour, with inlaid mahogany, silk brocade and Rose du Barri floor coverings; the morning-room character was 'dainty' with 'artistic decorations', fumed oak furniture, a gate-legged table and a bureau bookcase; the scheme for the best bedroom was pink and blue with a floral wallpaper, a mahogany Louis XV suite and a brass bedstead; finally, the other bedrooms were done out in schemes of blue and white, and pink and white.[30] At the 1912 exhibition, the hall of the Ideal Home was panelled with a half-timbered ceiling in a Jacobean style, and the dining-room also panelled Jacobean. The catalogue records that 'practically every period, design and style is represented, from the most modern and up-to-date examples from the factories to period designs, including Jacobean, Georgian, Sheraton, Hepplewhite, Adam and other styles'.[31]

The stylistic schemes in ordinary homes broadly followed the ideal schemes described above, with a heavier style dining-room and a lighter drawing-room, marked by the style of the fireplace and, perhaps, also by the overdoor and ceiling designs. Speculative builders tended to follow well-established styles rather than create new trends, hence the preference for eighteenth-century and, less often, Jacobean styles. Such tried and tested solutions, which gave home-owners a sense of confidence in their status in society, suggest a fashionable, yet essentially conservative, approach to the decoration of the middle-class house. The Arts and Crafts style, long established for architect-designed houses, also percolated down to the houses of the middle classes in the use of high panelled dadoes topped with a plate rail and decorative or plain frieze above, leaded lights and Voysey style doors and fireplaces, along with Arts and Crafts or art nouveau-inspired light fittings and door furniture.

As one would expect, the greatest stylistic accuracy and coherence of scheme appeared in better-quality houses, for example a top-quality house in Cardiff built in 1901 has a Jacobean breakfast- and dining-room and an eighteenth-century style drawing-room, where the original ceiling, wall and door coverings and fireplaces form a coherent whole. But the builders of smaller houses, in particular, paid less attention to accuracy or integral approach in decoration; a mixture of styles, for example, 'Adam' tiles in an Arts and Crafts fire surround, or a baroque overdoor and Arts and Crafts stained glass, was commonplace. Here, economy and practicality overrode questions of taste, and identical fire surrounds might be put in reception rooms and/or bedrooms, or overdoor designs were mixed and matched according to what the builder had in stock. The way in which fashion was pursued in the smaller house was thus in the use of details rather than an overall, coherent and integrated scheme. Compare, for example, Mr Pooter tacking a Japanese fan on the wall of his house in Brickfield Terrace[32] with Owen's 'Workin' drorins', drawn from *The Decorators Journal* for Mr Sweater's big house:

> 'It seems when he [Mr Sweater] was over in Paris some time since he saw a room that took his fancy.... This 'ere's a photor of it: it's done in a sort of *Japanese* fashion.' He handed the photograph to Owen as he spoke. It represented a room, the walls and ceiling of which were decorated in a Moorish style.... He threatened, 'But if it's goin' to cost a lot it won't come off at all. 'E'll just 'ave a frieze put up and 'ave the room papered in the ordinary way.'[33]

Another major difference between the houses of the wealthy and those of the vast bulk of the middle classes lay in the historical accuracy of decorative details and individual pieces of furniture which frequently bore little resemblance to the stylistic labels attached to them.[34] Furthermore, there was a time lag between fashions for the wealthy and their adoption and fall from favour in smaller houses. The Japanese style, for example, fashionable among the well-off in the 1860s, remained popular in a scaled-down and simpler version for the middle classes through into the twentieth century.

EXTERIOR STYLES

The style of the exterior of the middle-class house likewise broadly followed those in fashion for grander houses, as discussed earlier.[35] Italianate and Gothic revival styles, in vogue among speculative builders in the 1860s and 1870s, gave way to the influence of the Queen Anne and 'Old English' fashions by the 1880s and 1890s, and then to the vernacular-revival look after 1900. In middle-class housing of the 1870s, the Italianate and Gothic styles were indicated by means of features such as Italianate stucco wall surfaces, stucco quoins and classical pilasters, Gothic-inspired polychrome brickwork, ecclesiastical pointed arches with carved capitals, and elaborate Gothic style bargeboarding to porches and gable ends. Irregularity, domestic revival turrets, large tile-hung gables, mullioned, transomed windows, half-timbering, and stucco revivals in the form of elaborate vernacular pargetting and plain roughcasting, together with Queen Anne red brick, moulded brick or terracotta sunflowers, Dutch gables, semi-elliptical, segment and circular windows, and increased exterior woodwork, all characterised speculative housing of the late nineteenth and early twentieth centuries. Pioneering efforts in this style included Elsworthy Road, Hampstead, by William Willett in the 1890s, which with its red brick, gables, tile hanging and white-painted bay windows 'put Norman Shaw on the production line'; Downleaze, Bristol, of 1893 is also a good example of the use of these styles in standard housing.[35] In the Edwardian period, builders began to use large half-timbered or tile-hung gables, stone mullions, Voysey-style wooden porches, pebble dashing and leaded lights, casement windows with small panes, all arranged asymetrically in the manner of the larger houses of the later Arts and Crafts architects (see figs 3.6 and 5.4). The emphasis on height in the 1870s and 1880s, under the influence of the neo-Gothic and Queen Anne styles, gave way to a trend towards horizontality under the impact of the vernacular revival.

As with the interior, exterior styles were often translated into speculative housing more in terms of superficial, individual detailing, rather than profound spirit and meaning, particularly in the case of cheap houses, and features were often far from an accurate rendition of the original source of the style. In the case of the smallest houses in the range, 'style' would be applied in the form of a bay window, architectural decoration such as coloured string courses, eaves details, ceramic tiles and coloured-glass door panels. Indeed, many house fronts show the builder's eclectic use of style, combining elements of several different styles and periods within the same façade. Most builders of the 1860s built houses in a roughly classical style, for example, Belsize Park Gardens, Hampstead, London, but those built slightly later might also include Gothic ornamental brickwork, Gothic pointed window arches or a medieval-style porch alongside classical details. The time-lag in the filtering down of styles meant that there was also variety in style within the middle-class housing market at any one time. Some styles continued to be used at the lower end of the market long after they had disappeared from the best houses, as in the case, for example, of Gothic-revival-inspired features, which were universally applied to small houses well into the new century.

Mechanisation, the standardisation of components and their decreasing price, improved transport and changes in the structure of the building industry towards uniting various trades under one enterprise produced an overall increased amount and variety of materials and decoration on the exterior. For example, late-nineteenth-century houses in Leicester have lintels of Bath stone, window sills of Derbyshire grit and steps of York stone. As S. Muthesius says 'No other period of English building witnessed a greater variety of materials than the years 1870 to 1914.'[36] However, local preferences are evident also, such as the

39

use of stone in York and ornamental brick in Birmingham.[37] A style might persist in an area also due to a local factor, such as the Gothic revival style in Cardiff which was heavily influenced by the presence of William Burges' architecture in the city.

THE GARDEN

If the width of the road, types of trees, street names and elaboration of façade and front door were devices used to draw social distinctions between localities, the status of an area was further confirmed to visitors by the space, designed to secure privacy from onlookers, provided between house and street at the front, and the distance from houses which might overlook it at the back. By the end of the century, it was standard speculative building practice to provide for the majority of new, even fairly modest, houses, a small front garden or paved forecourt, and a garden or yard at the back which was generally about twenty feet wide and twice as long.[38]

How the space at the front of the house was filled in was important. The typical suburban front garden, with its wall, railings or hedge, gate and curved or straight path, emulated the grandeur of approach and walled privacy of large houses, and marked the house out from those which opened directly onto the pavement. Winding paths were considered inappropriate for the smaller front garden, as they 'make butcher-boys giddy, and perplex the stranger … and compel … the visitor to make half a tour of the grounds, when his chief object is to get inside the house'.[39] Instead, a straight tiled path commonly led from the garden gate to the front door, and sometimes the same pattern of pavement was continued on the door-step and into the hallway, which increased the effect of spaciousness. High-quality houses might have a flight of steps, flanked by terracotta urns, leading up to the front door, to give an impression of grandeur.

With the change in focus and orientation of the house away from the public front towards the private back of the house, and the emphasis on health, the back garden became elevated in importance and 'nature' an increasingly key feature of the house by means of connecting french windows which led into the garden from the back of the house. The back garden became less practically oriented and more concerned with recreation and decorative effects as amateur flower gardening became a popular pastime, particularly with the growth of home-ownership. Books on gardening for the middle classes came out from the 1850s, along with magazines, such as *Gardening*, aimed at new suburban dwellers. In particular, Edward Kemp's advice was very influential among the middle classes and the elements of his style of garden came to typify the suburban garden in the nineteenth century, with its square of grass incorporating one round bed of geraniums, two clipped holly bushes, a mixed evergreen shrubbery, two urns joined by a ballustrade fifteen feet long, and white rockery at one side.

2.9
Front cover of Havart's
The Back Garden Beautiful, 1909

2.10
Doulton, advertisement for
ceramic products, ranging
from garden ornaments to
fireplaces and bath fittings,
1909

DOULTON & CO. LTD.
MAKERS OF
ALL KINDS OF CONSTRUCTIVE
:: AND DECORATIVE POTTERY ::

MANTELPIECES AND FIREPLACES
IN STONEWARES AND FAIENCE.

WALL TILING IN NEW DESIGNS.
HIGH-CLASS SANITARY FITTINGS.

GARDEN POTTERY IN GLAZED
STONEWARES AND TERRA-COTTA.

ROYAL DOULTON POTTERIES
LAMBETH, LONDON, S.E.

The form of the suburban garden derived from two schools of garden making,[40] the formal and the picturesque, based on old formal English gardens using native English plants on the one hand, and ideas imported from abroad in the eighteenth century about landscape gardening and exotic foreign plants on the other. Even in smaller suburban gardens, J. C. Loudon noted that the fashion for foreign plants was well established by 1838: 'No residence in the modern style can have a claim to be considered as laid out in good taste, in which all the trees and shrubs employed are not either foreign ones, or improved varieties of indigenous ones.'[41] Other importations into Britain also included the first garden gnome introduced from Germany in the 1840s. Gertrude Jekyll, one of the most important influences on the suburban garden and a popular writer on gardens, combined formal and informal in her designs by using pergolas and trellising near the house, to contrast with a woodland garden with pools, walks and natural clumps of flowers and ferns beyond.

The prevailing trends were taken up in cheap books of basic instruction such as *The Back Garden Beautiful*, 1912, by Harry Havart, which was written specifically for the new occupants of the typical small suburban house with its 'tiny back garden … just free from the tender mercies of the builder's men, a mass of brick-and-mortar refuse enclosed by a wooden lath fence, with a patch of lank, weed-choked grass in the centre … or … a neglected wilderness enriched by waste cardboard boxes and scraps of oilcloth, the legacy of the last tenant.'[42] Havart complained about the orthodox and unimaginative plan for the average back garden, which comprised a flower border all round the garden, edged by a gravel path, surrounding a central plot of grass. He presented four solutions to laying out a garden which used the following formal and informal elements in different combinations according to aspect and personal requirement; wide mixed border with shrubs and climbers and stepping stones, shady border with shady climbers, ferns, trees, lawn with singular rose bushes, square or rectangular beds of roses and pansies, circular bed of flowering or ornamental shrub, straight gravel path with rustic arch, trellis-work screening off dustbin, freestanding or lean-to greenhouse, ornamental stone vase containing plants.[43] *The Woman's Book*, 1912, suggested that a secluded garden 'cosy corner' might be formed at the end of the garden from a five-foot trellis, an arch, a summerhouse, rustic bench and one or two trees.[44]

Manufacturers capitalised on the growing popularity of the suburban garden as a place of recreation. Often substantial sections appear in trade catalogues devoted to garden requisites. Gibbon's of Cardiff claimed in 1909 to stock everything for 'the garden beautiful'. Ceramic garden ornaments, descended from the idea of the formal neo-classical garden in the 1830s, were in demand; Doulton, for example, supplied female figures, urns and flowerpots, pedestals and ballustrades for every size of house from the stately home to the suburban villa.

Doulton also manufactured fountains for conservatories, garden seats, jardinières and garden edging, in terracotta, coloured stone ware and majolica glazed wares (see fig. 2.10). Wooden and cast-iron garden furniture was available, such as 'The "Sociable" chair with folding umbrella canopy', shown in Barnard, Bishop and Barnard's 1884 catalogue, priced £8 10s. Richard Redgrave had been critical of a lot of the cast-iron designs in the 1870s, warning that:

> We frequently come across garden-seats and chairs in cast-metal, which are principally to be noticed from the great want of due consideration of the material evidenced in their design: thus sometimes they are ornamentally constructed of branches and foliage naturally imitated, or of branches alone; while in others, carved and flowing lines are given to the back, arms, and legs of the seat, adding nothing to the comfort of their use, and sadly detracting from the form properly belonging to such works.[45]

CONSERVATORIES AND INDOOR PLANTS

The fashion for rearing exotic plants in conservatories derived from the huge importation of tropical plants into Britain by the 1840s, which needed special growing environments in the unfavourable British climate. Over the course of the century the function of the conservatory in large country houses shifted away from the 'gardener's conservatory', designed to provide an ideal environment for greenhouse plants, to the 'architect's conservatory', which gave priority to the social uses of the conservatory and confined planting to small, movable groupings around the edge.[46] The fashion for the conservatory filtered down into suburban housing (see fig. 3.8); here, French windows often led from the back drawing-room into the garden through a small lean-to conservatory, or 'fernery', built on the back of the house. Havart felt that the lean-to conservatory, while being the best sort of greenhouse, also had its drawbacks:

> one disadvantage of the lean-to built out from the house is that thoughtless visitors are apt to use it as a sort of smoking annexe to the room from which it leads, and, whatever the value of tobacco as a fumigator, it is possible to have too much of a good thing, while the presence of fag-ends of cigarettes, carelessly flung down into flower-pots, is by no means conducive to the welfare of the inhabitants of those pots.[47]

Quality conservatories were available from specialist greenhouse and conservatory manufacturers such as Messenger and Co. of Loughborough. Conservatories were also available at a range of prices from wood and metal firms with separate greenhouse-building departments. C. Jennings and Co. of Bristol offered a 'smart-looking conservatory' for between £26 5s and £44. A smaller lean-to greenhouse cost between £4 15s and £11 10s. This firm also had for sale small freestanding

PLAN

PLAN

2.11
Edwardian conservatory at
The Highlands, Winshill,
Burton upon Trent,
Staffordshire, by Messenger
and Co., Loughborough

2.12
Conservatory at
Collingwood, Davenport
Park, Stockport, Cheshire,
by Messenger and Co.

44

shelters 'suitable for the treatment of Consumption', and square and octagonal summerhouses, including a design with removable sides and hinged roof which could double up as 'a tabernacle during the annual Jewish Festival'.

Window boxes and other receptacles for plants and flowers were advised for those in small houses without much garden. In 1909, Walter Wright commented that 'Window boxes play an important part in house decoration in Suburbia, where capacious creeper-supporting borders are often difficult to provide.... Hanging baskets on porches, and specimen plants on terrace walls and window ledges, will also brighten up house fronts'.[48] The contemporary preoccupation with nature was evident too in the popularity of indoor plants, such as bulbs in bowls, hyacinths in glasses, and 'pot plants' for the hallway or the parlour window such as the india-rubber plant and the 'parlour palm' or aspidistra. The aspidistra, a hardy plant which was one of the few which could survive in cold and draughty Victorian houses, became identified with middle-class, and later working-class, respectability, as C. H. Rolph, writing about life in Finsbury Park around 1906, recalls,

> At Corbyn Street our front parlour for some years contained nothing, although the windows were decently curtained; and for this there was the highly practical reason that there was nothing to put in it. I think its furnishing began eventually with the acquisition, in exchange for a vast collection of trading stamps, of a jardinière, in which was placed a big flower-pot containing – of course – an aspidistra. After that the curtains were slightly parted in the daytime so that passers-by could just see that we too had an aspidistra, but not the emptiness beyond.[49]

2.13
Verandah at Holly Dene, Bromley, Kent, by Messenger and Co.

Indoor plants could be bought from nurserymen or even from door-to-door salesmen, though it was not advisable; in the suburbs of London and other towns and cities,

> the itinerary vendor of parlour plants is a familiar figure, so familiar, indeed, that the fiction of the young wife, exchanging her husband's best nether garments for a 'pot plant' has been immortalised in the humorous journals for a long time past. Most of these plants are simply large cuttings or branches ruthlessly torn from mature plants and stuck in pots without boasting the vestige of a root.[50]

Itinerant flower-selling earned a similarly bad reputation; Mrs Panton spoke of 'those engaging gentlemen who frequent the suburbs with a supply of blossoms, warranted to fade and die utterly within the space of twenty-four hours'.

DESIGN CHOICES

The question of whether people received the houses they wanted is difficult to answer. In such a speculative building system, rarely did the middle-class customer have any direct say in the fitting out of a house, except in the case of the top end of the market, where the builder might build the shell of the house and leave the internal arrangement, fittings and decoration to the customer, or if the purchaser was found while the house was in the process of being built, when the owner might be taken by the builder to the builders' merchants to make a choice from within a given price range. The amount of control the individual tenant had on building and decoration fluctuated in line with the general economic situation, where, as pressure was put on existing stock in times of depression and rising real income, tenants could afford to shop around, in contrast to occasions when 'tenants are willing to enter almost before the plasterer has finished the walls and ceilings'.[51] The balance of power remained in the tenants' favour throughout the 1880s and early 1890s, but swung in the landlords' favour in the late 1890s. The level of vacant properties fell again in 1904-5 but rose again the following year.[52] Only when improved deals from building societies began to encourage home ownership after 1900 was tenant control affected, and it has been suggested that the most modern designs were most evident in houses built for sale.[53]

The increasing emphasis in house advertisements on customer choice suggests that in times of tenant power or favourable mortage terms, the builder had to woo the client with promises of choice over decoration and in some cases, building. In *Where to Live Around London*, 1909, tenant choice in decoration was frequently advertised, in relation to top-quality houses, for example in the £50 to £130 rented houses on the Bromley Park and Hill Estates where houses were 'built to suit purchaser's or tenant's requirements'.

46

Home manuals suggest some dissatisfaction with what the builder and landlord provided, thus *Cassell's Household Guide*, 1912, criticised sculleries in most houses and commented that 'most houses in the garden suburbs are not "ideal homes", but honest attempts to give the best accommodation for a given sum of money, which is not quite the same thing'.[54] But on the whole writers tended to be realistic about the constraints of living in rented accommodation and suggested ways of overcoming the obstacles and achieving something approaching an ideal home. Mrs Panton commented that it was 'usual for the landlord to allow a certain sum for the decoration of a house; but rarely, if ever, does that sum allow of anything like really artistic papering and painting'[55] and recommended that 'brass bells, brass locks and handles to doors, and finger-plates must replace the china abominations provided by the landlord … replace the brass ones again when Angelina's lease is up, or she will feel that her money has gone into the landlord's pocket'.[56] The degree of the landlord's control over decoration is clear from records of repairs to houses owned by the Lower Norwood Cooperative Building Society, where exact instructions were given to repair-men on price and colour of papers and paints to be used, and the tenant was offered little or no choice. Nevertheless, house styles remained fundamentally market-led, simply through the builder's need to sell or let the house. The basic conservatism of the market and the building industry generally produced a non-innovatory solution to house form and decoration which was a step behind the latest fashion, a scaled-down and debased version of architect-designed houses, obtained from trade journals or from designs drawn up by architects for builders.[57]

3

MIDDLE-CLASS
SUBURBS

3.1
Edwardians outside a
standard bay-fronted house.
Note the Venetian blinds
and lace curtains

Semi-detached house, Manchester

PLATE 4

Suburban house, Brighton,
1908

Top-of-the-range housing,
Lakeside, Cardiff

PLATES 5 & 6

The miles and miles of little red houses in little, silent streets.... Each boasts its pleasant drawing room, its bow-window, its little front garden, its high-sounding title – 'Acacia Villa' or 'Camperdown Lodge' – attesting unconquered human aspiration.... The women, with their single domestic servants ... find time hangs heavy on their hands. (C. F. G. Masterman, *The Condition of England*, 1909)[1]

While people had always sought to live out of the towns from the seventeenth century, suburbia, as we generally understand the term, was substantially a product of the period from 1815 to 1939.[2] It was a response to effective demand, from a middle class sufficiently coherent and significant by the early nineteenth century, for houses away from the crowded and grimy city centres. The first English suburb was St John's Wood, developed from 1815 by John Shaw on the Eyre Estate; the detached and semi-detached houses became the blueprint for later suburban houses.[3] Suburban development round other major cities began in the 1820s and 1830s, for example, Liverpool's Everton, Birmingham's Edgbaston ('the Birmingham Belgravia'), the 'numerous mansions and villas of superior class'[4] of Headingley Hill, Leeds, and Manchester's Victoria Park, which boasted detached and semi-detached villas 'free from any possible nuisances that may arise from the vicinity of smoke and manufactures'.[5]

By the middle of the century every town with over fifty thousand inhabitants had its suburbs, for example Cottingham near Hull, Kemp Town and Hove near Brighton and Gosforth and Jesmond near Newcastle.[6] In London, St John's Wood was followed by suburban expansion in other areas such as Kentish Town, Hackney and Camberwell. During the last half of the nineteenth century, the population of London rose from 2.3 million to 6.6 million.[7] In 1850, the edge of the urban area had been three miles from Charing Cross; by 1900, London's outskirts stretched to five to ten miles away from the centre. By 1881, W. S. Clarke listed 89 suburbs of London. One of the fastest-growing suburbs was Willesden: between 1851 and 1891, the population of Willesden grew from 3000 to 114,000, while that of West Ham grew from 19,000 to 267,000.[8] The population of Ealing rose from 3349 in 1847 to 61,222 in 1911, and the numbers of houses from 657 to 12,959 over the same years.

The process of suburbanisation happened somewhat later and was more protracted outside London, the suburbs of a provincial city typically extending to a few miles from its centre. Unlike London, by the late nineteenth century, in the new industrial towns the upper and middle classes lived in villas in the suburbs rather than in a terrace or the centre of town. The hilly outskirts of Brighton saw the development of the Preston Park area. The single-class exclusivity of Bristol was located in Clifton, Cotham and Redland; the Edwardian middle-class suburbs of Leicester were to be found just to the south of the city, while Nottingham's best addresses were in Wollaton to the west, Mapperley Park to the north-east and the Park in the city centre. Late-Victorian and Edwardian middle-class suburbs sprang up around Manchester at Didsbury to the south close into city centre, at Alderley Edge to the south-east, and at Hale and Bowden further out to the south-west. Liverpool expanded with Prince's and Sefton Parks and Grove Park and Fulwood Park suburbs. With the growing popularity of the seaside, an estimated fifty-five per cent of the population visiting on day trips by 1911,[9] vigorous late Victorian and Edwardian building occurred in the north, for example in Southport, and in Blackpool, with its middle-class enclaves like St Anne's, echoing the middle-class resorts of Eastbourne and Bournemouth in the south.

INFLUENCES ON SUBURBAN DEVELOPMENT

What role did new forms of transportation play in the development of the suburb? The wealthy had private carriages and benefited from improved roads, but the so-called 'Railway Mania' of the mid-nineteenth century had great implications for mass transit. By 1914, the railway network reached 23,000 miles. The development of London's outer suburbs depended on railways. Bromley of the 1850s and west London of the 1860s and 70s were clearly boosted by new railway links.[10] Contemporaries held the railway responsible for the social deterioration of an area, as in the case of Croydon in 1876:

> Monotonous streets and lines and lines of villas are fast encircling the town, the neighbourhood of which being pleasant and picturesque, and within easy reach of the City, is a favoured residence for men of business, who may be seen flocking to the morning train in surprising numbers.[11]

The London Underground was also important in the growth of London's suburbs, beginning with the Metropolitan Line, opened in 1863; the first electrically operated tube began in 1890, and by 1914 other electrified underground lines had reached such places as Hampstead, Shepherd's Bush, Finsbury Park and Clapham.

But rail was not always the deciding factor; Liverpool, Manchester, Birmingham, Leeds and Sheffield were all suburbanised before mass cheap transit, and it was not until 1883, when the Cheap Trains Act brought in workmen's fares, that it was feasible for the working classes to travel by rail. Furthermore, the railway was largely irrelevant to the development of inner suburbs, such as those north of Leeds; areas too close in for rail were dependent on horse-drawn trams, introduced from 1861.[12] Horse trams were resisted in Edgbaston (Birmingham), Hampstead and Ealing (London), Kemp Town (Brighton), Kelvinside (Glasgow) and Victoria Park (Manchester) because residents held that they would bring in a lower class of resident.[13] By the 1890s horse-drawn trams and omnibuses were playing a key role in mass transportation. The electrification and municipalisation of the electric tram around 1900 was also very important in the development of suburbia; by 1914, electric trams were established in nearly every large town and city. Districts around Sheffield, such as Meersbrook, Millhouses and Sparrow, boomed as a result of access to the tram from 1896, and rapid building occurred in artisan suburbs, such as Sherwood near Nottingham, built at the ends of tramlines.[14]

Besides the role of transport, various other factors played an important part in establishing the overall character of a suburb. The character of an area could be determined before its full-scale development by the class of housing added early on to the existing village. In London, for instance, the lower-middle-class housing built in Acton in the 1850s secured this as the character of the area in the 1880s, and the 1880s and 1890s superior villas in Bexley maintained its high class status in the 1930s.[15] Geographical location and proximity to areas of work also affected whether an area developed as largely working-class or preserved as mainly solid middle-class housing, with a carefully graded hierarchy of houses aimed at different social groups. In the latter case, though the aim might have been to create an entirely single-class suburb, it should be remembered that in reality it was always more mixed because of the trades and services needed to support the middle-class residents.

The overriding influences in many cases (which will be dealt with in greater detail in the following chapter) were the system of land ownership and the nature of the building industry in an area. Most London land was leasehold on ninety-nine years. Some major provincial towns like Sheffield and Birmingham also used the ninety-nine-year lease system, but many provincial towns had a freehold system entailing the sale of land.[16] The impact of regional differences can be seen earlier in the century on the Eton College estate at Chalcots in Hampstead, where the landlords tightly controlled development and created an exclusively middle-class area, compared to the Norfolk estate in Sheffield, where the landowner's control was looser and the estate grew as an industrial working-class area in response to local needs. G. Calvert Holland recorded in 1841,

> the town has extended widely in all directions.... All classes, save the artisan and the needy shopkeeper, are attracted by country comfort and retirement. The attorney, – the manufacturer, – the grocer, – the draper, – the shoemaker, – and the tailor, fix their commanding residences on some beautiful site, and adorn them with the cultivated taste of the artist.[17]

Portsmouth responded to the late-Victorian build-up of the Navy by building impressive streets of two-storeyed, richly decorated terraces, such as Laburnham Grove, 1905-10, nicknamed 'brass button alley' after the petty officers who lived there. [18]

51

The creation of a middle-class suburb can be perhaps best illustrated by looking at some detailed examples, Muswell Hill in north London, Herne Hill in south London, and Roath in Cardiff, where landownership and the building trades played a large part in ensuring that these areas developed as largely homogeneous middle-class suburbs, confined to a particular type of house, and thus clientele.

ROATH, CARDIFF

During the second half of the nineteenth century, Cardiff grew from a small market town to a major port and its population rose ninefold from 1851 to 182,000 by 1911.[19] Its wealth was founded on coal. Indeed, Cardiff was known by the 1890s as 'the coal metropolis of the world'.[20] *The Cardiff Times* of 1905 spoke of 'an impression of modernity and progressiveness, of spacious streets and buildings, of docks and ships and of great commercial activity which well merits the epithet "the Chicago of Wales"'.[21] The number of houses built reflected the expansion, rising from 327 in 1801 to 20,476 in 1891.[22] These houses were built on land leased out to builders by the landowners on ninety-nine year leases. There were three large estates – Windsor to the south and west as far as Penarth, Tredegar to the east and north, and Bute with land dotted all over Cardiff. The large estates were built over from the 1860s to accommodate the influx of workers, creating homogeneous areas of working-class housing in the south, such as Splott, physically separated from upper-class Tredegarville with its large villas and adjoining stables on the north side of the main thoroughfare into town, and working-class Grangetown segregated from high-status Cathedral Road to the west. *The Cardiff Tide Tables Almanack* said of this road in 1880, 'the residences of its more opulent inhabitants display great architectural merit... in no considerable degree due to the example set by the late Mr Burges in his admirable and artistic restoration of Cardiff Castle'.[23] Gradually these smart areas were infilled with the working-class and lower-middle-class houses of Canton in the west and south Roath in the north, so those who could afford to do so moved further out to north Roath or west to Penarth, where ship- and coal-owners lived in houses on Marine Parade overlooking the bay. The building of south Roath spans the 1870s to 1890s and north Roath and Penylan from the 1890s to 1914 (see fig. 3.2). Roath as a whole was heterogeneous in character, much of it working-class and lower-middle-class houses, with pockets of older upper-middle-class housing in the south, and mainly middle-class, with some upper-middle-class roads in the north. North Roath, the last area in Cardiff to be developed, was homogeneous and spanned the range of middle-class housing, and the inhabitants had a 'district centred' lifestyle (see Appendix 2).[24]

What part did the landowners play in the formation of north Roath? Houses in north Roath were built on Tredegar and Bute land. The ground landlords defined the characters of different areas in Cardiff

3.2
Roath, Cardiff, from an
Ordnance Survey map of
1922

3.3
Houses in Ninian Road,
Cardiff, built in the early
1890s, which originally cost
£830 to build and had a
rateable value of £39 10s
in 1909

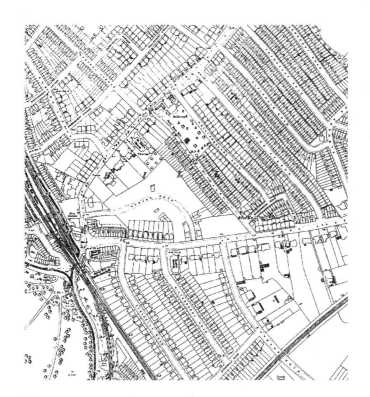

as 'respectable', that is, middle-class, or 'artisan'. The policy of all these landowners was a refusal to sell land; instead they let land on a ninety-nine-year lease, with strict control over development enforced by an army of estate officials. Lord Bute, for example, employed an estate architect, E. W. M. Corbett, brother of the estate solicitor, to design all houses on the estate. This guaranteed the high-status quality of houses facing Roath Park (see fig. 3.3). Tredegar imposed similar restrictions, using W. Scott as architect, to ensure that the Penylan area near Waterloo Gardens and Roath Brook Gardens was maintained as a high-quality residential area. Due to the desire of the landowners to maintain a high standard of housing even in working-class areas (Bute dictated that even the plainest of housing should have a bay and a small garden, rather than have the building line up to the street), there was a constant under-provision of working-class housing and an over-provision for the middle classes in Cardiff. The presence of an estate architect helps explain the homogeneity of design in this area, for, although several builders may have built a street in Roath, it is sometimes impossible to tell from the outside of the houses where one builder's work ends and the next begins. But it was the landowners rather than the dominance of one or two builders which resulted in such homogeneity. Local builders, for example Venning and Leonard, were all governed by estate policy in terms of type and size of house. At the mid to upper end of the housing range in north Roath, builders, while adhering to a basic form and size, could add 'individual' details to distinguish builders' blocks from each

3.4
Herne Hill, London, from an Ordnance Survey map of 1916

3.5
Houses on Herne Hill built in the 1890s

54

other in a road.

The fact that the same features crop up frequently in varied combinations in different builders' work also demonstrates the influences of local suppliers on house form. A builders' merchants popular with builders in Cardiff was D. Morgan and Sons (founded in 1874), which had 'a very extensive collection of the most modern and up-to-date designs', and 'everything requisite for the fitting up of a cottage or a mansion'.[25] Their office and showrooms were situated near the railway station serving the Welsh valleys. Sessions and Sons, also a prominent Cardiff builders' merchants, was founded in 1838 in Gloucester, and opened a large branch in Cardiff in 1857. Sessions' reputation was built on their early business manufacturing enamelled slate chimney-pieces, in which respect they were considered 'pioneers', doing a large trade at home and particularly abroad. The business included the 'latest patents and novelties' in roofing slates, also timber, joinery, laths, terracotta goods, cement, grates, fenders, baths and other sanitary goods and iron goods.[26]

SOUTH LONDON; HERNE HILL, DULWICH AND NORWOOD

Herne Hill in south London, straddling the parishes of Lambeth and Camberwell, was largely built up between the 1890s and the First World War. While parts of Lambeth and Camberwell were covered rapidly during the nineteenth century, particularly in the 1860s,[27] some areas, such as Herne Hill, Norwood and Dulwich, remained untouched until the late nineteenth century and maintained a reputation for health and exclusivity. The Herne Hill of the 1820s was known as the 'Belgravia of South London', populated with 'tradesmen of the better class … [with] a cortege of footmen and a glitter of plates, extensive pleasure grounds, costly hot houses and carriages driven by coachmen in wigs', and writing in 1885 John Ruskin added 'the leafy seclusion remains unchanged to this day'.[28]

The extension of the railway network to Herne Hill caused its eventual transformation from a retreat for the very wealthy to a middle-class enclave.[29] Estates lining the main thoroughfares were demolished over the course of the late nineteenth century, particularly after 1897, to make way for new residential roads (see fig. 3.4), for example, Deepdene Road replaced the Fairfield and Elmswood estates, 'The Cedars' was demolished to make way for parts of Gubyon and Woodquest Avenues and the upper part of Poplar Walk was built on nursery ground. The Dulwich College estate was sold in eighteen lots; Springfield estate made way for Stradella Road and Winterbrook Road and Dulwich Hill House was replaced in 1894 with Sunray Avenue by the Red Post Hill Land Co. Ltd which began building fifty semi- and detached houses costing £700 to £900 on Sunray Avenue. The estates governors of Dulwich College exercised strict qualitative control through leases over the development of streets and the houses built on them, preventing the population of Dulwich from rising above ten thousand, and thus translating the desire for an exclusive social suburb into reality. Uniformity was maintained on the estate by Charles Barry, architect to the estate, whose job it was to supervise all building.[30] On the Dulwich House estate ten mansions on Herne Hill, Half Moon Lane and Red Post Hill were auctioned in eight lots which were to be transformed into the roads from Danecroft Road east to Ardberg Road and south to Ruskin Walk; for example, Carlton House was demolished to make way for Danecroft Road, and neighbouring large houses made way for roads such as Frankfurt, Elmwood and Beckwith Roads[31] (see figs 3.5 and 5.1).

Herne Hill was well served by the large number of firms based in south London. By 1900 there were fifty-five builders merchants based south of the river and sixty-four based in the north. Local firms such as H. Tryer and Co. supplied the builders of Herne Hill, along with large concerns like Young and Marten. This firm, founded in 1872, had expanded by the late 1890s to create many specialist departments including paper-hangings, kitchen ranges, stoves and chimney-pieces, sanitary goods, and leaded cathedral and stained glass.

The strict qualitative control exercised by the estate governors was responsible for maintaining Herne Hill as a desirable residential area. Residents in the new roads where rents were £60 to £90 were considered 'comfortable' or 'well to do'.[32] Advertisements in local newspapers confirm the respectable, servant-keeping character of the area: 'Servant – £14. Good Cook, General or useful help wanted for plain cooking and housework – £16-18. Apply Burbank, 12 Sunray Ave, Herne Hill', and 'A tall capable House parlour maid. Plain needle-woman. Apply before 1 or after 6 at 4 Stradella Rd.'[33] Few took in lodgers on Herne Hill itself and, speaking of the detached villas in De Crespigny Park off Denmark Hill, George Gissing in *In the Year of Jubilee*, 1894, commented that 'in this locality, lodgings are *not* to let'.[34] While detailed information about residents was not forthcoming as most were listed simply as 'Court', a term reserved for those who saw themselves as middle-class, an impression emerges from Charles Booth, who records that the inhabitants of Herne Hill were 'not natural churchgoers and it is very difficult to get to know them ... regarding church attendance as by no means a necessary condition of respectability'.[35] He went on to report that they spent their Saturday afternoons bicycling and playing cricket and tennis and their evenings indulging in music and dancing, while they rose after midday on Sundays and strolled in nearby Brockwell Park. The ridges of Herne Hill, Denmark Hill and Brixton Hill were populated by well-to-do City people while the surrounding roads in Herne Hill were regarded as solidly 'servant-keeping' middle class.[36] Nearby North Dulwich was also a high-status area; aside from Richmond and Hampstead, *Where to Live Round London*, 1909, described Dulwich as the most beautiful London suburb, where rents could reach £300 per annum.[37]

Hornsey represents a different case in terms of land development, where builders and the local board, rather than the landowner, shaped the area. The homogeneous high-quality housing in Muswell Hill is similar to that in Herne Hill and Penylan and thus would confirm the similar interests of landowner and builder. Hornsey developed slightly later than Lambeth and Camberwell and had a greater percentage of clerks than any other part of London by 1900. Its population rose from 19,387 in 1871 to 85,000 in 1905. It developed in phases, with Stroud Green as the first area to be developed in the 1870s and 1880s, then Crouch End particularly from 1895, and lastly, Muswell Hill, built up between 1896 and 1910 (see figs 3.6–3.9). Hornsey's popularity was in part founded on its reputation as a healthy suburb, 'full of wide tree-lined streets'.[38]

In contrast to those in other areas of north London, landowners in Hornsey, Tottenham and Wood Green sold rather than leased their land to developers. In most cases, large land companies such as the Imperial Property Investment Co. were the purchasers; they then sold plots individually to small builders, who might each erect two or three houses. The quality of Hornsey as a whole was strictly maintained by the Hornsey Local Board (established in 1867) and by the dominance of one or two builders. 'Unscrupulous' builders attempted to gain influence on the local Board but failed, enabling the Board to maintain the strict building laws which were the envy of the rest of London in the 1890s. Any 'jerry-built' properties were immediately demolished. A sanitary museum was established to encourage builders to adopt only the best class of appliance, a development 'opposed tooth and nail by the builders'.[39] Materials and products used in the building process were also tested at the museum and it ran courses for builders and residents. The importance attached to health is shown by the attendance figures, which reached nine thousand within the first seven months of opening.

In 1906, Hornsey was described in *Where to Live round London* (Northern volume) as one of the most popular residential areas in north London, boasting 'high-class houses'. The most exclusive area was Muswell Hill, whose hilly terrain and consequent relative remoteness prevented its earlier development into an industrial and working-class suburb like neighbouring Tottenham. In 1835, *Pigott's Commercial Directory* described Muswell Hill as 'one of the most agreeable districts around London, and is inhabited by persons of the first respectability'.[40] Muswell Hill was intended to become as sought-after as south and west London and *The Suburban Homes of London: a residential guide*, 1881, suggested that Muswell Hill could even become superior to desirable Upper Norwood. Between the 1870s and 1901, the population of Muswell Hill expanded last of all, from 900 to 5230, as it developed into a solidly middle-class district.

3.6
Edwardian housing in
Woodberry Crescent,
Muswell Hill, London,
about 1905

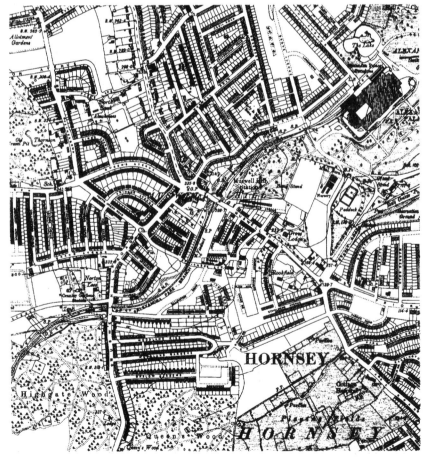

3.7
Hornsey, north London,
from an Ordnance Survey
map of 1920

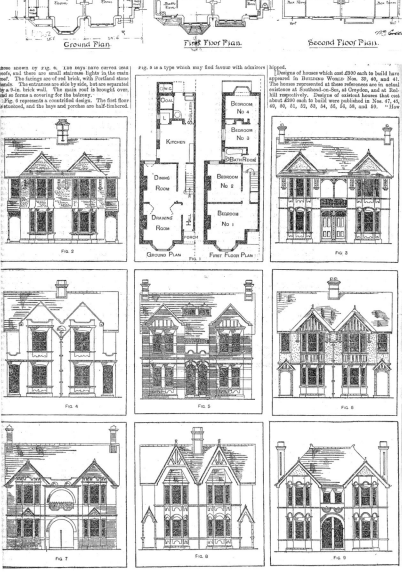

3.8
Elevation and plan of houses
built by W. J. Collins in
Muswell Hill in 1897

3.9
Plans and elevations of villa
architecture, *Building World*,
1897

The quality control and evident architectural uniformity of Muswell Hill was therefore due not to the influence of a local landowner but to the local board and to the dominance of two firms of developers, W. J. Collins and his two sons, and J. Edmondson and son. By the turn of the century, these two firms had between them purchased all the original estates in the area for redevelopment. Edmondson demolished the Limes and Elms estates and, from 1895, built up Queens, Dukes and Princes Avenues, St James Parade, Queens Parade and other roads on the land. Collins' firm bought up the Firs, Midhurst, and Fortismere estates, developing Church Crescent from 1897, and a block of six roads, Collingwood, Leaside, Fortismere, Birchwood, Firs and Grand Avenues; subsequently, W. J. Collins, and later, his sons, built the Rookfield Estate (1906-26). These firms were well served, not only by large merchants elsewhere in London, but also by local firms, Bond and White Ltd and John Knowles and Co. Collins and Edmondson intended to ensure that Muswell Hill remained a homogeneous, desirable area. *The Hornsey and Finsbury Park Journal*, 1905: 'High class, Substantial, Doublefronted and Semi-detached villas. Quite up to date. From £550 to £1000. Rentals from £50. Charmingly situated and 350 feet above sea level. 25 minutes to City. Variety of designs, some with full size Billiard Rooms and Electric Light.'

Similarly, the quality of Edmondson's houses, particularly on Queens Avenue where rents were £100 in 1914, suggest that he was aiming at a high-quality area. *The Alexandra Palace Magazine*, 1902, recognised the contribution of this firm,

> The firm of J. Edmondson and son has lined Muswell Hill with rows of houses so varied in style and so picturesque in architecture, that even the most exclusive of cognoscenti in such matters would not disdain to live in one of them … a series of flats … that are not only picturesque from the artists' point of view but can boast of every convenience which the most exacting housewife could demand.[41]

Politically Hornsey as a whole was a safe Conservative seat from 1885 (when the parliamentary borough of Hornsey was formed) until 1918. Even after the Liberal landslide of 1906 a Radical urging people to vote Liberal was told, 'Remember this is Muswell Hill.'[42] As in the case of Herne Hill, little is known of the residents' occupations as they were simply recorded as 'Court', but the class of resident is suggested by house advertisements offering conveniences such as electric bells and speaking tubes and by advertisements for servants such as the following in *The Hornsey and Finsbury Park Journal and North Islington Standard*, 13 January 1905: 'Houseparlourmaid. Wanted. Middle of January. Age 25. Wages according to reference, small family; no basement, early dinners 4 Woodlands Crescent, Muswell Hill Rd.'[43] Many houses in Muswell Hill had maids living in, though they were frequently fourteen-year-old girls from the local orphanage, and residents recall that the letting of rooms met with disapproval from neighbours. The area as a whole was nicknamed by its own residents, 'Pride, Poverty and Pianos' and 'Plus Fours and No Breakfast'.[44]

Such localised studies highlight the issue of regional variation in house form and decoration. There are clearly features, for example in house frontages and plans, particular to different regions and towns. To what extent can this be due to cultural differences in the social make-up of an area? This is difficult to know.[45] The mobility of the middle classes in particular would seem to suggest that this is not the main factor involved in regional differences of form. Rather, variations, where they exist, can be explained by the local system of landownership, bye-laws and supply network and the time-lag involved in the spread of fashions from, say, London to other towns. But what is equally remarkable is the degree of repetition of house details so far apart, a tendency which was most noticeable from the 1890s and for which the revolutions in publications for builders and manufacturers and in transporting methods in the late nineteenth century were responsible.

Tenant, landlord, landowner, builder and manufacturer all played vital roles in the production of the late-Victorian and Edwardian house. Middle-class speculatively built houses were the result of a combination of social, economic and technical factors, the final outcome a careful balancing act between fulfilling desires as they were perceived by the builder within the constraints imposed by external forces and within his own needs for practicality and economy, as will be shown in the next chapter.

4

LANDOWNERS AND
BUILDING TRADES

4.1
Front cover of early-twentieth-century catalogue of Messenger and Co.

Cultural factors were the initiating force behind market demand to be accounted for by house-builders, with other factors, such as the mechanisms of speculation and the economics of building, playing a vital role in translating market desires into shapes on the ground. For example, under the system of speculative building, whereby a builder bought or leased plots of land from a landowner, the landowner could exert substantial control on the builder's freedom. In the case of leasehold land, for example, the character of the area was frequently already determined before the builders appeared on the scene because the streets were laid out by the landowner. Furthermore, strict conditions laid down in the lease and the employment of an estate architect could determine the type and size of house and even the actual elevation and plan. Contemporaries like Charles Booth recognised the builder as merely a pawn in the game, exercising little effective control:

> Responsibility must be put on the right shoulders; many speculative builders who do the worst work are simply men of straw, the puppets of the real capitalist; who may be the ground landlord, the building company, or, to quote the glossary of the Labour Commission, the 'money-lending solicitor'.... The builder waits on a demand that he has little or no power to create. Other trades and other interests determine the growth of London. He may to some extent exercise a directing influence, but his first task is to carry out instructions and to control labour.[1]

But even freehold ownership did not necessarily give the builder more freedom than leasehold tenure as to the type of house he was allowed to erect, because restricted covenants, establishing the standard of house, were often contained in the contract for the sale of the land.[2] The builder's response to market forces had, in any case, to take account of the invisible force of bye-laws and local board policy, which might permit or ban a particular style of house in a certain area; 'a special form of interference to which the building trade is subject – that resulting from regulations of Local Boards, Bye-laws of Municipalities, and Acts of Parliament – may be noticed here', Booth wrote.[3] But whether land was freehold or leasehold was of secondary importance; there was often no need for the landowner to impose restrictions on the builder because they usually had the same aim in mind – to build the best houses possible. The controls therefore operated primarily to protect landowners from impecunious builders putting up cheap houses. Natural factors also played an important role in the development of an area. Hilly ground such as Muswell Hill and Herne Hill in London was regarded as desirable because of the health-giving fresh air and the views it offered.[4]

THE BUILDING INDUSTRY

However much control the landowner and other forces might exert over the standard and form of a house, the builder still played an enormous role, at least in so far as the choice of details was left up to him. The total number of houses built in Britain, the vast majority produced speculatively, rose from 3,432,000 in mid century to 7,550,000 by 1911, an 11.6 per cent annual increase during the 1880s and a 15 per cent annual increase during the decades of the 1860s, 1870s and 1890s.[5] Thus, a period of overall increase in building was punctuated with short-term fluctuations, such as the boom in the late 1870s and early 1880s, with the peak of building occurring in the late 1890s. In the years running up to the First World War, the house-building industry entered a depression. The state of the building industry in 1911 is indicated in statistics for houses in the course of erection, 38,178, as compared with 61,909 in 1901.[6] How did the building industry cater for this overall upsurge in demand from the mid nineteenth century? What changes had to be made to its internal structure, organisation and methods to achieve this, and how were such changes likely to affect what houses looked like?

Firstly, demand prompted a growth in the industry which mirrored the rate of house-building. Examining labour figures in more detail, the building trades, classified in Census records as 'bricklayers and labourers, masons and labourers, carpenters and joiners, painters, plasterers, paperhangers, decorators, plumbers, glaziers, etc.', rose from 831,394 in 1881[7] to 1,130,425 in 1901.[8] By 1911, the total employed in the building trades had fallen again to 946,127.[9] Numbers involved in house-building alone followed a similar trend.[10] The minute increase among those in the building trades between 1881 and 1891 was matched by an actual decline in the building materials supply industries, defined in *The Census of England and Wales* as 'the brick and tile, cement and plaster makers, stone and slate quarriers and dealers', from 105,544 to 103,926.[11] Likewise, the decline in the building trades after 1901 was matched by the reduction in the number of brickmakers and stone and slate quarriers, cutters and dressers, and by the decline of membership of trade unions from a peak of one member in every five building workers in the 1890s.[12]

The power of the building trade unions secured an increase in wages which, added to a price depression, amounted to a rise in real terms for building workers in the late nineteenth century. Wages rose as a proportion of the total building costs from a quarter in 1850 to a half in 1914.[13] The trades' hierarchy, reflected in earnings, comprised interior decorators at the top, and then, in descending order, grainers, plaster modellers and smiths, founders' engineers, slate masons, plumbers and smiths, then stone masons, bellhangers, plasterers, gasfitters and glaziers, and then slaters, carpenters, joiners, painters, paperhangers, bricklayers and tilers and, below them, a hierarchy of the trades' labourers. The annual wage of an average trade such as carpentry in 1906 was £98, slightly above skilled trades in other fields.[14]

The rising cost of labour, coupled with practical and economic necessities involved in meeting the demand for housing, led to fundamental changes in the structure and organisation of the building industry, namely, a growing professionalism. One of the key changes was that the size of the average firm expanded, cutting out the small builder as a greater and greater proportion of houses was concentrated in the hands of a few large firms. For example, in 1899 only seventeen firms, less than two per cent of the total number, built over forty per cent of new houses.[15] The traditional practice of subcontracting was popular with unscrupulous builders as it shifted the responsibility from the main contractor in the event of an accident and it encouraged the adulteration of materials. This practice declined with the concentration of building in a few firms' hands. Firms employed men for regular trades directly instead of subcontracting work and only subcontracted for specialist work.[16] Consequently, specialist firms emerged where a need for a particular skill was created by the development of a new material or a new technology, as seen, for instance, in the spate of new electrical firms and expert firms of grainers, carvers, composition moulders and interior decorators set up in the early twentieth century. As John Elliot, author of *Practical House Painting*, 1910, summed up, 'We live in an age of specialists. Every profession or trade is split up into many branches, and each branch has its man who is proficient in that.'[17]

The tendency of diversification and specialisation within the building trades also applied to the manufacture and sale of building requisites. Before 1870, as transport was expensive and difficult and distribution of materials limited, builders made their own materials on site, and supplied them also to other builders. Specialist showrooms existed for high-quality fittings, and ironmongers provided certain requisites. After 1870, the use of bulky machinery in large-scale production and the revolution in transporting goods by rail and steamship meant that manufacture and supply moved away from the building site.

A whole network of manufacturers and middlemen emerged to supply the builder with materials and components. The main source of these was the builders' merchants, whose numbers rose from 100 in 1870 to 1300 by 1910.[18] Builders' merchants varied greatly in size, from the small corner shop, which was advised to hold a small, varied stock[19] supplied from manufacturers, to the large firm which could be frequently involved in the whole process of import, manufacture and sale of goods and materials. Many of the largest suppliers were long established and promoted a speciality on which their reputations had originally been founded, for example, the main merchant for builders of the ornamental villa residences springing up in the fast-growing Croydon of the 1890s was Chapman and Sons, which had been founded in 1838 and had built a reputation on its rendered laths. Chapman's also serviced the rest of the south-east of England, and became known as 'one of the best-known wholesale building firms in the south of England, having large business connections in all principal towns, all the principal builders in the south-east of England being on its books'.[20] Outside

London and the south-east, leading builders' merchants included Mitchell and Son, Exeter, established before 1820, who specialised in marble and slate goods and manufactured them in their extensive sawing, dressing and polishing sheds. In the west Midlands, John Gough Noake, of Wolverhampton, founded in 1850, was a substantial concern, while the main supplier for Durham and Northumberland was Steel and Co., founded in 1879 in Sunderland, renowned for sanitary and tile ware, who had a special shop where tiles 'of considerable taste and beauty'[21] were slabbed up for grates and ranges.

Large firms such as these tended to be based on several sites, with many departments and showrooms (see fig. 4.2), and with facilities for fast delivery of goods in bulk. John Knowles of London, for example, had ten depots in London by 1898 and operated a delivery radius of fifteen miles from Charing Cross, with offices in Sheffield, Nottingham and Glasgow; indeed it was claimed that there was 'scarcely any part of the civilised world where their goods are not known'.[22] Thomas O'Brien, specialising in iron goods and claiming the biggest showroom for chimney-pieces in London, guaranteed same-day delivery by 'express vans, with quick trotting ponies or cobs'.[23]

4.2
Interior of Barnard, Bishop and Barnard's showroom in Norwich in the late nineteenth century

As competition increased between firms, those which were able to do so developed a large apparatus of publicity, discount terms for bulk orders, and extensive and profusely illustrated catalogues, made possible by cheaper printing methods and new modes of illustration, designed to appeal to different markets (see fig. 4.1). Many catalogues were undated so that manufacturers could reissue them year after year with only minor changes or additions. Such trade literature gradually superseded price and pattern books, which contained illustrated plans to be copied by the builder and had dominated until the 1870s. Larger firms went to great lengths to sell their manufactures; thus, a special new building material sample or a range of paint colours might be included in the catalogue. Catalogues provided invaluable price comparisons for a whole variety of designs and products. To impress their professionalism on readers the manufacturers included lavishly illustrated designs and views of premises and facilities, along with detailed delivery schedules. Trade journals, for example *The Builder* and *Furniture Gazette*, were a source of the very latest information on general trade concerns, imports, exports and new machinery. Builders could also gain advice from a growing number of technical books covering domestic sanitation, lighting, and carpentry and joinery.

AMATEUR WORK

Amateur work, the equivalent of today's 'DIY', became very popular in the Edwardian period as a result of the rising cost of professional labour, increased leisure time and purchasing power and general changes in social attitudes, prompting a greater range of books for amateurs. Some series were associated with a particular journal with which readers were familiar, for instance the 1914 'Decorator' series of practical handbooks edited by A. S. Jennings, the founder and editor of *The Decorator* journal. The intended audience for these books was often ambiguous, with many books being aimed at both amateurs and professionals. Publishers also brought out books specifically for the amateur on various aspects of home decorating, particularly carpentry and fretworking. Firms such as Hobbies of Norwich, set up by Jewson's in 1897, began to manufacture special fretwork kits, with the claim 'Fretwork – cuts out dull evenings', in response to demand from readers of *Hobbies Weekly* (see p. 69). The pioneering book in the field of handbooks on the applied arts and forerunner of many successful books thereafter was William Bembrose's *Manual of Woodcarving* published in the early nineteenth century. Many similar books followed, including Ward Lock and Co.'s *Every Man his Own Mechanic*, an all-in-one volume with sections on all the trades, aimed solely at amateurs, and their subsequent *Home Carpentry for Handy Men*.

The effect of the diversification and specialisation in the building industry described above was to intensify the problems of displacement and overlapping of trades. Disputes about task demarcation within trades were common, as in the case, for example, of the plasterers and specialist tile fixers who vied for the job of fixing tiles.[24] There were similar problems of overlapping where manufacturers sold direct to the public, and builders sold direct to other builders, rather than through a merchant.[25] Conflict also occurred in cases where manufacturers competed with local tradesmen when they operated as jobbing tradesmen as well as making goods.

Machines were introduced into almost every sphere of building work to a greater or lesser extent, and considerably undercut the cost of work done by hand. Such was the strength of feeling that machine workers could find themselves ostracised by the trades unions in the early 1900s. Where machines were not criticised was in helping in jobs which were laborious or where absolute accuracy was needed, for instance, in timber jointing. But despite the increased role of the machine in the production of materials and components, hand skill remained the basis of most trades on site. Even where machines were used in the production of materials and components, skilled workers were still needed to guide them by hand.

Of all the trades involved in the production of fittings for the late-Victorian and Edwardian domestic interior, the wood trade probably played the greatest role. The industry met and stimulated demand for wood, first, by developing ways of ensuring sufficient supply of cheap material, and second, by arranging production and retail distribution in such a way as to maximise the use of this material. This involved creating favourable conditions for importing, both in terms of economic measures and in terms of port facilities to accommodate imports. Wood was imported in increasingly large quantities from non-Empire as well as Empire countries, and by the Edwardian period Britain had become totally dependent on imports to satisfy home needs. Facilities such as the Manchester Ship Canal, opened in 1894, became crucial to the importation of large quantities of wood to supply builders' needs in central and northern areas of England; in 1883 it was said of the Manchester Ship Canal that,

> A vast increase will take place in the building trade of Manchester and all its outlying dependencies; ... when Manchester becomes converted into a wood depot, it will distribute a large amount of timber to the Midlands. The bulk of the supplies which will be sent out from Manchester, however, will be distributed in Lancashire and the West Riding of Yorkshire.[26]

One effect of the economic measures encouraging imports of non-Empire timber was to create fierce competition for British firms, which was in turn to have implications for the organisation of domestic manufacture of wood goods. They responded by implementing factory mechanisation and labour adjustments to reduce costs and increase output. Diversification and professionalisation within the organisation of the wood industry were found to be necessary in order to compete effectively in a growing market which constantly demanded novelty in design, and specialist branches increased and sophisticated retail and distribution networks were established. The scale and precise nature of the demand in the latter decades of the nineteenth century prompted a period of intensive development and improvement of woodworking machinery. Indeed, while woodworking machines had been in existence since the late eighteenth century, the period 1870-1900 could be said to be the greatest period of woodworking machinery development.[27] The direction that these machinery innovations took, governed by the increasing and diverse needs of industries such as house-building, followed the path of diversification and specialisation. This specialisation enabled industry to satisfy the late-nineteenth-century preference for ornateness, variety and the imitation of expensive hand techniques.

These new woodworking machines imitated the actions of hand tools. A new type of saw, the fretsaw or 'jig-saw', was brought on the market which could do 'internal cutting' or fretworking, which neither the circular saw nor bandsaw could do. Internal cutting made it possible

4.3
Joiners' shop at H. Gibbon Steam Joinery works, Cardiff, early twentieth century

to produce a comparable decorative effect to carving at a fraction of the cost, and any style could be reproduced simply by cutting the appropriate outline. Certain styles, such as eighteenth-century trellis and Moorish lattice motifs, lent themselves particularly to this process. Fretwork thus became a cheap substitute for hand carving and was affordable by the middle classes. Ultimately, the market saturation of machine goods caused a backlash; high-class specifications in 1899 say 'no stock mouldings'. An alternative aesthetic to the ornate look emerged, the rustic hand-made look. The irony was that there were quickly on the market machines capable of emulating the hand-crafted look.

The marble and slate trades responded in much the same ways as the wood trade to the increasing demand for their goods at low prices. Much of the British demand for marble was supplied from abroad; indeed, Britain relied totally on imported rough marble and finished marble goods from countries such as Italy and Belgium. In 1887, the Italian marble industry, based around the towns of Carrara, Massa and Serravezza, produced one hundred and seventy thousand tons of Sicilian, Vein and Statuary white marbles. Its main destination was the United States, which, together with Canada, consumed one quarter of this output; Great Britain purchased eighteen thousand tons.[28] By 1898, Britain had taken over as Italy's largest customer, more than doubling imports of marble from Italy in twelve years; that year, Italy exported 161,259 tons of marble, 40,089 tons of which was sent to the United Kingdom and 39,857 to the United States.[29]

From 1880, Belgium also stepped up the production and export to Britain of St Ann's, Rouge and Belgian black marble.[30] The Belgians supplemented their indigenous marbles by importing a large quantity of rough French and Italian marble, working it and exporting it as 'Belgian' marble. Many of the ready-made marble goods produced went to Britain; 'a considerable trade is done in manufacturing marble goods, the principal market for which is found in England'.[31] In addition to Italy, France and Belgium, major sources for marble by 1915 included Greece and Africa, which all together provided a vast range of qualities and colours of marble.

Meanwhile, the huge marble resources in Britain remained largely unexploited; 'the bulk of the coloured marbles used in England find no employment for home labour'.[32] The explanation for this lay partly in Britain's Free Trade policy. Her position as the only duty-free country meant that other countries such as Italy could export to Britain more cheaply than elsewhere. Transport costs favoured foreign manufacturers: for example, whereas French and Belgian quarry owners paid very low rail charges in their own countries, the equivalent of 4s 5d per ton to transport rough marble on Belgian rail, British owners had to pay 12s 6d per ton by rail in Britain. Furthermore, foreign firms received preferential treatment in Britain itself, which led British manufacturers to complain that 'British railway charges effectively destroy all chance of developing the home industry'.[33] These disincentives for the development of a large British marble industry were set against the strength of a well-established, age-old tradition of marble working in countries like Italy. The commercial attitude of France and Belgium further reduced the need for the British to develop their trade: 'Both French and Belgians have shown persistence and energy in securing a market for themselves in this country'.[34] In effect, it was more economical and convenient for British manufacturers to import rough marble or ready-made goods.

Along with wood, the late-Victorian and Edwardian period saw a marked increase in the employment of metal for a host of old and new uses, its convenience, practicality, versatility and potential for varied and highly ornamented design ensuring its popular appeal. The price of iron fell to its lowest point in the 1890s,[35] which encouraged a proliferation of cheap cast-iron details for middle-class houses. The other metal trades also contributed greatly to the look of the Edwardian home. Stamping and other processes enabled the brass industry to produce ornate light-fixtures and fireplace and door furniture at reasonable prices by the end of the nineteenth century. When fashion swung under the impact of the Arts and Crafts Movement from glittering brass to homely, softer-toned copper, the industry responded with machines designed to achieve a hand-beaten effect on that metal. This process was commonly applied to light fittings and to door and fireplace furniture, and was described as the 'antique copper' look in trade catalogues. In the case of the steel industry, the decorative potential of stamping designs on sheet steel was to have major implications for the casting process, since a similar effect could be achieved at a much lower cost (see Appendix 2).

NEW TECHNOLOGY

Technical innovation created new substitute materials and products designed to save time and labour over traditional methods of working (see fig. 4.4). These innovations, however, displaced and de-skilled traditional trades and initiated a torrent of attack by the trade unions and resistance from workmen. Indeed, the success or failure of a new product depended on its acceptance by the workforce, as in the case of the sheet-metal ceiling (see pp. 139-41).

The decline of costly apprenticeship was another factor which threatened skills. London and the south-east were particularly affected and builders were forced to recruit from outside London, where a good system of training still operated. The traditional master/apprentice relationship became replaced by a technical-school system. For example, John Eliott writes in 1910 that 'During the last few years there has been a growing desire on the part of employers ... to improve the capabilities of young men in the painting trade. All over the country classes at technical schools have been established.'[36]

Although the technical processes of mass manufacture, use of machinery and importation of goods and materials enabled industry to meet market needs, standards of craftsmanship were generally perceived by certain sections of the press and other vehicles of public opinion to have fallen in comparison to the workmanship of previous centuries. Those inspired by the writings of Ruskin, Morris and others were highly critical of much speculative building. In 1882, Lucy Crane complained that 'most of our houses, have as little convenience, comfort etc., and as much pretension, ostentation, insecure workmanship, and inadequate material, as can be got into the contract'.[37] Mrs Panton also criticised the 'dilatoriness

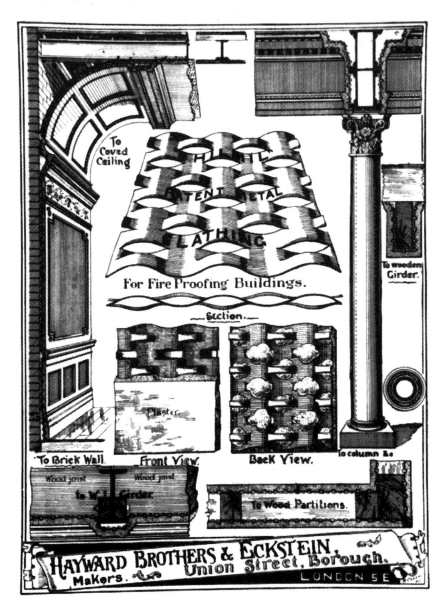

4·4
Advertisement for patent metal lathing, 1899

and utter worthlessness of many of the British workmen we are forced to employ, painters, as a rule, being the most unsatisfactory of all', and suggested that men who 'starve genteelly as clerks' would make much more honest workmen.[38] Where standards of work were poor, restrict-ive terms of employment, working conditions and training opportunities must have borne some reponsibility. The Socialist-Idealist Robert Tressell in *The Ragged Trousered Philanthropists*, 1906, described the demoralised workforce of a painting and decorating firm, Rushton and Co. of Mugsborough, working under a foreman who prepared the estimate and worked out how to 'scamp' on materials and labour in order to compete with firms like 'Smeeriton and Leavit'. Tressell described how slow, though thorough work, or the sudden availability of cheaper labour, could result in one hour's notice. This passage from Tressell argues the effect that employment pressures had on standards of work,

> In other parts of the same house the ceilings, the freizes, and the dadoes, were covered with 'embossed' or 'relief' papers. These hangings require very careful handling, for the raised parts are easily damaged; but the men who fixed them were not allowed to take the pains and time necessary to make good work: consequently in many places – especially at the joints – the pattern was flattened out and obliterated.... The ceiling of the drawing-room was done with a very thick high-relief paper that was made in sheets about two feet square. These squares were not very true in shape: they had evidently warped in drying after manufacture: to make them match anything like properly would need considerable time and care. But the men were not allowed to take the necessary time, The result was that when it was finished it presented a sort of 'higgledy-piggledy' appearance. But that didn't matter: nothing seemed to matter except to get it done.... These costly embossed decorations were usually finished in white; but instead of carefully coating them with specially prepared paint of patent distemper, which would need two or three coats, they slobbered one thick coat of common whitewash on to it with ordinary whitewash brushes, [which] ... filled up all the cracks but also filled up the hollow parts, the crevices and interstices of the ornament, destroying the sharp outlines of the beautiful designs and reducing the whole to a lumpy formless mass.[39]

But while the public generally held a poor view of the speculative builder and frequently equated him with the term 'jerry-builder', and while some bad housing certainly existed, Edwardian housing today bears witness to the very high quality of workmanship accomplished by speculative builders in this era. Charles Booth supported the view that much of the spec. builder's work was sound: 'uniformity of style and a resulting architectural dullness is the charge to be laid at his door, rather than inferior workmanship or the use of bad materials'.[40] Criticism of standardised design, prompted by the needs of large-scale production, abounded; for example, Walter Crane judged that 'the mass of modern London consists of the erections of the speculative builder – miles of absolutely uninteresting house fronts, composed chiefly of the repetition of one pattern, and that of the meanest and most uninventive kind, crowded together.'[41]

The writer Aldam Heaton laid the blame with the manufacturers, 'Each branch of manufacturing submits for selection a set of patterns at fixed prices, and it is vain to ask for anything outside the pale of "regular stock". We must choose what is made for the million'[42] and argued that, 'architects ... should ... design the ceiling, the frieze, the dado, the chimneypiece, the grate, the electric fittings, and not leave all these things to dribble into the hands of a set of uneducated shopkeepers, whose only interest is £. s. d.'. 'Novelty' is a word which crops up frequently by the late nineteenth century as a manufacturer's ploy to sell more goods, and many writers were wearily critical of it, 'Commercialism, perceiving a demand, brings out what it calls art-furniture, art-colours, and so on', 'a vain show of so-called "novelties" every season, whether they are really new and better than the old or not'.[43] There had been a huge upsurge in applications for patents after the 1852 and 1883 Patent Acts, which reduced dramatically the cost of protection. By the Edwardian period, renewal fees had to be paid for each year after the first four years to keep the patent in force. The copying of designs caused irritation among manufacturers, for instance, Young and Marten Ltd's catalogue of 1898 advises: 'we are obliged by the compliment paid us by competing houses in copying our previous issues of catalogues. We, however, trust that for the future they may strictly adhere to the lines of their own originality.'

But while the structural and organisational changes within the building industry, which had been necessary in order to meet the growth in demand for housing, certainly resulted in repetition and standardisation on the one hand, the developments in manufacturing methods also led to a greater variety of products overall and to increased possibilities of varied combination on the other hand and thus ultimately to greater diversity. Nowhere is this more apparent than when we look at the changes which occurred in the materials and components in late-Victorian and Edwardian housing.

THE HOUSES:
INTERIORS
AND
EXTERIORS

As suggested earlier, the late-Victorian and Edwardian period witnessed an unprecedented explosion in the amount and variety of decorative detailing inside and outside middle-class houses and in new technologies introduced into the home. There was also an overall increase in the types of decorations available over the period; while some items, such as ceiling roses, began to go out of fashion, many more new product types were added to the builder's repertoire, for example, overdoors and cosy corners. The 'new' products were often adaptations of past styles which were new only in the sense that they were applied for the first time at a mass level. There were also changes in the popularity of certain materials, with, frequently, an association between particular materials and styles, for example, the increased use of wood reflected the influence of the Queen Anne revival and Arts and Crafts styles. House fittings, or fixtures,[1] were more widely available from the 1890s, with more choice within each product type to suit different needs and pockets, and, while standardisation was necessarily a response to cope with increased demand, the possibilities of unique combinations of features brought ultimately greater variety in the decoration of houses. Overall, a tendency towards increased complexity and ornateness coincided with a strong counter-tendency towards simplicity at the top end of the market, which eventually became the dominant trend after the First World War.

The following chapters take you through the exterior and interior of the Edwardian house, detailing reasons for the particular design choices made – either by the home owner or the builder – and outline the many varieties of decoration that were on offer.

5

EXTERIORS

5.1
Middle-range housing in
Herne Hill, late 1890s

Fluctuations in the use of various materials for exterior walling and external decorative detailing throughout the period related to swings in architectural fashion, regional preferences, cost and availability.

The stone industry generally declined over the period 1850 to 1914, due in part to a growing preference for processed rather than natural materials.[1] Stone was widely employed for housing in some areas, notably York, Bath, Bristol and Weston-super-Mare. Following the example of William Burges, Cardiff made particularly elaborate use of stonework, for example, medium-sized Edwardian houses combine rubble with pressed-brick facing and polished granite shafts.[2] Ready-made details in Bath stone were transported by rail to Winchester, Portsmouth and Southampton, and identical designs can be found in all three areas.[3]

Unlike the stone industry, the brick trade expanded dramatically in the Victorian and Edwardian period: it superseded all other walling materials by the First World War, and it accounted for nearly one half of the total building costs.[4] Its popularity was due in part to the availability of brick earth close to most large towns, and even where stone was readily available, brick was often used in preference.[5] Brick production in 1907 was more than double that of fifty years before.[6] Taking the price of bricks over the nineteenth century as a whole, it did not alter much, the price of bricks in the mid 1890s not being very different from that of the 1820s – £6 per thousand for high-quality products for arches.[7] The Fletton brick industry developed in the 1880s, undercutting the small traditional brickyards, and capitalising on the increase in the level of housebuilding which began in the early 1890s and grew in intensity until 1898. Between 1895 and 1900, demand led to the establishment of no less than nine new brick companies in the Peterborough area, in addition to the expansion of already established firms, in response to panicky press reports such as that in the *Peterborough Standard* of 1897, 'A brick famine threatens London. The Grand Central Railway, the new City and Waterloo Railway, and the Electric Railway from the City to the West End have used up nearly all the available stock. Prices have risen 2s and 3s a thousand, much to the consternation of the speculative builder.'[8]

Perhaps more than any other material, brick sums up the look of the late-Victorian and Edwardian speculatively built suburban house. Brick fell from the status position it held in the seventeenth and eighteenth centuries to a low point between 1820 and 1840, when better-class houses were faced with stone substitutes such as stucco. Brick was revived by the architects of the High Victorian period, who used different coloured bricks together to form decorative patterns, flush to the wall surface in keeping with Gothic revival ideas about 'honesty' in

5.2
Top-quality housing in
Penarth, near Cardiff

materials and construction. In the 1870s, bright red brick was used by the Queen Anne revival architects for large houses and thereafter filtered down to be universally used for middle-class houses. The colour of brick was often chosen, not only according to availability, but also in relation to class of house or status within the house; for instance, cheap red bricks might be used for the less important back of the house. The more expensive grey 'stock' might cover the front, with windows and doorway arches trimmed with top-quality yellow 'malms', as in London houses of the 1880s.[9]

While red brick remained the most common colour of brick outside London, there were many local variations, for example, the white-ish bricks of Cambridge, Lowestoft and Ipswich, the silver-grey bricks of Reading and the grey-purple bricks common to Luton.[10] Builders especially in the later nineteenth century used different coloured bricks to denote fine degrees of status between houses, even smaller ones. Examples of the polychromatic use of brick include Reading's combinations of silver grey, red, yellow and black and Luton's purple/dark grey bricks used with red trim.[11] Some of these areas' local preferences persisted despite the fashion for uniform red brickwork which dominated most of the rest of the country by the twentieth century.

Regular, machine-made bricks were normally preferred to uneven hand-made ones.[12] Mechanical brickmaking had begun in the 1820s and was commonplace by the 1850s. Pressed brickmaking, which produced a smooth finish similar to dressed bricks, began in 1831, and the process was later cheapened through mechanisation. Firms in Ruabon, near Wrexham, produced the bright red and buff yellow pressed bricks used in Reading, Cardiff and Newcastle.[13] Cities such as Liverpool, Manchester and Birmingham also used pressed brickwork on a large scale. With the growth in the employment of pressed brick, by 1900 some firms were advertising hand-made bricks for high-class work, and better houses in Cambridge, for example, were faced on the front with such bricks while cheaper pressed bricks were reserved for the back.[14]

Terracotta and moulded brick typified the middle-class house of the late-Victorian and Edwardian period, following its place as an important feature of the Queen Anne revival style. With the manufacture of moulded brick by firms such as Prosser of Birmingham in the 1840s, the use of ornaments became available to a wider market. Leicester witnessed the use of ornamental brickwork on a wide scale, beginning with the better houses in the Walk of the 1860s. Liverpool, Birmingham and Nottingham also favoured ornamental brick, as in Princes Avenue in Liverpool of the late 1880s.[15] Similarly, elaborate panels of flowers or cherubs can be found between bays or above doorways of medium-sized houses in late-Victorian and Edwardian Brighton. Terracotta, developed from Coadestone of the late eighteenth century, came into its own from the 1860s. It was sold by firms such as Blashfield's of Stamford, and Hathern Station Brick and Terracotta Co.,

Top-of-the-range house,
Manchester

PLATE 7

Detached house, Manchester

PLATE 8

Detached house, Manchester

PLATE 9

Semi-detached houses,
Manchester

Detached house,
Manchester

PLATES 10 & 11

Leicestershire, and by the very end of the century cheap kinds of terracotta were in common use around doors and windows of medium-sized houses especially in the south east.[16]

One of the materials to enjoy a flowering in the late-Victorian and Edwardian period was stucco. Stucco had slipped in and out of favour in a dramatic way over the course of the century. Its peak had occurred in the 1830s, and, under the impact of the fashion for the Gothic revival which shunned stucco, its use fell to a low in the 1870s and 1880s. It was revived at the end of the century as part of the Queen Anne revival and Arts and Crafts styles. The appeal of stucco lay in the fact that its cost was only one-third that of stone.[17] It was very popular in the early nineteenth century in London and on the south coast; about mid century it spread to other parts of the country, for example Bristol;[18] and by the third quarter of the century areas like Cheltenham, Plymouth, Eastbourne and Hastings were dominated by stucco-covered houses.[19] It was used for wall surfaces, as in 'rusticated' frontages in London, or for corner 'quoining', as in Brighton. Frequently, stucco was used in the form of small heads, figures or scroll brackets to doors and windows. The stucco revival at the end of the century involved, on the one hand, the imitation of older vernacular methods such as pargetting, as can be seen in Muswell Hill houses (see fig. 5.3), and on the other hand

5.3
Good-quality housing in Muswell Hill, built in 1903 by Charles Rook

5.4
Houses in Woodberry
Crescent, Muswell Hill,
about 1905

5.5
Houses built around 1908 in
Poplar Walk, Herne Hill

roughcasting, using cement and coarse sand, used, for example, with mock half-timbering in Brighton and Southend from the 1890s.[20] After about 1910, roughcasting using cement and small stones, that is, pebble-dashing, used in combination with brick, tile-hanging and exterior woodwork, became popular and superseded all other surface treatments, for example, houses on the Rookfield estate in Muswell Hill. Pebble-dashing went on to epitomise speculative housing of the period between the wars all over Britain. Such trends are vividly described by H. G. Wells in *Ann Veronica*, written in 1909:

> Morningside Park was a suburb that had not altogether, as people say, come off.... There was first the Avenue, which ran in a consciously elegant curve from the railway station into an undeveloped wilderness of agriculture, with big yellow brick villas on either side, and then there was the Pavement, the little clump of shops about the post office, and under the railway arch was a congestion of workmen's dwellings. The road from Surbiton to Epsom ran under the arch, and, like a bright fungoid growth in the ditch, there was now appearing a sort of fourth estate of little red-and-white rough-cast villas, with meretricious gables and very brassy window blinds.[21]

DOORWAYS AND WINDOWS

The most prominent and often the most decorated area of the exterior was the doorway, which echoed general architectural trends on a miniature scale, while in some cases maintaining local traditions concerning materials and styles. The wooden, brick, stucco or stone porticoes of Regency houses gave way in the mid nineteenth century to the positioning of the porch inside the doorway following the disappearance of the basement area. The door-surround was often decorated with stone or terracotta ornaments, as in the case of larger houses of the 1890s in Cardiff and London. Smaller houses used moulded-brick or cement details, foliage and heads, or later on broken pediments after the Queen Anne style, which were then stuccoed or painted.

The front-door area had become generally less pretentious than the middle of the century, if no less decorated, as builders took on more modest motifs from the Arts and Crafts and art nouveau styles. Medium-sized and even small houses in Cardiff also had doorcases of carved stone in the form of a flat Tudor arch, surrounding angled and tile and stained glass decorated side parts connecting the frame to the front door. Porches or doorcases were revived around 1900, inspired by the Queen Anne style or the picturesque cottage ornée, for example, Bedford Park houses of the 1880s. Queen Anne style canopies, incorporating shell motifs, can be found in the best class of house in Muswell Hill, for instance. Prefabricated wooden porches were available from large joinery firms; those on Edwardian medium-sized houses in Cardiff had simple Arts and Crafts motifs cut out in a cottage style shielding an inner porch richly decorated with a floor-to-ceiling tile panel design. Elaborate tiled porches to dado or ceiling height were common in Cardiff houses, particularly after 1900, and the decoration on the tiles, with Aesthetic Movement, classical revival or art nouveau motifs, offered the builder a cheap and easy means of lending a house an up-to-date appearance (see plate 19). Large and medium houses in Herne Hill have very elaborate cottagey wooden porches with brackets and spindles and red-tiled hip or pitch roofs; varying sizes either single, for detached houses, or double, for terraces, were clearly obtained from the same merchant. In Muswell Hill, builders used wooden porches inspired by exotic styles, using fretwork and other decorative effects, in large and medium houses between 1897 and 1905. Thereafter in this area simpler wooden porches in the manner of Voysey were used instead. Porches were also manufactured in cast iron, such as John Russell Ltd's (about 1910) single cast-iron porch at £9 19s; a double porch spanning two house doorways cost £14 5s. Small cast-iron porches, often in the art nouveau style, roofed with glass or tiles and arranged singly or spanning two adjoining front doors, were common in small and medium houses in Cardiff and the south-west by the Edwardian period.

5.6 *left*
Edwardian doorways with wooden canopies and tiled porches, Cardiff

5.7
Design for a porch by Paul Hasluck, 1910

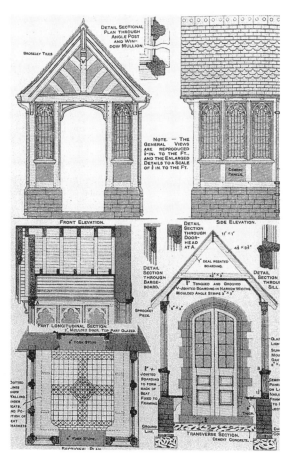

5.8
Top-quality housing in
Muswell Hill, late 1890s

5.9 *right*
Design for a cast-iron porch
by William Pryor and Co.,
1913

Balconies had gone out of fashion in the nineteenth century with the withdrawal from participation in the life of the street, but, following the popularity of balconies and verandahs in seaside towns as part of the Sanitary Movement, enjoyed a revival at the end of the century. Part of a general move towards the greater employment of wood inside and outside larger houses, encouraged by the 'Old English' style, timber features dominated larger houses around 1900 in Ramsgate, Southend, Brighton and Bournemouth.[22] After 1900, balconies combined with doors and windows assumed a new importance, as can be seen in large houses in Cardiff where the increased width of the house allowed for a door opening on a balcony in the centre of the house. The vogue for fresh air and country views inspired firms to offer combination porch and balcony features, such as Young and Marten's model costing £9 7s 6d. Some writers, however, while noting that, 'balconies are sometimes useful, especially when opening off a landing and taking a good view', cautioned 'it is well to avoid anything of a brittle construction, and to steer clear of the amazing and uncomfortable-looking fretwood treatment affected by some speculative builders'.[23] Smaller houses of this period, for instance in Cardiff, frequently had small balconies, although they were often purely decorative, not actually performing any practical function.

With the increasing width of houses as the internal plan of the average house began to change, front doors of medium and large houses often acquired side windows, frequently leaded, on one or both sides of the front door. The front door itself on a top-quality house might be teak or oak, while smaller houses would tend to have a soft-wood door, painted green in the Victorian period and a wider selection of colours after 1900. Following the lead by the Queen Anne revivalists, white paint was particularly fashionable. While smaller houses would lead directly into a hallway from the front door, top-quality houses often had a vestibule leading to double inner doors and a hallway inside the porch and its ornamentally glazed and heavily panelled front door. Prices of these inner doors, or 'vestibule screens' as they were called, varied; C. Jennings' of Bristol offered a selection ranging from £2 to £13 depending on the design and quality of wood used (see fig. 8.1).

The most archetypal Victorian and Edwardian window form was the bay window. Technology and economics had a major impact on window form between 1880 and 1914. With the abolition of the Window Tax in 1851 and the repeal of the duty on glass in 1857, the twelve-pane eighteenth-century sash windows had been superseded around mid century by four or six upright panes.[24] The most widely used type of glass was sheet glass introduced in 1838. Later, Patent Rolled Rough Plate was also used widely. The price of glass fell between 1840 and 1910 by two thirds; in the 1890s sheet glass cost 4^{1}/$_{2}$d to 1s 8d per square foot.[25]

The new large window pane was commonly used for sash windows, which were often then grouped together to form a bay window. Jennings sold eighteen different designs for sash pairs by 1914, comprising varied combinations of plain and leaded-light designs, plus square, 'segment', or semi-circular-headed windows. The bay window had been introduced in the late eighteenth century by Gothic architects for their country houses and villas.[26] As with the balcony, the bay's revival was linked to the fashion for fresh air, especially in seaside resorts, and around the mid 1860s the bay covering one or more storeys became popular for suburban housing, partly because it made more space available at the front of the house. The large bay window came to epitomise middle-class status, and was regarded as an asset worth mentioning in advertisements for fairly well-to-do houses even in London in 1905, long after it had come into common use. A range of complete bay windows could be bought from large firms ready for fixing, for example Jennings' various designs costing from £2 7s 6d to £3 15s a pair of bay windows over two storeys with panelling between cost £9.

As the bay spread to smaller houses, the architects of the domestic revival, in seeking to create a new cosy domestic ideal, reintroduced small panes and sometimes used the old-fashioned casement frame. The fashion spread and by the Edwardian period small panes and casements were in common use in all fashionable housing schemes, such as the Rookfield Estate in Hornsey, built by the Collins family in the early twentieth century. 'Casement bay' windows were on sale from Jennings of Bristol in 1914. Norman Shaw had also used the sash window in his architecture of the 1870s, and windows for standard housing generally represented a compromise between a large single-paned lower sash for vision and light and small, divided upper lights to create a cosy image, often with leaded lights in medium and best houses. The bay window area, in particular, was often highlighted by decorative detailing, such as elaborate polychromatic brickwork or cement-rendered dressings combined with brick on the piers even on small houses. Queen Anne broken pediments appeared above such windows in Cardiff and Herne Hill. Local traditions died hard: for example, elaborate carved wood was widely used to decorate bay windows in houses in York, Grimsby and Hull, because of the strong shipbuilding tradition in these localities.[27]

The bay continued to be used in all sizes of houses in the Edwardian period, although in larger houses it widened and divided into more sections, which might be seperated by heavy stone mullions, as can be found in Cardiff, for example. Looking beyond the bay, sash and casement trends, other types of window were added to the repertoire in the later nineteenth and early twentieth centuries; these included the oriel window, (costing £5 5s from Jennings of Bristol), which can be seen in Edwardian houses in Herne Hill, and under the influence of the Arts and Crafts movement small, triangular-sectioned windows became popular, along with the irregular arrangement generally of windows. Edwardian housing of a medium or good standard also used the 'bow' (curved bay) window. One finds examples of bow windows in Penylan, Cardiff, and very elaborate examples on top-quality houses overlooking Roath Lake, Cardiff, and in Penarth near Cardiff.

The introduction of the bay window called for new solutions to the roof to cover the bay. By the 1870s and '80s the heavily bargeboarded gable had percolated from the cottage ornée to the villa and semi-detached house in places as far apart as Harrogate, Sheffield and Bristol,[28] and by the new century the most common solution for the standard house was to use an enlarged gable, topped with an elaborate terracotta finial, bounded and supported by decorative wooden bargeboarding and large brackets, and filled in with red-tile hanging, or roughcast with mock half-timbering. The use of slate on roofs reached a peak at the very end of the nineteenth century; pantiles were rejected in favour of slate and thus can be found on less desirable parts of a building, but in the early Edwardian years slate itself faced stiff competition from coloured asbestos-cement tiles.[29]

6

LIGHTING, HEATING
AND PLUMBING

THE CHARM OF ELECTRICITY

Electric light is the only light for a really neat and comfortable bedroom.
Electric heat (from a luminous radiator) is the only suitable source of warmth.

6.1
Advertisement for electric
lighting and heating in the
Watford Bulletin, early
twentieth century

One important characteristic of the late Victorian and Edwardian middle-class house was the introduction of new technologies into the home. They revolutionised the life-styles of those inhabitants who adopted them and generally ushered in the potential for massive changes in decor in the new century. Most people did not have access to these innovations until much later, as many landlords were unable or unwilling to up-date their homes. But new forms of lighting, heating and plumbing were in theory within reach of the middle-classes, certainly after 1900, and they became regarded as highly desirable status symbols to be shown off and demonstrated to visitors. Coinciding with the rise of home ownership, the falling cost of installing these new technologies must have had a major impact on their inclusion into the home. The stress on health and convenience ensured the popularity of such services. Mrs Peel in 1902 reflected, 'it is more important for a house to be sanitary than to be beautiful'.[1] She went on, 'It is only of late years that it has been fully recognised how much sunlight affects our health', and advised readers to let in the light and avoid heavy drapes and thick window blinds and to keep the house dust-free, for 'therein the microbe is most likely to abound',[2] a reference to current thinking about how germs were carried.[3] While servants were easily available to do the work of cleaning and carrying water, the incentive to install new systems might have been reduced for some, but the 'servant problem' after 1900 necessitated the introduction of labour-saving systems and materials into the home.

ARTIFICIAL LIGHTING

The period 1880 to 1914 saw the widespread introduction of gas lighting and, towards the end, serious competition from electric lighting. Gas lighting began to be introduced into homes in the 1830s, and by 1885 there were two million consumers in England and Wales.[4] Following the introduction of the one-penny-slot gas meter by the 1890s, the market broadened and by 1918, half a million houses were connected.[5] The main advantage of gas over conventional methods of lighting by candles and oil was the greater efficiency and convenience afforded, as gas produced five to ten times the amount of light and could be fixed in every room.[6] But despite the increased benefits of gas, it was still rather wasteful, unreliable and dirty; its fumes ruined books and pictures and blackened ceilings, which, together with smuts from coal fires, made annual spring-cleaning a necessity; this process involved massive upheaval which lasted a week, even with a charwoman employed specially to do the job. For health reasons, gas was considered unsuitable for use in bedrooms.[7] 'There is a widespread dislike of gas-lighting in England, where nobody is prepared to use gas-lights anywhere except in halls and domestic offices for fear of the dirt caused by soot and recognition of the danger to health that arises from piping gas into the room.'[8] Mrs Haweis, when comparing gas to oil and candles, pointed to a further problem encountered with gas, that of managing unflattering cast shadows; 'Gas is the cheapest and the least trouble, but it is the most destructive to furniture and pictures, the least healthy, and the least becoming.… The main light then should come from above so as to ensure some shadows somewhere, but minor lights should diffuse a comfortable and becoming clearness, sufficient to cheer, but not impertinently criticise.'[9]

The popularisation of electric light was looked forward to eagerly; Mrs Panton referred to 'the present odious system of lighting by gas' and urged readers 'never to have gas anywhere where they can avoid using it, and to pray heartily for that bright day to dawn when the electric light shall be within the reach of all'.[10] After independent discoveries of the electric carbon-filament lamp by Swan in 1878 and a longer-lasting version by Edison in 1879, the first public supplies were established in Brighton and Holborn, London, in 1882. Its potential appeal to consumers lay in the fact that a lot of the problems encountered with gas were potentially solved; in 1914, one writer declared 'In the way of convenience, hygiene, and beauty, electric light is undoubtedly the best illuminant.'[11] Electricity was arguably more economical due to 'the extreme facility with which the switches can be turned off and on',[12] compared to gas where small jets had to be kept on or the matchbox searched for in the dark.

The cleanliness of electric light saved the labour of continually repapering, repainting and cleaning curtains and carpets, an essential attribute of the future servantless house. Indeed, the cleanliness and increased brilliance of electric lighting were major factors in the feasibility of lighter colour schemes promoted for room decoration in homes in the Edwardian period. Mrs Haweis predicted this in the 1880s:

> a revolution in dress-colours and wall-colours will doubtless follow its [electric light] introduction in private houses, for some of our now fashionable colours, especially intended for use by the yellow light of gas, are greatly altered under the electric rays.… Blues and peacock-greens become painfully vivid; while yellow, which nearly disappears under gas, keeps its natural colour.[13]

Now that paler colours were practically possible in the electric house, people were persuaded that money could be saved on lamps because less illumination was needed than for the previous darker room schemes; for example, in 1909, a room with a white ceiling and cream walls was calculated to be as light with thirty-three candles as the same room with eighty-seven candles if the walls were covered in brown oak panelling or maroon paint.[14] Even so, by our standards, the light was still weak, the most popular lamp being 16 candle-power, the equivalent of a 25-watt bulb today.[15]

There was much contemporary excitement about the potential of this new technology; *The London Globe*, 15 February 1882, reported on the Electrical Exhibition at the Crystal Palace, 'its universal adoption must be held to be an absolute certainty', although it provoked resistance from some in fashionable society, prejudiced by their encounters with the stark blue light of the electric arc lamp used in ballrooms and other public places in Britain in the 1870s; as R. Hammond reported, 'two or three noble ladies preferred to sit in the shade during the whole of the evening, rather than dance in the full effulgence of the arc light'.[16] Notices from the time indicate that fears about electric light were quite general and remind us of the strangeness of this new technology at the time:

> This Room is equipped with *Edison Electric Light*. Do not attempt to light with a match. Simply turn the key on the wall by the door. (The use of electricity for lighting is in no way harmful to health, nor does it affect the soundness of sleep.)

Despite initial acclaim and the enthusiastic predictions of writers on the home, the spread of electric light in homes was slow before 1900 on account of its cost and the difficulty of installation. In the 1890s, electric-light installations varied widely in price, the average for a fifty-lamp system for an office or larger house being £100. (But if there was no access to a public electricity supply, a private generator with dynamo, cables, fittings, accumulator and steam, gas or oil engine could add another £300 to the cost.)[17] The price fell as more areas were connected and the increase in the number of consumers reduced the average cost. By 1904, it was reported that electric light was 'becoming more and more general'.[18] By 1913, most new medium to large houses had it installed, as the price had fallen to one ninth of the 1891 price.[19] Despite the fall in the price of electricity, however, gas was still cheaper (though some sources suggested that, if managed economically, electric lighting was no more expensive than gas).[20] Lighting thus became a class issue; those who could afford it seized on the advantages offered by electric light, and it became a fashionable status item, as house advertisements show.

The gas industry fought back. A new technical innovation in 1885 which was on the market two years later was the more efficient Welsbach burner and incandescent mantle using silk or cotton fabric impregnated with chemicals (thoria and ceria) rather than metallic substances. This became the main weapon in the fight against electricity in the 1890s. The problem of shadows cast on the ground by the upright gas mantle was also solved at that time with the invention of the inverted mantle, 'a downward light free from shadows'.[21] Additionally, in an effort to compete with the convenience of electric light, the gas industry brought out gas switches, such as the pneumatic gas switch, which relied on a gas pilot light to work the gas valve from a switch on the wall by the door instead of turning the light on manually.

The battle between these two industries and the move from gas to electric lighting among the middle classes is illustrated well if we consider Hornsey, north London, which, until 1903, was lit by the Gas Light and Coke Company, the Hornsey Gas Company, and the Borough Council. The gas industry began to lose consumers to the Hornsey Electrical Supply Board as established roads were connected to electric supply (initiated by written requests received from individual residents or after builders had canvassed a road). Electrical installations began in 1903 and users of electric light in Hornsey grew rapidly from 126 in 1903 to 1113 in 1907.[22] Electric light became a major selling point for houses and was clearly associated with the better class of house. Speaking of Park Road in Hornsey, the Hornsey Supply Board commented, 'generally, the houses in the road are not of a class to take a supply'.[23] *Healthy Hornsey*, 1905, argued that electricity cost no more than gas, was cleaner and more convenient and did no damage to pictures and rooms;[24] 'nearly every house now built is wired for electricity, a large and growing number of householders are substituting the light for the gas which had previously darkened their ceilings and wallpapers'. The electricity board determined that advertisements would take place 'before the spring decorations commence'[25] to attract those who dreaded the annual spring cleaning necessitated by gas lighting.

The gas companies fought a rearguard action, issuing pamphlets and offering premiums to builders who would pipe for gas in the process of building. The Hornsey Electricity Supply Board similarly began a campaign of offering premiums to builders who would wire houses for electricity rather than pipe for gas. Builders, estate agents and wiring contractors were also sent information, advertisements for electricity were put in the local papers and the Board put on local exhibitions of electrical fittings, lamps and appliances. A hire-purchase system was also launched to increase the number of consumers, free technical advice was available and satisfactory installations were guaranteed, a reference to the significant number of notoriously untrained 'electricians' in Britain.

Even by 1914 the majority of houses still had neither gas nor electric lighting. To the lower-middle classes living in Tottenham, gas was still sufficiently novel to mention in house advertisements. C. H. Rolph records how, to a policeman's family living in a house in Stroud Green on £1 8s a week in 1906, gas light was a luxury, and, even then, how many households used naked jets rather than gas mantles.[26] This class of householder was aided by the introduction of the penny-slot meter, and it was not until 1914 that fierce competition between gas and electricity began to affect this market.

Designs for gas and electric fittings were the result of technological imperative, convention and fashion. A common gas fitting type was the ceiling-pendant, either single or with a crossbar holding two burners (one with three or more arms was called a 'gasolier'). Billiard-rooms had a three-light pendant, while hallways usually had a central single rod pendant. Wall brackets, often either side of a fireplace, were either at a right angle to the wall, fixed, swivelled or jointed to extend out into the room, or were curved in a sideways-on 'S' shape. The dining-room usually had a centre light above the table, while brackets on side walls were common in the drawing-room and the study. The technical characteristics of gas determined the design of the fittings: for instance, adjustable pendants, to be lowered when needed, were introduced to get around the problem of insufficient light for some tasks, and what light there was shining upwards on the ceiling rather than downwards on the task. By 1900, adjustable pendants had become so popular that 'rise and fall' pendants were introduced, which operated on a counterweight principle, with either a movable joint on the down rod connected to a crossbar with the lamp on one end and a sliding weight on the other, or a spring-reel device holding a flexible extending tube.[27] With the invention of the inverted incandescent mantle, 'swan neck' fittings became common. The design of lampshades was governed by the dual need of increasing lighting levels, yet diffusing and softening it. The typical shade of the 1870s and 1880s consisted of a large globe with an open top, the surface either clear rippled glass, or various combinations of clear, frosted (acid etching, stencil etching or cut) and opaque milk glass. The range of shapes used for shades expanded as the technology changed and new materials, such as supastone, were used to soften the light. Holophane (prism) shades became very popular as a means of increasing the light. The force of tradition was evident in the popularity of fittings designed to resemble candles and oil lamps.

The early electroliers provided direct light in the manner of a chandelier or gasolier, but the electric light bulb brought potential new freedom for designers of electric fittings. Designers did not take up the challenge immediately; rise-and-fall mechanisms, chandeliers with three or five arms, wall brackets and even combination gas and electric fittings illustrate the newness of electric light and the power of the familiar. Also the novelty of the early electric bulb led designers to expose it or incorporate it as the stamen of a flower fitting rather than shield it. But the bright light of electric lighting compared to gas meant that direct light seemed too glaring. In the later nineteenth century, W. A. S. Benson recognised the need to diffuse the light using reflectors, screens and shades. He developed his innovatory, simple, Arts-and-Crafts-inspired designs in brass and copper to fulfil the need for fittings which would direct strong but not glaring light for specific tasks, as well as fittings which would create general lighting in a room. He had little faith in 'the ordinary builder … with little enough regard to enduring safety, with still less to economy of use, and least of all to artistic effect'.[28] His influence at home and abroad was huge, with many manufacturers and designers bringing out designs along similar lines. In 1915 a writer commented that, 'Of late years a great deal of attention has also been devoted to the design of fixtures with a view to the distribution of light

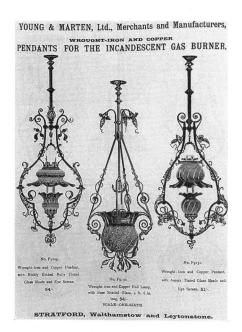

6.2
Gas fittings by Young and Marten, about 1898

6.3
Wm Whiteley, electric light fittings, about 1910

94

in the most efficient manner.'[29] Direct lighting thus gave way to other methods of lighting, which created softer and more diffused effects: 'The indirect and semi-indirect systems of lighting represent a typically modern development.'[30] The material and decoration of lampshades also moderated the light emitted; rectangular lanterns were thought to diffuse light better than a globe, and a shade of clear crystal with facets worked best of all; clear glass obstructed eleven per cent of the light, engraved glass fourteen to eighteen per cent, ground glass thirty per cent, and plain opal was the least effective, cutting out fifty-five per cent of the light.[31] Catalogues show fittings in a range of styles, including classical revival styles, art nouveau and Arts and Crafts (see fig. 6.3). *The Illuminating Engineer* was concerned about appropriate design: 'in dealing with interiors of a distinctive period the appearance of the fixture is just as important as the illuminating efficiency', arguing that the fixture should be considered for its appearance when lit as well as by daylight and its colour should harmonise with the walls of the room, and suggested that 'the incongruity is lessened if the modernity of the source can be concealed'.[32] The future course of domestic lighting was thus set in our period, where developments led W. Shaw Sparrow to declare in *The British Home of Today*, 1904, that 'the most modern of decorative essentials is the electric light fitting'.

THE BATHROOM

At a pinch it might be possible to live a tranquil, and even a useful, life without a drawing room. It might be possible, under stress of circumstances, to make one room serve the purpose of both breakfast room and dining room. But there is one room which no self-respecting householder can do without, and that is the bathroom.[33]

In the 1870s, most small and medium-sized houses and about one half of larger ones were built without a bathroom. As S. Stevens Hellyer remarked in 1877 in *The Plumber and Sanitary Houses*, 'Instead of a bath in a house being the exception, it ought to be the rule.'[34] Portable baths were the norm, commonly the iron hip-bath, which was painted to resemble marble on the inside. This method of bathing was acceptable as long as there were servants to do the work of carrying the water back and forth. In addition to this, from the late eighteenth century, the bedroom would have a free-standing marble-topped washstand, to which a tiled splashback was later added; a servant's version would have an oilcloth-covered top rather than marble.[35]

With the arrival of running water after 1870, the bath and wash-stand became fixtures, contained in a seperate bathroom. In the 1880s, the possession of a bathroom was regarded as a status symbol. Most better-class new houses in inner London of £100 rental or more and those of £50 rental in the suburbs were built with a bathroom. After 1900 all but the smallest London houses and six- and seven-roomed

houses in the provinces were built with an upstairs bathroom. Initially, many bathrooms were simply converted bedrooms, and those which were purpose-built had comparatively large floor areas, similar to regular bedrooms. The bathroom was treated as a furnished room, with ornamental woodwork, wallpaper, stained glass, curtains and carpets. Catalogues show fixtures spaciously arranged around the room. A bowl was recessed into the marble top to create a wash-basin and the front was wood-panelled to disguise untidy pipes, so it still looked like a piece of furniture. The early fixed baths, available only to the well off, were again encased in panelled woodwork and had a wood-framed tiled splashback and sometimes a shower cabinet.

The bathroom was increasingly in demand by the middle classes also and firms such as Jennings, Twyfords, Shanks, Adams and Bolding produced lavish colour catalogues showing bathroom designs to suit a range of pockets. A washstand from John Russell Ltd in about 1910 cost £3–£5, while Wm Whiteley Ltd's porcelain enamelled shower and bath combined cost £25. The well-equipped bathroom in the early Edwardian period had a 'bath, shower-bath, wash-basin, hip-bath, heated towel-rail, mirror, clothes-hooks, a shelf for towels and a receptacle for used towels',[36] in contrast to the simplest basic schemes. Catalogues also often showed a toilet in the scheme, but in practice, when a house was large enough to have an indoor toilet, it tended to be

6.4
Design for a well-equipped bathroom of 1904 by Beaven and Sons, London

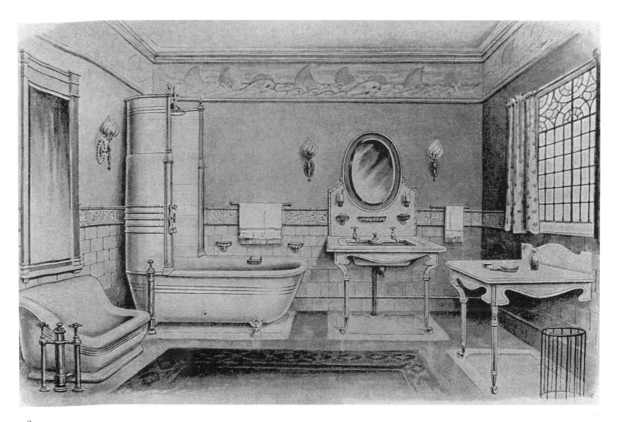

housed in a separate room; 'a lavatory is practically never found in an English bathroom',[37] said Hermann Muthesius in 1904. He praised the industry, 'English fittings are celebrated everywhere.... The continuing development of this field in England is in the hands of a few influential manufacturers.... Shanks at Barrhead and Doulton in London, whose catalogues are the best guide to the present state of development of the bathroom.'[38] Beaven and Sons, sanitary-ware makers of London, concluded the same year that 'perhaps few trades connected with the essential comforts of British homes have shown more rapid advance than that which is noticeable in Modern Plumbing'.

The needs of cheap, large-scale production brought about changes in materials and design. In particular, cast-iron brought bathroom fittings within reach of a wider market. The wash-stand developed into an earthenware basin set into an iron frame, either free-standing on metal legs, or attached to the wall on brackets. As with other cast-iron fixtures in the home, here was an opportunity to decorate, and so iron frames and legs, often 'enamelled oak, rosewood, walnut or marble', appeared in fashionable styles from baroque revival to art nouveau. Young and Marten's catalogue of 1898 showed a range of wash-stands, or 'lavatories' as they were known, in various designs to suit modern and more conventional tastes, from the wood-cased scheme incorporating an earthenware sink with a tiled back and a mirror, to elaborate cast-iron art nouveau designs.

The cast-iron bath was introduced around 1880,[39] bringing the fixed bath within reach of a wider market, so that by 1904, 'enamelled cast-iron is frequently used in cheaper bathrooms'.[40] To begin with, its top edge was flat and surmounted with a wooden rim; later on the roll top without a wooden rim was introduced. Until enamel paints were improved around 1910, the bath needed continual repainting, as the enamel could not withstand the heat. In *The Diary of a Nobody*, Mr Pooter illustrates vividly the disastrous consequences of having a bath before his red enamel paintwork was properly dry:

> Bath ready – could scarcely bear it so hot. I persevered and got in; very hot, but very acceptable. I lay still for some time. On moving my hand above the surface of the water, I experienced the greatest fright I have ever received in the whole course of my life; for imagine my horror on discovering my hand, as I thought, full of blood.... I looked like Marat in the bath, in Madame Tussaud's.[41]

Marble veining was a common interior finish, as it had been for portable baths, but the outside was now available in a wider range of colours and decorative patterns (see plate 12). It was recommended that, while the porcelain bath was more luxurious and comfortable, cast iron was preferable, especially where water was drawn from the kitchen range. The standard bath which became available to the mass market by 1910 was the cast-iron single shell bath, enamelled on the inside only and painted on the outside or boxed in. For those without a fixed bath or bathroom, John Russell Ltd's 'Tala' tip-up bath for 'Villas, bungalows and artisan dwellings' folded away into a cupboard when not in use.

After 1900 the size of the bathroom shrank and took on a design identity of its own. Even in large houses, it became preferable, instead of having one bathroom to be shared by all, to have several small bathrooms to cater for the family and servants separately. The elaborate furnishings of the earlier bathrooms disappeared, to be replaced, even in large houses, by simple, unadorned, white enamel fittings all fixed to one wall,[42] and, if affordable, by walls covered with marble facing, tiles, washable wallpaper in a tile design or waterproof paint, and by a marble, tiled, cork or tile-design linoleum floor. An example of a scheme for the bathroom of 1909 comprised 'Dado of white tiles; pink-and-white paper above; pale-green or white paint, and green cork-carpet.'[43] What underpinned this change was the concern that homes should not only be healthy but should also *appear* healthy. 'In good bathrooms in the past the bath used regularly to be encased in wood; but the custom has now [1904] ceased entirely and all parts are expected to be accessible for cleaning purposes.'[44] Householders were being advised by 1914 to choose fittings which were 'simple in construction and easy to clean ... modern sanitarians condemn woodwork enclosures to any of these fittings'.[45] The easy-to-clean fireclay pedestal basin replaced the 'composite' form and the all-metal combined shower and bath replaced the wood-encased version, with a trend towards separating the shower and bath altogether. Such an image would have been previously thought appropriate only for servants' quarters.

Increasingly, new technology and a technological aesthetic were not merely becoming acceptable in a domestic environment, but embodied status and a matter of pride; 'a modern bathroom ... is like a piece of scientific apparatus', Muthesius marvelled in 1904.[46]

HEATING

'The result of a "smokey house" is a "scolding wife".'[47]

New heating technologies were tardy in their adoption. In 1880, there were various methods of heating a house available, including the closed stove and central heating by hot air, hot water or steam, but by far the commonest method of heating was by means of the open fireplace. It was not an efficient form of heating; it consumed vast quantities of fuel (an estimated seven-eighths of the heat produced went up the chimney), while at the same time producing smoky and draughty rooms and entailing constant dirty and laborious work in laying and keeping the fire going. Mrs Haweis complained:

> It is horrible to have a cold nose and a burning hand; it is more horrible to have a burning nose and cold hands. Fried toes alone are small

comfort, so is one hot ear, yet it is really not possible to be equally warm all round beside a fire.[48]

Nevertheless, for practical and emotional reasons the open fire persisted. First, the open fire performed a function believed to be crucial to health, that of aiding ventilation; Mrs Haweis thought that 'a sitting-room over 55 degrees Fahrenheit is unhealthy, and extremely likely to induce colds'.[49] Furthermore, while fuel and domestic servants were cheap and available, and many houses were still rented rather than owned, there was no incentive to change the system. The popularity of the open fire lay also in its function as the decorative focus of the room, as will be seen in the next chapter, and in its appeal to tradition and to the notion of the home, a point not lost on the American domestic reformer, Harriet Beecher Stowe, who in *Sunny Memories of Foreign Lands*, 1854, admired the 'Bright coal fires, in grates of polished steel, … the lares and penates of old England', and regretted the passing of the open fire in America and its replacement by the airtight stove, 'that sullen, stifling gnome', a trend 'fatal to patriotism … for who would fight for an airtight'.[50]

The typical grate of the 1870s, held responsible for many of the problems encountered, was cast iron and round arched, with spandrels intended to radiate heat into the room and an adjustable register trap at the chimney opening to regulate air, smoke, etc.; the back of the grate was cast iron and was inclined towards the front at the base. There were many patents, brought out in response to the complaints of contemporaries, which claimed to solve the problems of smoke, draughts and loss of heat. These involved incorporating radiating surfaces into the design to reflect the heat out into the room, building in a chamber or false back where air could be warmed before passing into the room, along with schemes for pull-out drawers, revolving grates, and blowers or canopies to consume the smoke.[51] The design of the standard grate was improved following the work of T. P. Teale in the 1880s, who drew on late-eighteenth-century ideas of Count Rumford, and argued for a smaller but deeper grate opening, a firebrick back inclined towards the front at the top, and an 'Economiser' box below the grate. The resulting standard grate by the 1890s had a narrower opening than its circular predecessor, a brick back, splayed sides lined with tiles, a canopy hood and a shield below the grate. Mrs Haweis perceived the change. 'Modern science is seeking to provide a thin, vertical fire…. Most people are giving up the large circular burnished eyesores which drive a conscientious housemaid wild.'[52]

The Edwardian period saw the continuing quest for an efficient firegrate and also a growing challenge from other forms of heating, particularly gas and electric fires. Although gas fires had been on the market for some time, the adoption of new technology in this area had been slow, for reasons discussed above; its eventual success was predicted by the British Commercial Gas Association advertisement in 1918:

After the war domestic labour will probably be both scarce and dear, and the servantless home will, through force of circumstances, tend to become the rule rather than the exception ... convenience, cleanliness, economy, efficiency, and comfort, without unnecessary labour, are signs of progress which no woman can afford to disregard.[53]

Gas was thus promoted on grounds of progress and the ideal home was increasingly seen as one run 'on modern labour-saving lines'. Of all the alternatives to the open fire, gas and electric fires were the forms of heating which 'lend themselves most readily to the absence of servants'.[54] People were unfamiliar with how the new appliances worked, as they had been with new forms of lighting; an advertisement in 1912 for a Belling electric fire warned 'This fire is warmed by electricity so do not use a poker'. The appeal of tradition for middle-class consumers was reflected in the popularity of the up-market Berry 'Magicoal' fire, with artificial flame simulating a real coal fire, introduced in 1920.[55]

Even so, in 1918, it was judged that 'for continuous heating, the coal fire, with modern grates, is still the cheapest method',[56] although in rooms used only for a small amount of time each day it worked out cheaper to use gas. Competition from gas and electricity spurred on significant improvements in the design of the fire-grate early in the new century, for example, the 'barless' fire and the 'Well' fire, which used up less coal and were much easier to clean and tidy. Such improvements were supported by 'the strong affection of the British householder for a bright coal fire and its accompanying dancing flames'.[57]

7

FIREPLACES

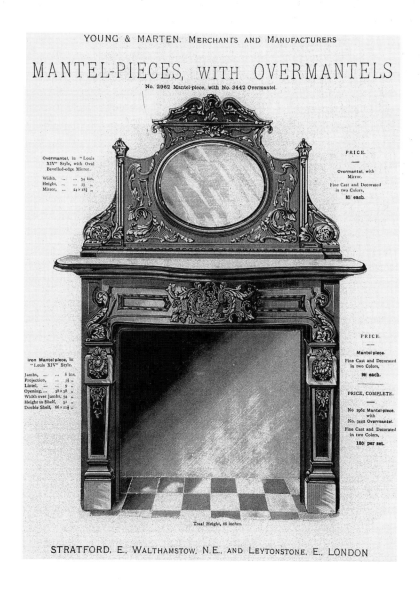

7.1
Cast-iron mantelpiece by
Young and Marten, 1898

Perhaps more than any other aspect of fixed decoration, the open fireplace lent character and style to an interior and symbolised traditional notions of hearth and home. Moreover, as W. Shaw Sparrow pointed out in *The British Home of Today*, 1904, 'the fireplace, perhaps comes first in importance.... Always a centre of attention in our climate.' Its design was therefore of the utmost importance to contemporaries and probably evoked more passionate comment than any other detail of fixed decoration.

MARBLE CHIMNEYPIECES

The fire surround in standard use in middle-class houses in the 1880s was made from marble. Its style, deriving from the Greek and Roman classical tradition, was plain, often arch-shaped around the grate opening, with severe, monumental trusses, often acanthus leaves or volutes, supporting a shelf which was frequently surmounted by a large mirror. *Furniture and Decoration* recalled that this style of chimneypiece had been first fashionable in the period 1800 to 1850: 'the early Victorian era of fireplace evolution was characterised by the introduction of cold white marble chimneypieces and cold steel embellishments'.[1]

The colour of the marble, rather than any difference in style, marked out room differences; for example, black, and later red and brown marbles also, were frequently used for dining-room chimneypieces and white marbles for those in drawing rooms. Marble was available in varying qualities and prices, for example, Thomas O'Brien's top-quality white fireplace in Bastard Statuary marble cost £5 1s 6d, while the same design in white Sicilian marble (the more usual type used in middle-class houses), cost £4 0s 3d.[2] For a superior house, Young and Marten Ltd, a builders' merchant, in 1898 advertised good-quality grey and red marbles in four designs for use in dining-rooms, all available in St Ann's marble with black mounts at £3 6s to £5 2s, depending on the size, or in Rouge or Griotte marbles with black mounts, from £3 to £5 2s.[3] Reception rooms in upper-middle-class houses of the same date in Herne Hill, for example, were furnished with chimneypieces made from superior brown marble. Such was the ubiquitous use of colour as a device for room differentiation that its appeal was wearing thin by the late 1880s. Mrs Panton felt that 'the possession of a large and hideous white marble mantlepiece and a tiled hearth to the ugly, wasteful grate says "drawing room" too plainly for the ordinary mind to rise above the builder's dictum'.[4]

Criticisms of the marble mantel multiplied during subsequent years, so much so that advice on how a 'funereal and unsentimental chimneypiece of uncompromising insipidity'[5] could be disguised, using drapery, fans and tassels, became a recurrent theme among architects and others writing in home manuals and journals (see fig. 7.2). Mrs

Humphry advised on how:

> *To Hide an Ugly Mantlepiece* – Perhaps the thing that most frequently exercises the mind of the modern house-seeker is the fire-grate, with its white or black chimney-piece. A really good, bold, white statuary marble one is best left alone, but Sicilian marble with its yellowish stains, which grow and increase with every year, especially on a clay soil, is distinctly unsightly…. There are two ways of disguising a chimney-piece of this sort…. A plain board, covered with cloth or art fabric…. Another plan is to have a complete wooden casing for the offending mantel-piece.[6]

The marble mantel was used in reception rooms on the ground and first floor in middle-class houses. While it was going out of fashion in the journals, marble chimneypieces continued to be available from builders' merchants, and speculative builders in Cardiff, for example, still regarded it as a selling point even in upper-middle-class houses of the early 1890s, by which date cheap versions had also filtered through to lower-middle-class houses there. Likewise, in top-quality houses in Herne Hill, London, marble was still acceptable in 1896. In this area

7.2
Ways to disguise fireplaces, in Oetzmann's catalogue of the late nineteenth century

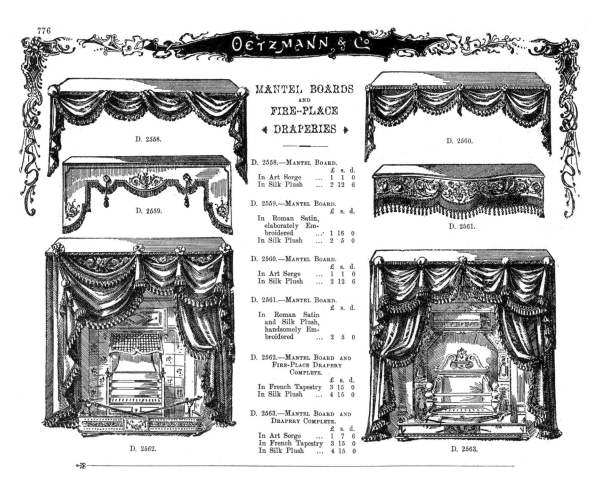

also, it filtered down to middle- and lower-middle-class houses, for example, a Sicilian marble chimneypiece design, identical to the one on sale at Thomas O'Brien's showroom at £4 0s 3d, appears in reception rooms of medium and small houses built about 1898. The widespread popularity of the marble mantel in the 1870s and 1880s rested on its ability to convey a sense of tradition and status, guarantees of respectability. As Mrs Panton observed in 1889, 'Of course, some people, even in a small house, regard the possession of the marble in the light of a patent of nobility – it is so handsome (odious word), so genteel; but these belong to the hopeless class, for whom little or nothing can be done.'[7]

The social status attached to ornamentation was the impetus behind the various attempts to invent a machine to carve cheaply, none of which proved very successful. In the end it was possibly the lack of good carving machines which determined the plain form of the marble chimneypiece and the use of different coloured marbles to distinguish between room types. A certain amount of decoration could be produced using moulding machines and lathes. Patterns could also be sand-blasted through a stencil on to the marble slab surface to produce limited, superficial decoration; this method was useful for ordinary fire surrounds. 'This process is useful for purposes in which a flat surface requires to be ornamented at a very low cost'.[8] Ultimately these technical limitations contributed to the fashion for the wood fireplace (and its imitations in cast iron), as these materials could be easily manipulated to reproduce desirable stylistic detail in a way not possible with marble.

Following fashionable advice, by 1900 the marble mantelpiece had fallen from favour in the best houses, which increasingly tended to use wood instead, while marble was still very much aspired to in middle- and lower-middle-class houses. By 1909, the white mantel only generally remained in use at the lower end of the scale, and even here its use was often limited to the front bedroom. Along with changing tastes, one of the main reasons for marble's decline in use in fashionable homes by 1900 was undoubtedly its dissemination to smaller houses.

IMITATION MARBLE: SCAGLIOLA, MAREZZO MARBLE
AND ENAMELLED SLATE

The demand for marble spawned a host of imitation marbles which undercut the real thing in price terms. One early form of counterfeit marble introduced in 1750 was 'scagliola'. By 1900, the scagliola industry had become a profitable industry. Scagliola possessed several advantages: it was not a varnish, but its polish was a natural result of friction and 'stoning' (as in the case of polished marble), and it was therefore claimed to be much more durable than other products on the market.[9] Although some scagliola was a very good imitation of marble, and 'cannot be told from the genuine by an expert at five paces', the quality was not uniform across all manufacturers; 'it is inferior scagliola which we should be on our guard against ... as at present made, about sixty-five per cent of it is inferior and worthless'.[10] The main advantage of scagliola lay in its relatively cheap price: 'in our large cities you can summon to your office at twenty-four hours notice a suave gentleman, who will blandly offer to duplicate in scagliola, or counterfeit marble, a row of columns which would cost you a small fortune if done in marble'.[11]

In 1868, the Patent Marezzo Marble Co. Ltd had brought out an even cheaper product: 'The cheapness of Marezzo (about one-tenth the cost of real marble) brings its application to decorative purposes within the reach of all classes.'[12] Marezzo was 'applicable to all the uses of ordinary life – as slabs, chimney-pieces, washing stands and tables'.[13] As the colours went through the entire thickness of the material, it was sawn, dressed and polished like ordinary marble and was 'so accurate as to defy detection, even by an expert'.[14]

By far the most common method of imitating rare and expensive marbles, which could not normally be afforded, even in good-quality houses, was by means of enamelling slate. The Magnus Enamelled Slate Works in 1862 advertised that they could make twenty chimneypieces marbled to resemble Italian and British marbles 'in a morning' by floating minerals together. Enamelled-slate allowed builder and occupant to escape from the colour range of real marbles available within their budget and give the impression of a more expensive home. The wide range of enamelled-slate chimneypieces on offer by the late 1890s is demonstrated by Young and Marten's catalogue of 1898, which advertised four designs available in four different imitation marbles, black and Italian griotte, black and malachite, black and pyrenees spar, and black and serpentine with plain gilt lines. Each design was also sold in three sizes at prices ranging from £1 3s 9d to £2 14s. Complexity of design went hand in hand with cost; the cheapest of the four designs had panels of the imitation marble on a plain black surround, while a slightly more costly design had more elaborate panels and 'triglyphs' at the top of each jamb or side piece; a superior design to this had carved trusses rather than the triglyphs, while the most expensive of the surrounds on sale had both trusses and triglyphs. The same catalogue showed four more expensive designs which comprised highly complex arrangements of panels, trusses, triglyphs and mounts, available in black and porphyry spar with gilt lines costing from £2 14s to £3 6s, waulsort (a brown marble with fragments of white, black, red and pink) with black mounts, dove and limestone with black mounts priced from £2 5s to £2 17s, and green serpentine and spanish brocatella with gilt lines from £3 15s to £4 10s. On the whole, even elaborate enamelled-slate designs were cheaper than marble chimneypieces, about half the cost in the case of St Ann's marble.

The use of enamelled-slate fireplaces tended to vary regionally in line with material availability. They were used in medium and small houses in Cardiff, for instance, from the late 1890s through to 1910, and were less often found in top-quality houses. Such surrounds were normally combined with the new narrow style of grate, with the tiles and canopy mentioned in the previous chapter. In other areas, enamelled slate was used in a wide range of middle-class houses, for example, in Herne Hill, south London, where they continued in use in small houses well into the Edwardian period, identical designs suggesting a local supply source. In other areas, by contrast, they were largely absent, for instance, in Muswell Hill, London, where other materials were used instead.

The designs for the surrounds themselves, which were variations of the styles used for marble chimneypieces using derivations of classical motifs, changed little and continued to be readily available through to the end of our period. They were produced in a variety of colours, especially reds, imitating top-quality Griotte, and, more occasionally, imitation green or shell marbles. Slate surrounds were also enamelled to resemble wood; for example, Dibben's Catalogue of about 1910 shows a design in 'Imitation Oak, Walnut or Rosewood, with Cloisonné Enamel Enrichments'. These 'wood' designs were particularly popular in kitchen/living-rooms in Cardiff, for example, and were decorated with Arts and Crafts style painted motifs or inlaid woods and used in combination with a standard grate with mock eighteenth century hobs to each side. A house in Cardiff has a fireplace which combines both these imitation materials, with green 'marble' panels set into a 'wood' frame.

Standards of enamelling varied greatly between manufacturers, and cheaper-quality surrounds, used in smaller houses or in less important rooms in larger houses, caused concern. In 1896 M. H. Baillie Scott commented, 'In the average house the treatment of the fireplace is painfully ugly, and the coarsely modelled cast-iron grate, with its mantlepiece of enamelled slate, are things which one can only try to obliterate with drapery, while the stock overmantel with its bevelled mirrors and flimsy construction is hardly less objectionable.'[15] The widespread problem of surface damage contributed to enamelled slate's eventual fall from popularity.

Home recipes for imitating marble were very numerous; for instance, *Cassell's Household Guide*, 1868-71, advised a method of imitating marble using chalk and copal varnish. Entire books devoted to the subject emerged, and advice was also given to painters and decorators in general decorating books. The marble and enamelled-slate mantel declined in popularity in the years before the First World War. Whereas in the 1870s there had been more marble than wood surrounds displayed in catalogues, Nicholls and Clarke Ltd's catalogue of 1913 had only four designs for marble or enamelled-slate fire surrounds, far fewer than designs in wood and cast iron, and that of William Pryor and Co. Ltd, 1913, had only six designs compared with twenty-eight in wood and many more in cast iron. In the 1921 edition of Nicholls and Clarke's catalogue, this firm had stopped selling marble and slate surrounds altogether.

In 1900 *The Illustrated Carpenter and Builder* concluded,

Nothing will run a thing out of vogue so quickly as the placing on the market of cheap and tawdry examples of it.... With the miserably poor imitation marble mantel came the downfall of the marble mantel itself. Not that the marbleized slate thing half the time looked enough like the real article to libel it. Only that the plain, ungraceful marble shelf was not of itself beautiful, and to decorate it with carvings, and polish it to a tombstone finish, cost a quantity of cash. And so it came about that the mantel of hardwood pushed the mantel of marble out of vogue and fashion.[16]

WOOD CHIMNEYPIECES

By 1900, then, for upper-middle-class homes at any rate, as the Queen Anne revival and Arts and Crafts Movement focused attention on details such as the fireplace, fashion had swung towards the wood mantel away from those in marble under the impact of late-nineteenth-century taste. Influenced by the Arts and Crafts style, one writer in 1911 felt that there was an 'undue emphasising of the fireplace', and it was always the 'centre of the decorator's efforts' even though it was out of use for half the year.[17] The Arts and Crafts approach was rooted in the idea of the fireplace as historically the central part of the medieval house. Thus *Furniture and Decoration* felt in 1890 that 'the chimney corners of olden times are fashionable again, under the title of ingle-nooks and cosy corners'.[18] It was felt that, ever since the Jacobean revival of the 1870s, 'The gradual stages of progress that have marked the improvement in the designs of our modern mantel-pieces have all been, more or less, the result of our adopting forms and mouldings of an architectural character.'[19] Six years later, M. H. Baillie Scott commented: 'So much of the comfort as well as the beauty of a room depend on a well-arranged fireside that few will underrate its importance ... mentally picture the fireplaces of an earlier age, when the art of homemaking was so well understood.'[20]

At the same time, the eclecticism of the later nineteenth century and the early twentieth century meant that other styles, such as 'eighteenth-century' were also acceptable for the fireplace. Period-style fireplaces demanded a level of detailed ornament which could not be economically provided by the limited marble-manufacturing processes currently available. Processes available for wood, in comparison, enabled a specific style to be reproduced in minute detail. Thus the choice of a wooden fireplace offered the consumer a wider variety of styles with the potential to lend a recognisable style to an interior and put the middle classes within reach of the richly carved woodwork which had previously been monopolised by the wealthy. *Furniture and Decoration*, 1892, commented in relation to furniture that: 'A large section of the public, however, will not be satisfied with an absence of carved ornament, when they know that such work can be well and cheaply done. This is proved by the enormous demand which exists for cheap yet highly ornamented furniture.'[21]

The machine was used also to make a 'cut out' design (as the journals described it) of which, in about 1890, 'a great number of excellent designs … are at present being used by builders'.[22] The role of the machine in the production of the wood mantel was clear, as Thomas O'Brien notes in regard to a design for an oak or walnut fire surround with overmantel for £4 10s 6d, 'Prices Greatly Reduced…. They are made by Special Patented Machinery, which enables us to offer them at a price which defies competition.' The use of machines in this way invoked fierce debate, with many feeling, as Lucy Crane did, 'the superiority of hand-work to machine work in all kinds of things,'[23] while *Furniture and Decoration* argued that machine carving, although disapproved of by Ruskinites, was in fact superior to that done by hand.[24] Mahogany, whether top-quality South American or darker, slightly lower-quality African, were used on good-quality fire surrounds. Such woods were smooth and knot-free and so could be easily worked into complex forms and mouldings, and for this reason were considered prestigious. Other wood surrounds were made of pine, whose knotty quality meant that only simple bandsaw cut forms were possible. Whereas a mahogany surround would be polished, a pine one would be painted, frequently white, in the style of the Queen Anne revival. Arts and Crafts designers favoured oak, left plain, as opposed to exotic, polished mahogany; the technical limitations of working the grainy oak produced simple forms which were in keeping with Arts and Crafts ideals.

7·3
Wood fire surround with cast-iron grate and tiled panel cheeks, in a house built in 1909, which had a rateable value of £28 in 1914, Albany Road, Cardiff

The taste for ornament and style supported not only wooden mantels but a new style in overmantels, an idea derived in the late 1860s as an alternative to the overmantel mirror.[25] 'Art' overmantels with shelves and brackets were very popular by 1890 as they could up-date an old marble mantel and offered the consumer the opportunity to display ornaments and bric-à-brac. But the cheap end of the market brought criticism of this style of overmantel. *Furniture and Decoration* commented in 1891 that 'It is quite time that we had done with the spindled absurdities called overmantels which have been so long in vogue.'[26] Two years later, the same journal optimistically reported, that 'the beaded and spindled article of many shelves, are slowly but surely disappearing from the show-rooms of tasteful house-furnishers',[27] superseded by Georgian and 'French' overmantels, among others, in houses belonging to 'artistic people':

> the lingering influence of Aestheticism has lately encouraged our manufacturers to produce some curiously devised overmantels of a quaint and irregular order.... Side by side, however, with this more refined fashion, is the constant changefulness of popular taste, a changefulness which it is the business of the artist and the manufacturer to constantly study ... there are several styles in vogue which afford a sufficiently large scope for the fancy and tastefulness of the designer of overmantels. The Louis Seize, the Queen Anne, the Classic, the Italian Renaissance and the Aesthetic styles are a few of those which we might cite at random, and all of these are appropriate and fashionable styles which could advantageously be employed simultaneously with the garish Louis Quinze mode.[28]

The importance of the overmantel, in French styles in particular, in the middle-class interior in 1895 was apparent.

> The modern overmantel, with its many shelves and bevelled plates, is an attractive and up to date descendent of the chimney-pieces of Elizabethan and Queen Anne times. It continues, despite its commonness and increasing cheapness, to continue its hold upon public taste. An overmantel is still regarded as an indispensible item of furniture in middle-class houses.... Now-a-days the majority of overmantels manu-factured are 'in the French style', and hideous enough in all conscience some of them are too! Some are aesthetic in character and others are simple and somewhat classical in design.[29]

McDowall, Steven and Co. Ltd's range rose in quality and price from £9 14s for a combination pine mantel with mirror to £42 7s 6d for a white pine and composition mantel in an 'Adam' style with mirrors. The commonest wood design in catalogues and on the ground was Queen Anne. Besides neo-classical and Adam, rococo was also popular. Thomas O'Brien advertised a rococo design complete with overmantel in 1900. Another style which became very popular was a 'modern' style known as 'Progressive', often white-painted. Carron Co.'s catalogue of about 1910 advertised plain whitewood designs. Wooden fire surrounds increase in numbers in catalogues as marble and slate ones decline. In 1898 trade catalogues offered only a few wood mantels, yet in about 1910 William Dibben's catalogue illustrated the huge increase in production of wood designs. With names like 'The Windsor Well Fire' and 'The Scarborough Well Fire', the catalogue sought to attach a distinct character, and imply a life-style which the possessor might want to project. This device had not been used with marble and slate chimneypieces. Other designs in Dibben's catalogue were given stylistic labels, rather than names; there were three Adam designs, one Georgian, one Sheraton and a page of Jacobean style surrounds. There was also a page of 'modern' designs, in an Arts and Crafts style with inlaid mirror or copper repoussé panels. A very similar range, including some of the same designs, was available in Nicholls and Clarke's catalogue of 1921, with a number of 'Elizabethan' combination mantels added. The combination mantel was a design envisaged and manufactured all in one piece, often with a mirror incorporated and, as such, represented a major change in fireplace form as it superseded the separate surround and overmantel. Thus an alternative to 'the "wearisome" overmantel'[30] sought by *Furniture and Decoration* in the 1890s was finally being produced on a mass level nearly twenty years later.

Evidence drawn from catalogues about trends in wood chimneypieces is borne out by fireplaces which can be found in houses. South American and African mahogany chimneypieces were used in the best houses by 1900. For instance, the dining-room fireplace of a top-quality house in Cardiff was made in South American mahogany, hand-carved in a Renaissance style; other reception rooms of the house had wooden eighteenth-century-style fireplaces and a homely wood design with strapwork decoration, copper repoussé panels and a tiled hob grate. Another Cardiff house, built in 1907, has a fireplace in African mahogany with a large shelved and bracketed overmantel. A medium-sized London house of 1909 has a combination fire surround with details after Mackmurdo and a new-style tiled grate. The fashion for the wooden mantel was taken up by some speculative builders for use in medium and small houses by the late nineteenth century, but here pine was used rather than mahogany.

> The improvement that has, of late years, been made in the designs of our chimneypieces is happily apparent on every hand, and now-a-days, it is usual to see really tasteful little mantel-pieces, even in the second and third best bedrooms of modern suburban houses ... it has at last dawned upon the intellect of the speculative builder, and the demand for pine mantel-pieces as well as cast iron ones has consequently increased of late. (*Furniture and Decoration*, 1890)[31]

Rococo proved popular for wooden bedroom and drawing-room surrounds and overmantels, for example in Muswell Hill, but as usual often combined with other styles for other parts such as an Adam surround. Carved baroque examples can also be found in reception rooms of the largest houses of the late 1890s. Just as enamelled slate rarely appeared in Muswell Hill, the wood chimneypiece was noticeable by its absence in Herne Hill.

CAST-IRON CHIMNEYPIECES

A cast-iron version was the next best choice for those who could not afford a high-quality carved wood chimneypiece. Generally, cast iron was much more common than wood in medium and small houses, although cast iron was also, as will be seen later, sometimes clearly chosen in preference to wood in some large houses. By 1900, the cast-iron surround was widespread: one writer commented, 'Nothing in the building trade is more marked than the extended use of iron, cast and wrought, both in construction and decoration, during the last few years … [which has] culminated in the stoves and overmantles now made entirely of the universal metal' (see fig. 7.1).[32]

The appeal of iron lay in its versatility to reproduce styles originally executed in wood. It was cheaper than wood, because it was easier and quicker to cast a design all in one than to cut and mould the

7.4 *left*
Cast-iron mantelpiece by Young and Marten, 1898

7.5
Small cast-iron fireplace in lounge/hall, Wood Green, London, 1909

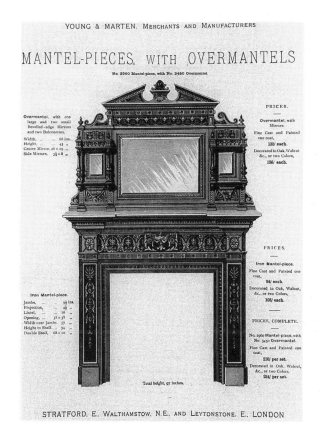

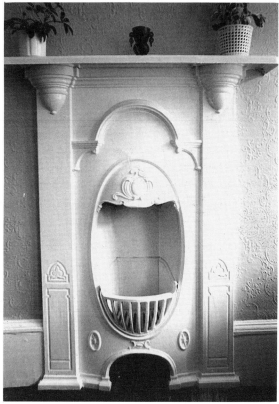

parts for a wooden fireplace, even though woodworking machinery had reduced the cost of these processes dramatically. The pattern for the casting was made from wood, and this was crucial to the final appearance of the product; in many cases, the texture and feel of wood can be detected in details on the final casting. Turned and carved wood forms were easily reproduced in cast iron – the only difference lay in a subtle distinction in the degree of sharpness of the forms. The detail made possible by the casting process was admirably suited to the convention for providing different styles to suit different types of room and thus giving the impression of wealth and status.

Generally, as already mentioned, the manipulation of cast iron to forms not compatible with the nature of the material, and its use to imitate other materials, met with violent abuse from theorists and designers from Pugin onwards. Charles Eastlake in 1878 condemned the 'curvilinear and elaborate monstrosities'[33] of Birmingham and Sheffield, with their coarse and clumsy ornament and concealed bolts, nails and rivets, and in 1896 Baillie Scott recorded that many 'art loving' people had been put off cast iron on account of the 'phenomenal ugliness'[34] of the designs currently on the market. Sixteen years later, *Cassell's Household Guide*, 1912, criticised the 'composition mantlepiece imitating marble, with wonderful panels of ferns and flowers let into the sides, or, what is nearly, though not quite, as bad, an iron mantlepiece imitating very richly-carved wood'.

Styles for cast iron echoed those in fashion for wood, but generally the range was narrower. Barnard, Bishop and Barnards, iron founders of Norwich, were at the forefront of the Aesthetic Movement in the 1870s and 1880s with their designs for grates decorated with Japanese-style birds, branches and flowers which contrasted with the regular curved grate with its baroque revival details current at the time (see fig. 4.2). Throughout the 1880s and 1890s, similar Aesthetic Movement motifs were used on tiles in the cheeks of the standard grate. Young and Marten's General Illustrated Catalogue shows how, by 1898, this style of grate came to be generally reserved for cheap mantel registers, in combination with a pedimented Queen Anne overmantel, and probably destined for bedrooms in all but the smallest middle-class houses. But by this date there was a greater number of small fireplaces on sale in a neo-classical or Adam style. The majority of the larger designs destined for main bedrooms or reception rooms were likewise loose interpretations of either the early-eighteenth-century neo-classical style or the later Adam style, and there was little deviation from these styles. Such a predominance of classical-revival styles suggests once again the conformity and conservative tastes of the solid middle-class market. D. Morgan's Cardiff showroom in 1907 revealed the persistence of classical styles, with 'artistic' designs with hammered copper, iron and brass ornamentation in styles ranging from Adam to florid Louis XVI. Later catalogues, for instance, that of William Prior and Co. Ltd, 1913,

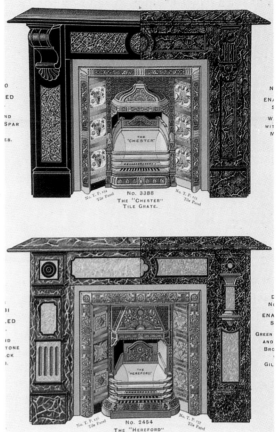

Young and Marten, designs
for combination baths

right
Young and Marten, designs
for enamelled-slate fire
surrounds and tiled grates

Young and Marten, designs
for leaded windows

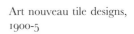

Art nouveau tile designs,
1900-5

Four transfer-printed tiles,
about 1885

PLATES 14, 15 & 16

Wooden porch, Crouch End

PLATE 17

7.6
Large cast-iron fire surround
in a reception room of a
house built in 1906 in Herne
Hill, which had a rateable
value in 1914 of £50

retained classical-revival styles for cast-iron mantels for reception rooms; indeed, some of the designs are identical to the Young and Marten catalogue of 1898. The fashion for Aesthetic Movement birds and flowers for small mantels gave way to Arts and Crafts motifs derived from Voysey, Mackintosh and Baillie Scott and to the art nouveau forms of Olbrich and others.[35] The generally simpler, low-relief, curvilinear forms associated with the Arts and Crafts Movement and art nouveau styles were particularly suited to the casting process, and small bedroom fireplaces could be mass-produced very cheaply, in one piece, without much undercutting.

Evidence from houses confirms that of the trade catalogues. Eighteenth-century styles, either neo-classical or Adam, were the most commonly used styles for the middle-class house, and by 1909 Adam was more common than neo-classical; rococo or baroque revival occurred less frequently. The use of the Aesthetic Movement details was common in the 1880s and 1890s, and New Art motifs after about 1905. Builders used styles eclectically, both in differentiating between rooms, and also within the fire surround itself, and a neo-classical surround with art nouveau tiles and an Adam canopy, or an Arts and Crafts design mixed with Adam tiles, was commonly used. Each design for a mantelpiece or mantel register was usually available in a range of sizes, and the cheaper the surround, the greater the range of sizes. In addition, mantels and overmantels could be 'mixed and matched' according to taste; most designs, even the cheap ones, were illustrated with overmantels in catalogues, each with its own order number. Prices were given for each part separately and for the two items combined. Such eclecticism was a result of the nature of the retail system. There was the potential for further variety in the choice of possible finishes for each design, with more choice the more expensive the fire surround. In this way, cast iron offered flexibility, individuality and variety to the consumer and convenience to the builder. Young and Marten's catalogue of 1898, for example, divided their fireplaces into 'mantel pieces with overmantels', 'mantel registers with overmantels', and 'cheap mantel registers'. The most basic finish was fine cast and painted with one coat; thereafter, in order of price, designs enamelled in two shades ('special' finish and 'best' finish), designs enamelled in imitation oak, rosewood, walnut, mahogany, or marbles (two finishes). There was an extra cost for ornamental parts to be picked out in 'colour', 'gold', 'colour and gold'.

The use of cast-iron chimneypieces varied regionally. Large cast-iron mantels were frequently used in upper-middle-class houses in north and south London, for instance, but they occur less often in Cardiff. Where a builder chose to use cast-iron for reception room chimneypieces, he tended to use cast-iron fire surrounds throughout the house, and in top-quality houses different designs were found in each reception room, at least. What is most noticeable is the standardisation of designs across different localities, many of which can be traced back to contemporary trade catalogues, such as those of Young and Marten, and a clear hierarchy between design and class of house and status of room within a house emerges. Fig. 7.6 shows one of Young and Marten's most expensive designs; it appeared frequently in reception rooms of predominantly top-quality houses across the country. Another design, the 'Malvern', a 'design specially suited for picking out in colours to suit the decoration of a room', had a rococo lithographed tile panel and hearth set, measuring 39" x 48½"; this design was put into the bedrooms of top-quality houses or in the reception rooms of the houses of the lower middle class. One of their cheap designs, the 'Milton', was produced in ten sizes, ranging from 18" x 36" to 36" x 42"; an overmantel was available only with the largest size of this design. It was found in minor bedrooms of large and medium houses, and in the reception room of the smallest houses.

The range of materials available for use on fire surrounds expanded dramatically between 1880 and 1914. By the Edwardian period, W. Shaw Sparrow spoke of 'a unity of materials welded into one intention by skillful manipulation, a charming combination of wood, metals, tiles or marble properly selected and fittingly used'.[36] Copper was increasingly popular, used with repoussé panels or enamel decorations, as it 'gives the minimum of trouble in the important matter of cleaning; unlike brass, it does not demand a high polish'. Such a consideration we find emerging again and again in relation to the internal fittings of the Edwardian home, as the middle classes prepared themselves for a future without servants.

8
DOORS
AND DOORWAYS

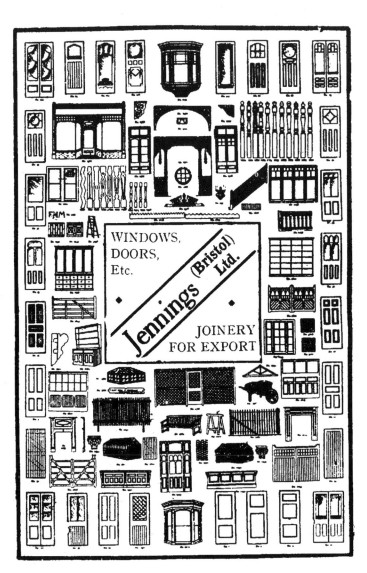

8.1
Catalogue cover advertising the range of wood products available at C. Jennings of Bristol, about 1914

Along with the fireplace, late-Victorian and Edwardian home manuals point to an increased interest in the design of the door and doorway: 'The importance that attaches nowadays to the decoration of doors renders it necessary that the house-furnisher should be ever prepared with new and tasteful fancies to submit to his clients.'[1] The roots of this lay in the revival of seventeenth- and eighteenth-century domestic architecture; In 1891, *Furniture and Decoration* signalled the renewed interest in the design of the door area.

> The ordinary room door is a much more important feature in our apartments than it is generally considered to be. In fact, the way in which it has been neglected by the house-furnisher, for at least a century, shows in what small esteem the interior door has been regarded in the past. Nowadays, however, this essential feature in every room is beginning to be looked upon as an object that must needs be taken into account, if we are to have our rooms completely furnished in good taste.[2]

THE DOOR

Door design had come under increasing attack in the later nineteenth century because of what was held to be inconvenient and poor design. R. W. Edis, author of *The Decoration of Town Houses*, 1881, remarked that in the average house, 'the doors are four panel, with weedy-looking mouldings'.[3] The correct arrangement of panels on a four-panel door, according to James Ward, was to have two shorter panels below, rather than to have four panels of equal size.[4] But, writing in *The Cheap Cottage*, 1914, George Allen felt that the location of the handle entailed by this arrangement meant that one had to stoop when opening it and complained in 1914 that 'many machine made doors, especially those from Sweden, are very badly proportioned'.[5] Writing in 1904, Hermann Muthesius also reflected the contemporary concern with details such as doors; he noted that, compared with the 1830s, there were fewer doors in the speculatively built house, false doors had disappeared, and the doors themselves lacked variety and were meaner, seldom measuring more than three feet in width. Muthesius complained, 'doors nowadays no longer stand out as architectural motifs, they simply fulfil their purpose and are no larger than is necessary'.[6]

These various influences effected an increased variety of standard doors on offer. The four-panel door remained the conventional door design throughout the period, but was joined by five- and six-panel doors from the 1890s and even more varied designs by 1914. The five- and six-panel doors derived from the fashion for eighteenth-century styles. Doors with five panels were arranged with one of the panels horizontally either at the top or in the centre of the door. A richer and more substantial effect even than this was given by a six-panel door, which had two smaller square frieze panels above larger middle and

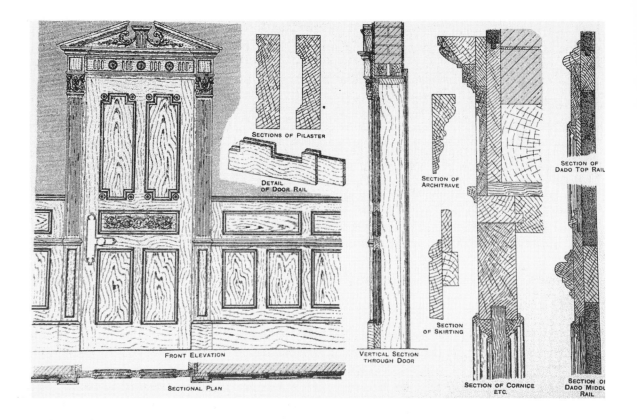

Front Elevation

Sections of Pilaster

Detail of Door Rail

Sectional Plan

Vertical Section through Door

Section of Architrave

Section of Skirting

Section of Cornice etc.

Section of Dado Top Rail

Section of Dado Middle Rail

8.2
Design for a doorway and wall area by Paul Hasluck, 1910

bottom sets. C. Jennings, general woodworkers of Bristol, around the year 1914, claimed to stock one hundred thousand doors at any one time and to manufacture five hundred doors a day (see fig. 8.1). The firm offered twenty designs for interior doors which had between two and nine panels each. These designs consisted of one or two designs for two- to three-panel doors, six versions of the four-panel door, three designs each for five- and six-panel doors and four types of nine-panel door. There was a rough equation between numbers of panels and cost of door, but in the final analysis the amount of wood rather than complexity of production governed the cost of the door. A wide range of panel mouldings were also available, from the dearest with both sides 'drop-moulded', those drop-moulded on one side only, to the cheapest where the moulding was cut as part of the frame. The most expensive mouldings were 'bolection' mouldings used on top-of-the-range doors, where the moulding was raised above the plane of the door and was extended to cover the join of frame and panel; usually, panel mouldings were sunk into the angle of the door panel and frame. Manufacturers offered matching doors and mouldings; Jewsons' catalogue of 1910-19 advertised two-, five- or six-panel doors and coordinated panel moulding, architrave and skirting.

The four-panel door was universal in all sizes of middle-class house

8.3
Plaster overdoor in a reception room of a 1909 Cardiff house which had a rateable value of £26

in the 1880s and early 1890s, but when the new designs of doors became used in the best houses from the late 1890s, the four-panel door became relegated to private or less important areas of this type of house, like the kitchen, bathroom and back bedrooms, and they were smaller and thinner than the doors used for the best rooms. Five-panel doors tended to be used by the Edwardian period for medium-sized houses, while doors with six panels and large bolection mouldings were reserved for top-quality houses. The influence of a local supplier can be seen in identical designs used frequently within an area; for instance, houses in north Roath, Cardiff, were supplied by Harry Gibbon, the nearest large general woodworking firm to the new house-building, which stocked over five thousand doors at any one time.

THE OVERDOOR

In addition to the greater attention paid to the number and arrangement of panels and size of the door, a device introduced in the 1880s to give the impression of a larger and grander door was the doorhead or 'overdoor', borrowed from eighteenth-century architecture. Manufacturers and writers seized on the overdoor with eagerness, as *Furniture and Decoration* noted in 1891: 'There has sprung up in the trade of recent years an almost distinct department in this direction, and nowadays no house furnisher's stock is replete unless it contains a goodly assortment of such articles.'[7] Mrs Panton was also in favour, 'The simple overdoors, sold by so many furniture houses nowadays, should be placed over the doors, in most houses, in the hall, or else pictures hung there.'[8] The overdoor was decorative, lending instant style to a room, and was also practical, as *Furniture and Decoration*, 1891, observed:

119

The architectural frieze and rigid pediment of former days has long since given place to a more attractive and fanciful class of fitment. Shelves and niches for bric-à-brac are now the fashionable thing, and the more 'broken-up' in arrangement the over-doors are made, the more popular and pleasing do they seem to become. The accommodation for pottery and nick-nacks, however, should not be the only purpose of an overdoor. It should be made to correspond with the rest of the furniture, and would thus materially help to complete the harmonious appearance of the apartment. Further, too, it should, in most cases at all events, be so constructed that it may serve as a portière holder.[9]

Overdoors were available from woodworking and furnishing firms. C. Jennings and Co. Ltd, in about 1914, offered twelve designs in deal, pitchpine, white wood, mahogany-oak, teak and Austrian oak. Most of the designs were hand-carved in relief, although the cheaper designs, while superficially looking complex in detail, were machine-pressed, which reduced the cost. Overdoors were also available in other materials besides wood, such as metal, papier mâché and, very commonly, plaster. For example, an averagely priced Young and Marten iron design appeared in the hallway above the entrance to the drawing-room of a top-quality house in Muswell Hill built in 1897, while papier-mâché overdoors were installed above each reception room door in the hallway of a similar house also in Muswell Hill. The overdoor proved popular in middle-class houses from the later 1890s, although regional variation occurs; for example, while overdoors were almost universally used in all sizes of house in Herne Hill from 1896 to the early 1900s, in houses of the same date in Hornsey they were included only in the largest houses. Overdoors were not general in middle-class houses, for example in Cardiff, until about 1904, and continued to be included as standard fittings through to 1910 (see fig. 8.3). On the whole they were used in larger houses first, but once the idea had percolated down the scale, it is significant that identical designs were used in large and small houses alike.

Overdoors usually derived in style from eighteenth-century precedents, although most were an eclectic combination of English neo-Palladian motifs such as the broken pediment and scallop, Adam-style swags and urns, and Chippendale rococo trelliswork. Eighteenth-century French styles were popular; *Furniture and Decoration* featured such a design in mahogany, describing it as 'a guarded tribute to the fashionable French style'.[10] The same magazine predicted that white enamel Louis Quinze overdoors would come into fashion. Detailed carved work was easily imitated in cast iron or plaster. Designers capitalised on quick machine operations available and produced overdoor designs with shelves and spindles in an Aesthetic mode. Designs were specified for different rooms in the house, for example, *Furniture and Decoration* mentioned a design suitable for a lady's boudoir.[11] Occasionally, a different design would be chosen for each room. Usually, the practical and economic demands on the average builder of middle-class housing meant that he generally bought in bulk and might put the same design above doors to all the reception rooms, on both the hall and the room sides.

Overall, the range of designs was very small. For example, one design which was especially common had a scroll broken pediment and shell forming the basis of the design. It not only occurs frequently in one area in a wide range of house sizes, but also can be found at opposite ends of the country. Basic designs using the same mould with minor variations or additions, such as a different top or panel or added shelf, were often used. Machine-pressed carving was also common and some designs incorporated platforms for ornaments.

DOOR DECORATION

For those stuck with the old-fashioned four-panel door, writers on home decoration prescribed expedients, such as painting decorations on the panels. A cheaper and more convenient version of this was to use ready-made paper panels, such as R. Tuc's 'Iris'. This type of device proved popular, for example, a medium-sized house of 1896 in Herne Hill, London, has classical figures on the insides of each of the reception room doors along with Japanese blossom twigs in the smaller panels of the door. Cheaper even than this device was to use Anaglypta or some other relief paper to decorate the panels of the door, with paper in a typical sunflower pattern. Doors could be made to appear larger and

8.4
Oetzmann, door drapery,
late nineteenth century

D. 2531.—Portière Drapery in the Renaissance Style.

For Prices, in various materials, please see page 774.

D. 2532.—Portière Drapery in the Renaissance Style.

grander using drapery designed for use with overdoors. Even so, as *Furniture and Decoration* of 1891 pointed out; 'The modern short-lease system is ever opposed to the employment and payment of decent art on landlord's fixtures, and even Japanese leather paper, although it forms a good and tasteful substitute for artistic painting, yet this does not altogether suffice to make the ordinary joiner's door congenial with its surroundings.'[12]

Drapery was considered by some as the best form of ornament-ation for a door (see fig. 8.4). A way (generally abhored by writers) of making a door appear grander was by means of 'graining'.

> Painters always beg to be allowed to 'embellish' at least the front door with the hideous but orthodox arrangement of yellows and browns, scraped mysteriously and agonisedly with a comb, or some such instrument, in a faint and feeble attempt to deceive callers into believing that the door is made of some highly polished wood, veined by nature in a way that could not deceive the veriest ignoramus.... Many people cling to it who dislike it as much as I do, because they are told nothing can be done to it, unless all the paint is burned off; never was there such a greater fallacy![13]

Despite the reaction against the practice from some quarters, trade books frequently contained a chapter on graining and, indeed, entire books were written on the subject. By 1904 Hermann Muthesius suggested that doors were normally no longer painted to imitate wood and instead tended to be painted white,[14] influenced by the Queen Anne revival and Arts and Crafts style; but in the type of housing we are concerned with, graining was still widespread by 1910.

In the medieval period a lock was a very valuable item and was regarded as a tenant's property and taken with him when he moved. Locks were usually made of brass, occasionally copper or aluminium, or silver in wealthy houses. Door-furniture production expanded dramatically in the late-Victorian and Edwardian period, in line with manufacturing techniques and the demand from the public for these simple indicators of style. John Russell Ltd's range in about 1910 included Arts and Crafts designs in antique brass and pewter, art nouveau designs in copper, antique bronze and repoussé, and Georgian in polished brass. Muthesius, writing in 1904, did not recommend pierced finger-plates because dirt could easily collect. Porcelain and glass tended to be used as they did not need cleaning, although Muthesius regarded these materials as 'alien' on a door. Styles for door furniture broadly echoed the architectural styles in fashion, for example, Aesthetic Movement, art nouveau, Adam and baroque, and elaborate examples can be found in better-quality houses in particular (see fig. 8.5).

8.5
Door plate to front reception room of a substantial house built in 1906 (rateable value £60 in 1914) in Tydraw Road, Cardiff

9

WINDOWS

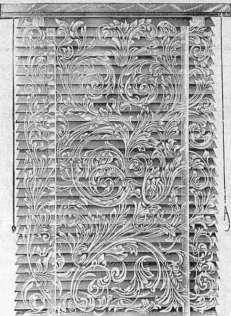

9.1
Advertisement for the Lux
Venetian blind, which was
designed to match the decor
of the room, 1897

With the abolition of the tax on glass and technical improvements in sheet-glass manufacture, mass housing in the Edwardian period was characterised by its unprecedentedly large window area. The bay window, seen as a symbol of respectability, was a crucial device as regards the design of the interior; W. Shaw Sparrow wrote in 1904: 'After the fireplace, coming next in importance among the decorative essentials is the bay window'. While large windows were welcomed because they let in plenty of light, they were also often criticised for undermining the house's privacy from the street, for giving unwanted views of the street and houses opposite, and for causing furniture and furnishings to fade in the sun. Lucy Crane complained about the current trends in window design and furnishing in 1882: windows were 'too large, too low, and ill-placed, so that they look from both inside and outside, like large holes made only to be filled up again in some way, veiled in large muslin curtains, and within these again larger and heavier ones, wire or wicker blinds also perhaps, and linen or else Venetian ones as well, and tables with plants.'[1] (see fig. 9.2).

BLINDS

Blinds were one solution to the problems described above, screening the interior yet allowing light through. Contemporary photographs often show windows decked out on the outside with sun blinds, together with blinds, drapery and lace curtains on the insides. A sun blind or curtain on a rail might be attached to the outside of the front door. Writers argued about their worth; while Mrs Humphry regarded blinds as 'among the first things to be considered in the furnishing of a house', and described outside blinds as 'absolutely needful',[2] Mrs Panton considered that 'ordinary blinds are not necessary, and are never useful; if the house has very much sun, *inside* blinds are no use at all'.[3] But the continuing popularity of blinds is clear from *Kelly's Post Office Directory* of 1910,[4] which listed several columns of window-blind manufacturers and revealed the vast range of indoor and outdoor blinds available. Janes and Son, established in 1789, for example, sold Venetian and dwarf Venetian, heraldry or wire blinds, silk festoon blinds and cane blinds. Another long-established firm, Tidmarsh and Son, founded in 1829, made spring roller blinds, glass blinds, Florentine, Spanish and Helioscene blinds and Canaletti door blinds.

Designs for outdoor blinds had to accommodate the need for regulating light and heat and yet allowing ventilation. At the top end of the market were shutter blinds or jalousies which operated on an adjustable louvre system. The Helioscene blind, a series of hoods on an iron framework, worked on the same principle, as did the spring-roller Spanish blind, which had a single hood at the bottom. Both these blinds were recommended also because they promised 'pleasant views'. The

D, 2527.—Window Drapery in the Anglo-French Style.   D, 2528.—Window Drapery in the Anglo-French Style.

For Prices, in various materials, please see page 774.

FOR CONDITIONS UNDER WHICH GOODS ARE SENT CARRIAGE PAID PLEASE SEE PAGE 3. ALL CARPETS MADE UP FREE OF CHARGE.

9.2
Oetzmann, designs for window drapery, late nineteenth century

most popular blind of this kind was the Florentine blind, a large hood which filled the whole window area; the Oriental blind was its counterpart designed for circular-headed windows. A simple and cheap outside blind was the spring-roller blind, which fixed into a boxing with extending irons to let in air, a device also often used on doors.

The Venetian blind was originally an outdoor blind but became common for indoor use. Wood-lath Venetian blinds were available from Jennings and Co. of Bristol 'Painted any Colour, or Stained and Varnished' and were made to measure and charged by the foot. Manufacturers were keen to entice consumers by offering blinds to coordinate with one's room scheme. For example, the Patent Venetian Blind Co. Ltd of Birmingham advertised 'The Lux Patent Venetian blind', which was claimed to be 'the lightest, cheapest, most artistic and perfect blind in the world. This is the only Venetian Blind that can be

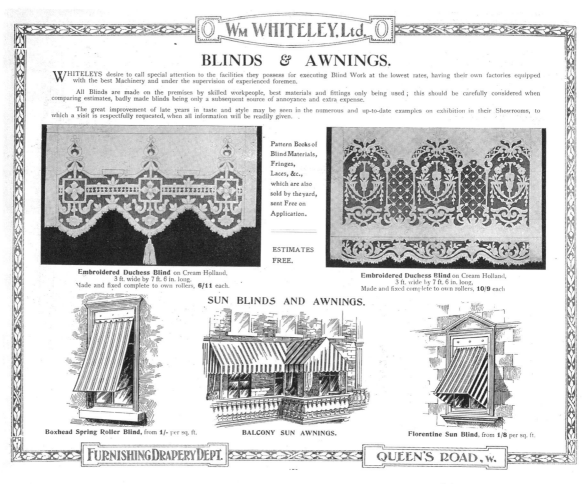

9·3
Wm Whiteley, awnings and blinds, early twentieth century

made to harmonise with the Decorating of the Apartment.' (see fig. 9.1).[5] Venetian blinds with coloured and ground-glass slats instead of the usual wood were also on sale, for example at Young and Marten's, builders' merchants. Iron Venetian blinds, japanned in bright colours, were also available. There were other types of indoor blind such as the Festoon blind, and related cheaper version, the Reefer blind, but the most commonly used by the end of the first decade of the twentieth century was the roller blind. There were several types of roller blinds in use; the by then old-fashioned plain roller and pulley, arranged on an endless cord and rack-pulley system; the single-line roller which comprised a single cord on a pulley which rewound itself, and the American and English spring-roller blinds (see fig. 9.3).

With the concern over public image, how blinds looked from the street was given a high profile in home manuals. Mrs Humphry advised in 1909 that 'in choosing the patterns and colours of blinds, it must always be remembered that they are seen from the outside as well as from the inside. In town houses it is often the custom to have all the blinds of the street frontage to match.'[6] *The Woman's Encyclopaedia* of 1911 noted that 'with regard to the colour of these blinds, the matter is always considered from the outside, and not from the inside point of view – that is, what looks best against the house'.[7]

Exterior blinds were expensive and their use thus restricted to 'the better class of houses'.[8] The possession of indoor and outdoor blinds was a ticket to middle-class respectability. For example, Keble Howard in *The Smiths of Surbiton*, 1906, mentions that in the summer Surbiton was bright with window boxes and sun blinds. Blinds were a frequent feature of house advertisements to entice prospective buyers or tenants, for example, four-bedroomed houses in Leinster Road, Hornsey, were 'fitted throughout with ELECTRIC LIGHT and gas, Art blinds and every modern appointment', while £300 houses on the Crabtree estate in Fulham in 1910 had 'blinds fitted to all front windows',[9] along with electric-light fittings and a tiled bathroom. Because of what blinds represented to outsiders, those families who could not afford the real thing improvised. C. H. Rolph, writing about living in Corbyn Street in Finsbury Park between 1906 and 1910, illustrates this: 'Some of our neighbours had a "false blind", a twelve-inch strip of lace-edged and cream coloured linen, tacked to the top of the window frame, for show. A tasselled cord hung from the centre of it, which you tugged at your peril – it didn't pull anything up or down and you had better leave it alone'.[10]

Repair ledgers from the period present us with a vivid cameo of exact types, prices, colours and locations of blinds in particular houses listed; for instance, J. and F. Grover of Ealing noted in 1875 that four crimson blind tassels were needed by a Miss Percival, along with green conservatory blinds and blinds for her billiard room.[11] Two years later, their ledger recorded that a green striped blind was needed for another client's kitchen, along with blue striped Florentine blinds at 9$\frac{1}{2}$*d* per foot for another room. Venetian blinds and roller blinds were frequently mentioned in records, for example, in those of the Lower Norwood Cooperative Building Society about 1905, and it is clear that by the 1880s they were incorporated into working-class houses on the Artisans, Labourers and General Dwellings Co.'s Shaftesbury Estate in south London[12] and their Noel Park Estate in north London, where it was noted that blinds of different colours were used in 'six shilling' (rent per week) houses as a device to break the monotony of the street.[13]

There was plenty of criticism of both Venetian and roller blinds. Mrs Panton commented on the 'expensive blind with its rollers, its cord eternally out of order, and its ugly effect from both inside and outside the house'.[14] Aldam Heaton, writing in 1897, said

surely never was anything uglier brought into our houses than the ordinary roller-blinds. Whether they are up or down, they are entirely hideous, even with cheap lace at the lower edge. They are particularly apt to go wrong, either in the way they roll up, or in their cords or other tackle. The last lap dirties far sooner than the rest, and, as they come down from above, they inevitably exclude the best light that comes into the room, when they are pulled down. No doubt they have been adhered to as being rather less cumbersome, and because their cords hurt the fingers less, than the terrible Venetian-blind; but in a well-furnished house they are today inexcusable. I hope to live long enough to see roller-blinds entirely done away with, or relegated only to the kitchen and office.[15]

In 1902, H. J. Jennings in *Our Homes and How to Beautify Them* noted the demise of both these types of blind: 'the old Venetian blind has completely gone out, and the roller blind is hurrying fast after it'.[16] The Venetian blind's downfall was explained by 'the craze for cheapness having led to the manufacture of a wretched article, the slats of common spruce roughly painted, with cotton ladders and jute cords'.[17] The style of blind which became fashionable instead by the Edwardian period was the fringed and braided silk or taffeta casement blinds, which were pulled backwards or forwards on a cord and pulley to cover the upper lights of windows and which it was claimed 'form better decoration and are cleaner than roller blinds'.[18] *Cassell's Household Guide* approved: 'many modern windows have an upper division either of decorative lead-lights or bull's-eye glass, or sometimes merely plain glass in smaller panes. Short casement blinds should always be provided for these upper windows, to be drawn whenever it is necessary to keep out the strong sunlight'.[19] They were on sale at furnishing shops, for example Wm Whiteley Ltd, where they were considered 'particularly suited to the Early English Style of Architecture with quaint casement windows, which have been recently revived'.

DECORATED GLASS

Cassell's Household Guide points to an important aspect of the late Victorian and Edwardian house, the use of decorative glass. Whether brilliant-cut, sandblasted, figured (textured), painted, transfer-printed, stained or plain leaded, decorated glass provided a good and permanent screen to the interior and shade from the sun and gave an instant, up-to-date appearance to a house. Mrs Haweis pleaded for the extended use of decorated glass in the 1880s: it was 'very useful as a screen, and often an ornament of considerable beauty',[20] thus

> in London and all large towns, where the outlook is so uninteresting or so ugly as to be commonly outside the question of taste – why do we use so little painted glass?... most persons will say, painted glass excluded the light, and all light that can be got is indispensible in a London street ... much of the good modern glass, such as the pale diaper-patterned kind provided by Clayton and Bell, Morris and Powell – and providable by any intelligent glass manufacturer – does not exclude light. In certain positions it occasionally even *adds* light, owing to the refractive property of uneven surfaces.

The effect of glass from the outside was often considered as important as the effect from within, especially with increased lighting levels in homes, as advertisements showed; 'high class leaded art glass window adds to the beauty of the interior of a home.... The leaded art glass designs as viewed from the street also add much to the appearance of a house.'[21]

Painted glass was expensive, but new techniques of decorating glass, affordable by the speculative builder by the end of the century, brought it within reach of the better-off middle classes. Glass with patterned surfaces was used in less important areas of the house. The processes included grinding or sandblasting, where sand was driven against glass by means of compressed air to produce a fine milky finish, similar to frosting. 'Embossing' involved treating the surface with hydrofloric acid to achieve a light satin-like finish, while etching with dilute hydrofloric acid produced a superficial white obscure look. Rolled figured glass was made from casting molten glass and rolling it into sheets; different patterns could be rolled into the surface during manufacture. Patterns were also commonly produced by sandblasting through a stencil, either on a clear background (Clear Enamel) or on a ground glass background (Obscure Enamel).

Leaded glass was a term which referred to method rather than a particular type of glass. Plain plate glass, semi-obscure or figured glass could be used, and the leading was done using lead, copper or zinc. 'Leaded glass' might refer either to clear leaded glass, over part or all of the window, with lead strips forming it into square or diamond patterns, or clear glass with coloured decorations, leaded one-colour coloured glass, leaded opalescent painted glass, or opalescent and cathedral glass.

The term 'painted glass', or stained glass, often did not mean glass with a painted decoration on it, but rather glass which was stained during manufacture; the paint used was similar to the glass in substance and in the process of firing became fused with the glass (in contrast to decorations which were painted on the glass, where one material was superimposed on another and remained separate). The colours for staining glass were mainly metallic oxides; reds were produced from oxide of iron, sub-oxide of copper, gold, and silicate of sodium; blues required cobalt, zaffre and copper; greens used oxides of iron, peroxide of copper and chromium oxide. Examples of trade names of tinted glass include Opal glass, Cathedral glass and Opalescent glass. Cathedral glass was cast and rolled in sheets with either a smooth or 'hammered' surface, while Opalescent glass had a •smooth surface finish. Figured rolled glass was also available in all standard colours.[22]

By the 1890s, in Hornsey, for example, large to medium sized houses made use of ornamental glass in vestibule doors, hallway and staircase windows, in the upper lights of main front-room windows, and in French windows and conservatory windows. Using stained, painted or transfer-printed leaded glass, elaborate scenes incorporating Aesthetic

Movement motifs such as birds and sunflowers could be achieved. These were particularly common in drawing-room windows at the back of the house and continued to be popular to the end of the Edwardian period. Front doors of such houses frequently also contained stained and figured glass, leaded to form elaborate patterns, and a small landscape scene, figure or head was often used as a centre-piece to the door design. Decorative glass in smaller houses of the same date usually consisted of a scaled-down version of designs for larger houses, often a mosaic of coloured pieces of glass set into the front door and side panels.

The suburban dweller's access to highly ornamental glass by the late nineteenth century brought criticism from writers and designers. M. H. Baillie Scott in 1895, while advising that the 'judicious use of leaded glass will add greatly to the effect of the interior', cautioned that 'the average stock patterns of the manufacturer are more suggestive of the gin palace than the private house, and should be carefully avoided'.[23] If colour was desired, he suggested that the best method was 'to introduce in a pane of plain squares or diamonds of clear glass a small heraldic or floral design in rich colouring, which in such a setting will have a brilliant jewel-like effect'.[24]

In the years after 1900, influenced by the Arts and Crafts Movement, the style of mass-produced decorated glass altered, employing instead simpler patterns created from plain and figured red, blue, green and amber stained glass, cut up into pieces to form stylised flowers, often a tulip or rose, or heart motifs after designers like Mackintosh and Voysey, or continental art nouveau 'whiplash' forms, set into plain leaded lights. This type of decoration glass was cheap to manufacture and thus can be found liberally applied to medium-sized houses, for instance in Cardiff, where identical or similar designs were repeated in front door, fanlights, side lights and side windows in the hall, as well as in reception rooms, conservatories, bedrooms and staircase windows. Even the smallest houses in the range had a coloured design in the clear leaded glass of the front door, which gave the house a cheap and instant 'modern' look.

For those who lived in houses without the much-sought-after decorative glass, amateur work was encouraged. Mrs Haweis urged 'young ladies at home' to trace a pattern on glass with enamel paint. In the Edwardian period, *The Decorator's Assistant* gave copious advice on how to paint glass in varnish colours to resemble stained glass, on 'Diaphanie' (the art of imitating stained glass for windows and conservatories using a pattern printed with glass colours which was varnished on the window), on etching glass using hydrofloric acid, fixing engravings to glass, and on how to imitate ground glass.[25] Manufacturers came up with substitutes for stained glass, such as Powell and Cottier's glass screen, designed to avoid the problems of altering a leasehold house. Also, Young and Marten Ltd introduced,

'Lithoglas' Transparencies in Imitation of Stained Glass for Window Decoration. 'Lithoglas' is used in thousands of Private Residencies, for the Panels of Front Doors; for Fanlights, Lavatory Windows, Staircase Windows; in Library, Bedroom or Bathroom. 'Lithoglas' is used to tone down excess of light, to brighten interiors, to prevent outsiders seeing through the Windows, whether night or day; and often to substitute a pleasing object for an unsightly one.

10

CEILINGS
AND CORNICES

10.1
Plaster ceiling rose in a
house built around 1880
(rateable value £34 in 1914),
Stroud Green, London

Of any fixed decoration in this type of house, possibly the clearest example of features that were declining in use over the late-Victorian and Edwardian period was that of plasterwork mouldings, or 'enrichments', which consisted of the decorated cornice, the ceiling 'flower' or 'rose' and smaller items such as trusses and small roses or 'paterae'. Enrichments and roses were fashionable from the early nineteenth century. The function of the ceiling rose was both ornamental and practical, in making a smooth transition from ceiling to light fixture, in the same way as the enriched cornice made the change from wall to ceiling. The rose also caught the smuts from the gas-lit chandelier or 'gasolier', preventing them from spreading more generally over the ceiling; when gas was first introduced, they had been seen as an essential part of a fashionable interior scheme. By the 1870s and 1880s, such decorative plasterwork was standard in medium-sized houses; those in Stroud Green in north London were typical, having often identical, decorated cornices and ceiling roses in the front room on the ground and first floor, and/or the room at the back on the ground floor, and trusses, paterae and small roses in the hallway (see fig. 10.1).

CEILING ROSES

From the 1870s onwards, however, a swing began to occur in critical opinion. Rhoda and Agnes Garrett, in *House Decoration*, 1876, condemned the 'coarse ornament'[1] in the centre of the ceiling; R. W. Edis in *The Decoration and Furnishing of Town Houses*, 1881, suggested plaster ornaments should be cut away;[2] and Lucy Crane in *Art and the Formation of Taste*, 1882, denounced the 'ugly and meaningless cornices and centre-pieces of the ceiling, looking like the ornaments off a wedding-cake'.[3] In the period up to 1914, plaster enrichments were increasingly the subject of criticism from those who were involved in the formation and dissemination of the latest ideas on what a tasteful interior should look like. For instance, Mrs Panton said, 'always insist on that ghastly round in the centre of the ceiling, above the gasolier, being removed. Workmen always say this is impossible, just as they say they cannot paint over graining.'

> There is absolutely no reason why our ceilings should not be as well and carefully coloured as our walls, if only huge and dreadful rosettes could be kept out of them … the frieze is to the constructional part of the room what the flower or fruit is to the plant … the absence of one nearly always results in the undue enlargement of the cornice, which becomes filled with 'enrichments' and becomes a slough of despond.[4]

Such practice persisted because decisions were too often left to the local builder or decorator. 'There is no more mischievous feature than the huge cornice which the builder always puts into his house. He thinks, I suppose, to make his room look "handsome".'[5] G. Cadogan Rothery, author of *Ceilings and their Decoration*, objected to the 'central bud, surrounded by radiating rings of foliage, each now of a different kind, the outer ring attentuated acanthus alternating with foliage spikes, terminating in a blossom the like of which nature has never produced … hideous travesty of the old rose (that ancient symbol of the sanctity of domesticity and joviality)'.[6] Enrichments were also condemned on grounds of health in the home. It was suggested that the plaster cornice could be avoided using a picture-rail below and whitened frieze above. The worst type of fixed decoration for trapping dust and harbouring germs was the deep cove and the enriched moulding which were regarded as 'expensive, dust-catching, and often unsightly'.[7] Moreover, one of the rose's functions, that of catching smuts from gas burners, became redundant in better-class houses after 1900 with the change to electric lighting.

CEILING   DECORATION

Along with the criticism of enrichments went complaints of the unpanelled or largely bare ceilings which accompanied them. G. Cadogan Rothery argued that plain ceilings looked glaringly white and became dirty quickly,[8] while Mrs Haweis in *The Art of Decoration*, 1889, protested that 'People seldom see ceilings now; they are so used to finding nothing there to see; yet this expanse of surface should never be neglected by the decorator.' Aldam Heaton, in 1897, said that 'the average citizen's ceilings consist of thirty to sixty square yards of plain whitewashed plaster … we pretend we "prefer a plain ceiling"'.[9]

A revolt took place from the end of the century, which led to a rejection of the rose and decorated cornice and 'the renewal of interest in the ceiling, even in modest houses'.[10] The revolt took the form of a return, on the one hand, to the flat ceiling treated as a surface to be decorated, and on the other hand, to boarded or plaster-panel ceilings with visible joists which were decorated with modelled plaster or stained.[11] The reassessment of the ceiling was due to several factors; in 1897, William Millar viewed the new treatments as 'partly due to the recent revival of the Queen Anne style, partly to the caprice of fashion, and partly to a more general use of panelled ceilings'.[12] The eclectic use of style in the 1890s and 1900s, generally, applied very much to ceiling decoration; indeed, the ceiling received new attention at the upper end of the market perhaps partly on account of its usefulness in conveying style forcefully by virtue of its sheer scale. For instance, in 1898, G. L. Sutcliffe described taste as having recently become more 'refined', using low-relief eighteenth-century details rather than heavy cornices and roses.[13] In 1908, *The Architectural Review* pointed to the contemporary vogue for Louis XVI, Empire and Adam styles in ceiling design, or naturalistic or conventional flower motifs provided they were given a

10.2

Detail of the back of a ceiling rose showing construction using a wooden frame to which would be glued individual casts to form a whole

'modern' flat treatment.[14] Whatever the style chosen, it implied a consideration of the whole ceiling area. The alternative style for the ceiling and its plasterwork was influenced by the work of the Arts and Crafts architect, Ernest Gimson, who, inspired by sixteenth- and seventeenth-century examples, hand-modelled plaster ceilings using metal tools. Such an approach was promoted by authors such as H. Muthesius in *Das Englische Haus*, 1904. This approach had its critics though, as Heaton demonstrates: 'There were three or four specimens in a recent "Arts and Crafts Exhibition" where the modern gesso work was cracked and going to pieces within a few months of its production. The saving clause is that these crazes are of short duration; and we are constantly learning that tradition is the only safe foundation.'[15] The move away from roses towards overall ceiling treatments occurred also because of the dis-semination of cheap mass-produced roses and cornices to small houses.

There were several ways of manufacturing ceiling roses for the speculative building market in common use until the 1890s. All methods involved separately cast parts; for example, plaster sections could be glued to a wooden frame or reinforced by means of a thin wooden stick running from the centre of the rose through each part of the rose (see fig. 10.2). William Millar, a leading contemporary authority on plaster-work, outlines a common manufacturing technique in use prior to 1897:

> Formerly, 'plate flowers' were greatly in use. The term 'plate' was applied to these flowers because the foliage was modelled and cast on a level plaster ground. Small centre flowers were generally cast on one plate, but large flowers required several pieces to complete the design. The enriched plates were let into the ceiling and made flush with the lime plaster, so that the plate formed part of the ceiling. This method was adopted to support the delicate foliage which was too weak to be cast separately.[16]

The manufacture of the rose itself changed in order to cope with large-scale demand and reduce costs, and the quality and range of designs fell as a result. One of the most important new processes which had a major impact on fixed decoration was gelatine moulding. The gelatine mould did not last as long as the usual wax mould and soon became hard and dry (a disadvantage with stock work), and the cast produced from all but the highest quality gelatine mould was not as clean, sharp and true as that from a wax mould. But the gelatine mould's major advantage was that it was flexible, which meant that undercut work could be produced from a single mould and fewer casts were broken when being taken from the mould. Roses of the 1890s tended to be smaller and cruder in design and construction compared to those of the 1870s and 1880s, with their eclectic, stylised versions of acanthus leaves, flowers and fruit motifs. The same few stock designs were frequently repeated across the country, regardless of class of house.

Solid plaster enrichments were imitated in other materials which claimed to be more convenient than solid plaster or compare favourably in price terms. The first substitutes were carton pierre, papier mâché and metal, and later, fibrous plaster. The price of a 24" papier-mâché rose at Young and Marten's builders' merchants was 4s 6d, compared to 3s for one in solid plaster; carton pierre was more expensive at 9s 6d.[17] Iron roses compared favourably price-wise; because of their weight they were less used in middle-class houses, although they were used in areas where there was easy access to cheap iron, such as Newport, Gwent. Fibrous plaster (plaster moulded with a canvas backing in a wax or jelly mould), on the other hand, was cheap and had a number of added advantages. Roses would be made in wax moulds and laid out flat to dry, and then some of the details such as fruit, foliage and flowers were undercut afterwards if necessary. Cornice mouldings would be cast in 'reverse' moulds[18] in lengths of ten to eighteen feet, or in sizes where two or three casts would make up the length of a room. Fibrous plaster could also be cast in sheets for ceilings and walls to any design or size. Its success was due to its strength, lightness, flexibility and convenience.

10.3
Modelled plaster frieze and
ceiling beams in the library
of a house in Jersey, by
Ernest Newton, about 1904

Compared to carton pierre and papier mâché, 'It is not only lighter and tougher than either, but it can also be made in larger sections, and adapted to more purposes.'[19] Fibrous plaster was less than a quarter of the weight of ordinary plaster and, for this reason, it was especially useful for centre flowers as, not only did it not pull down the lath and plaster, but it actually lent support to the ceiling when screwed to a joist. Moreover, fibrous plaster could be screwed to the ceiling by unskilled labour and the plastered ceiling did not have to be cut to key in the rose.

By the 1890s, roses and decorated cornices made from any material were no longer socially acceptable in fashionable houses. In 1897, Millar declared, 'The use of centre flowers, sometimes called roses … for ceiling decoration has gone out of fashion during the last decade.'[20] G. L. Sutcliffe pinpointed 1898 as the year when 'bold' or decorated cornices and centre roses went out of fashion,[21] although Millar conceded that 'When centre flowers are well designed, and the work is done direct by a qualified master plasterer, without filtering through the channel of a general contractor, centre flowers are still in demand, although in lesser quantities.'[22] Following this in the 1890s and 1900s, many of the upper- and middle-middle classes also began to reject enrichments and insist on houses with overall decorated ceilings. R. W. Edis suggested how the effect could be achieved using deal or canvas ribs laid over existing plaster to form the panels which would then be filled in with flock paper.[23] This method was apparent in Muswell Hill, for example, where from 1895 ceilings of reception rooms and/or hallways of top-quality houses were divided into panels using laths and fibrous plaster or other materials. Most of these houses also demonstrate a compromise between enriched and plain ceilings, in that they have panelled ceilings and boldly coved but unenriched cornices while still also retaining a simple flower, consisting of a series of plain concentric circles, in the centre of which was sometimes a small decorated rose. The trend towards black-and-white or modelled-plaster decorated visible joists was also greatly applied to 'the modern and rather uncertain but decidedly improved suburban villa'.[24] Nevertheless, variety within the middle-class market is clear; while writers were persuading consumers to shun the enriched cornice and ceiling flower, and many did, late-Edwardian builders' merchants' trade catalogues and views of showrooms still showed large stocks of roses which indicate their continuing popularity in certain markets. Certainly, builders, attending to aspirations towards social respectability, put roses into reception rooms in small houses up to the end of our period, while in some areas (for example, Herne Hill) enrichments also continued to decorate fairly substantial houses throughout the 1890s and early 1900s, in the hall and the main rooms on the ground floor, especially in drawing-rooms; in this particular locality, panelled ceilings were less common and decorated roses were used in preference in conjunction with all-over, very-high-relief ceiling papers.

As previously suggested, the middle classes kept up with the fashion for the overall decorated ceiling using substitutes for plaster (see fig. 10.4), such as fibrous plaster panels, or the more flexible high- or low-relief papers, such as Lincrusta, Cordelova, Anaglypta and Tynecastle. These papers were manufactured in squares or lengths suitable for ceiling or cornice, in a range of revival styles, and could be quickly assembled by the decorator. By these means, a rich and overall effect in a recognisable historical style could be achieved quickly and at an affordable price. It enabled the occupants to change their decoration at will to suit their taste and made them somewhat independent of builder's or landlord's preferences. Moreover, with the growth in home ownership, there was an increasing market for this type of product as people were prepared to spend money on their own homes in a way in which they could not when renting property. But such papers were still relatively expensive. Aldam Heaton suggested other ways to achieve a similar effect at less expense:

> Not enough use is made of flock paper. Ten or twelve flocks give a much bolder relief than 'Anaglypta', and nearly as much relief as the well-known 'Tynecastle', and cost less … a paper ceiling with printed borders

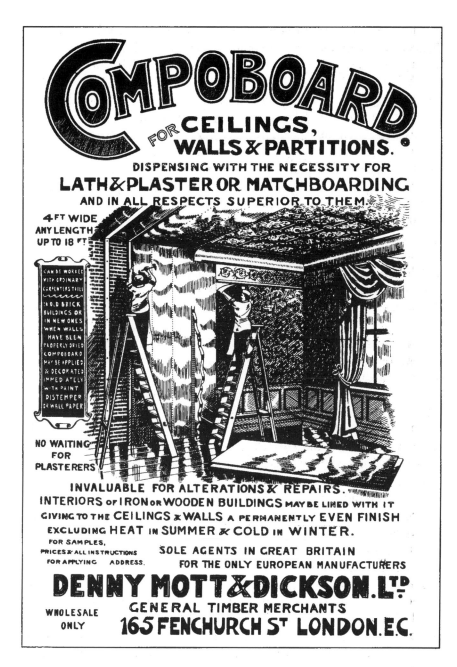

and hand-painted foliages and plaques can be executed at half the cost of a Tynecastle or moulded ceiling, and comes within the price that the average house-building John Bull can pay.[25]

Sheet metal, stamped with a design, often a period style or in imitation of decorative tiles or mosaics, was another substitute for the modelled-plaster ceiling. The stamped-steel ceiling, of American origin and commonly used in the USA, where it was manufactured by firms such as the Steleonite Metal Stamping Co. and Berger's Stamped Metal

10.5
Stamped-metal ceiling in a
1913 house (rateable value
£55 in 1914), London

Co., Ohio, was available in this country from companies such as Young
and Marten. These were advertised as 'highly decorative, incombustible,
inexpensive. Easily and quickly fixed, equally suitable for new or old
work',[26] and could be sold already painted white, or enamelled in
colours. They were considered 'excellent for bathrooms, corridors,
nurseries, and school-rooms, and kitchens, because they can be washed
regularly'.[27] Generally, their use in standard British houses appears to
have been relatively rare. Fig. 10.5 shows an example of such a ceiling in
London, where each room of the house had ceilings and cornices in
different designs in the Jacobean style. Identical designs to these were
manufactured by Young and Marten; the hall design, for instance, was
made in sheets 4 x 2 feet. Other examples of the use of stamped-metal
designs include a house in Muswell Hill with a Young and Marten frieze
in the hall and a Young and Marten cast-iron overdoor above the
drawing-room doorway in the hall. J. H. Elder-Duncan in *The House
Beautiful and Useful*, London 1911, p. 68, suggests stamped-metal ceilings
as an alternative to what most people had, that is, plain plaster or plaster
divided into compartments with mouldings and wallpaper or relief
decoration. The advantages of stamped-steel ceilings, resembling old

plaster patterns, he suggested, were that they could be applied in large sheets over old ceilings without removing them, and could not become water-damaged. Despite this, as Elder-Duncan notes, such ceilings were beyond the means of most people. Besides their high cost, there were also other trade reasons why they were resisted.[28] As *The Illustrated Carpenter and Builder* explained:

> A metal ceiling, while not so nearly artistic as a panelled ceiling in oak, cherry, or birch, or as a properly decorated ceiling in plaster, has a beauty of its own, and with the painter's aid may be made quite artistic; and, as it is less costly than any other ceiling having any claim to artistic beauty, and being fireproof, light, and easily applied, it is sure to become quite popular as soon as its good qualities are known, and the prejudices of old-fashioned workmen are removed.... The ordinary workman will find nothing very formidable in the putting up the sheet steel ceilings or wainscotings, and in the interests of good taste, to encourage a more extensive use of sheet metal than it is to discourage it, as is done at the present.[29]

With the impact of the Queen Anne revival, the upper- and middle-middle classes abandoned the ceiling rose in favour of panelling or overall ceiling pattern. The lower middle classes followed suit. Ultimately, their widespread use and change in tastes and priorities caused the demise of the rose and decorated cornice, along with the fall in the quality of design and the repetition of stock patterns. By 1914, the ceiling rose and enriched cornice were no longer used. A plainer look, which derived from recent trends, had emerged, with plain cornices and distempered ceilings. The revulsion felt in the 1920s for all things Victorian, classed as old-fashioned, was summed up in regard to ceilings in the 1927 edition of Millar's *Plastering Plain and Decorative*, where he described the central rose which was once 'the crowning glory of the plasterer's work' as 'the lowest form of degradation to which the plasterer's trade in this country ever descended and to which it succumbed; but the degradation did not stop with this feature only; it embraced the whole trade'.[30]

11

WALLS AND
FLOORS

11.1
Moulded plaster dado,
London, 1906, in a house
with a rateable value of £50
in 1914

A striking feature of the late-Victorian and Edwardian period was the dramatic increase in the use of mouldings, such as the skirting, dado and picture rails, architraves and panel-mouldings in the middle-class house, and their increasing complexity of design. The origin of mouldings was practical and aesthetic, for example, skirtings and dado, or 'chair', rails were used to protect the wall and dado, and picture rails supported ornaments and pictures. Skirtings, cornices, architraves and panel-mouldings covered joins and gaps and softened the transition for the eye between floor and wall, wall and ceiling, door and wall. Mouldings were traditionally available only to the wealthy few and this link with status underpins their usage in middle-class homes between 1880 and 1914.

DADOES AND PICTURE RAILS

The dado and picture rail in particular were typical late-Victorian and Edwardian features. H. Muthesius in *The English House*, 1904, explained how their introduction by the artistic avant-garde in the 1870s came about: 'In place of the Victorian papered wall that ran from floor to ceiling, they revived the dado. It became so important to aestheticism of the 1880s as to be found almost indispensible to an artistic room. No less importance was attached to the frieze.'[1] The impetus behind their use then stemmed from the taste for the Queen Anne revival style and the associated Aesthetic Movement. The position of such mouldings marked the areas of the wall which, in a room intended to be in a classical style of some sort, derived from rules of classical proportioning; the bottom of the pedestal was marked by the skirting, the plinth of the wall marked the dado (see fig. 11.1), the bottom of the frieze was marked by the picture rail and the classical cornice by a plain or decorated plaster cornice. The most common arrangement of mouldings in the middle-class house derived from the rules of classical proportioning. Whereas the fireplace indicated the style intended for a room, the fact that wall mouldings generally set the stylistic tone for the entire house offered the speculative builder a relatively cheap and quick way of making a house fashionable and saleable. The simple addition of a few mouldings could convey a sense of social respectability and status to others, thus ensuring that mouldings became an indispensable part of the middle-class interior. H. J. Jennings, speaking about the use of the dado rail in the 1870s and 1880s, said, 'No middle class house was considered perfect without it.... The lady whose rooms had dadoes looked down on the lady who had none.'[2] The picture rail, which marked the frieze from the filling, was also a vital ingredient of an up-to-date interior of the 1870s and 1880s, and offered a new solution to the problem of hanging pictures. The method of hanging pictures prior to the 1870s, by means of rings on iron rods which ran round the room just below the cornice, was replaced by a cheaper and easier solution, the wooden rail, which was adequate for hanging lighter pictures. By the new century, the picture rail had become 'a permanent feature of every English wall',[3] and possession implied ownership of middle-class trappings, such as prints and paintings. In particular, the dado was used in hallways and drawing rooms. The dado rail was more or less standard in the hallway in all sizes of house and many had both dado and picture rails. The picture rail was more common in reception rooms than the dado rail, with only dearer houses possessing both.[4] The dado rail could also have more practical functions; when it was strictly speaking going out of fashion among the arbiters of taste, Mrs Panton, writing in 1889, explained its usefulness. 'I must say I still hanker after a dado, because in the drawing room I like to hang all sorts of odds and ends upon it.'[5] The dado rail continued to be included in new houses long after the journals declared it old-fashioned, and this suggests the force of conservatism in the middle-class interior.

MOULDINGS DESIGN

Increased variety and complexity of the design of mouldings can be plotted through trade catalogues. For example, whereas early catalogues of Jewson's wood company often showed only a limited selection of designs for cheap houses, their catalogue of about 1910-19 reveals a vast selection of all sorts of mouldings for a wide range of markets; over one hundred designs for architraves were illustrated, each design often available in several sizes, along with thirty-three designs for skirtings and a similar range of dado and picture rails and panel mouldings. Their prices varied widely, depending on the design; for example, picture rails cost between 4s 9d to 15s, dado rails from 6s 3d to 12s 6d, and architraves from 3s 9d to £1 14s 6d.

Generally, complexity of design and top-quality mouldings were assumed to go hand in hand.[6] Skirtings varied from the short, narrow, and often simply cut type of skirting to the tall, deep, and elaborately moulded expensive skirting which comprised two separate sections, one slotted in on top of the other. The best houses had skirtings which were composed of two sections, while skirtings in medium-sized houses were high but made in one piece. Smaller houses had lower and thinner skirtings, although the profiles were often quite complex. The forms of the mouldings in the period 1880-1914 derived from classical, Renaissance or Gothic mouldings, and it was recommended that the form of a moulding should not be arbitrary, but should be determined precisely by its intended position on the wall.[7] But the ease with which machines could cut any profile led to an eclectic use of styles far removed from their origins, and manufacturers did not adhere to the plea for stylistic accuracy or for the form of the moulding to relate to its position on the wall; for example, H. Gibbon and Sons, Cardiff, advertised six sets of coordinated designs, consisting of architrave, dado

T. Parsons' washable
distemper paint samples,
1908

Decorative suggestions for
the drawing-room, dining-
room and study, in
Mrs Humphry, 1909

No 325A
No. 326A
No. 327A
No. 328A
No. 822
No. 330A
No. 331
No. 823
No. 824
No. 825

Tessellated floor tiles by
Gibbon, Hinton and Co.

PLATE 22

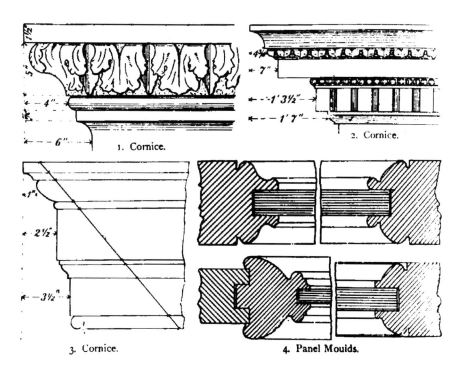

1. Cornice.

2. Cornice.

3. Cornice.

4. Panel Moulds.

11.2
Renaissance wood
mouldings by G. Ellis

and picture rails and panel mouldings, each pattern available in different sizes. The items in each set were almost identical in profile apart from minor alterations where practicality demanded, for instance the picture rail, which needed an upper part that the picture hook could grip. 'These mouldings which have been specially designed for use are arranged in series ... [which] ... enables you to have all mouldings alike throughout the house.'[8]

By the new century, as we have seen from the trade catalogues, the use of these mouldings had spread, provoking the same criticisms that were aimed at ceiling mouldings. George Ellis, writer on joinery, was among those who condemned the 'meaningless assemblage of hollows and rounds that do duty for mouldings ... thanks mainly to the exigencies of machine production'.[9] The dado became such a cliché for would-be middle-class households that it inspired the words of a music hall song:

Oh sweet adornment for the cottage wall,
Dado, dado;
Oh poverty's sure solace whatsoe'er befall,
Dado, dado, da:
To dream of thee all night,
To gaze on thee by day,
Is the proletarian's supreme delight;
Dado, dado, da.
When the grate is empty and the cupboard bare,
Dado, dado;

When the Briton's tugging at his wife's back hair,
Dado, dado, da;
How rapturous to mark Thy grades of green and gray,
Where the farthing dip dispels the dense, dim, dark;
Dado, dado, da.[10]

Such a widespread dissemination of mouldings prompted a change of taste in fashionable circles, as H. J. Jennings in *Our Homes and How to Beautify Them*, 1902, explained: 'It would have been no great wonder if, as a consequence of its appearance in the cheap suburban villa, the dado had by this time become as extinct as the dodo.'[11] The criticisms levelled at mass-produced mouldings by Arts and Crafts supporters, together with their use in cheaper houses, eventually led to the disappearance of some mouldings, such as the dado rail, from fashionable houses:

> The revival of the dado and the frieze at once made three wall areas available… . But this was decidedly too much and English wall decoration took a long time to rid itself of the excess… . It was finally recognised that a limitation was called for and that there must be a choice between dado and frieze. The frieze was preferred and the wall was divided into a shallow area at the top and a deeper one below. The dividing line is marked by a cornice at the level of the lintel of the door, which is also meant for hanging pictures.[12]

As in the case of ceiling enrichments, complicated mouldings generally were increasingly seen as an obstacle to health in the home, and their removal would, it was suggested, even alleviate the problems caused by the shortage of servants, thus, 'The servant difficulty would be largely resolved if all elaborate mouldings, ledges, and other resting places for dust and dirt were banished from the house.'[13] Randall Phillips, writing in 1920, complained, 'Many seem to regard a picture-rail as the acme of desirability in any room; but … it is a veritable dust-trap, very awkward to get at.'[14] Some were persuaded that there should be a return to simple mouldings as 'the old-fashioned nine-inch simple skirting … is far the best'.[15] By 1914, the Arts and Crafts Movement had ushered in a new fashion for simple mouldings of all kinds, and so we find that prices in the catalogues of this period are the same for simple or complex designs of identical wood and dimensions.

WALL PANELLING

The Arts and Crafts adherents and others also revived panelling for wall treatment in keeping with the new domestic ideal: 'this is a specifically English case – the wall may be panelled in wood from floor to ceiling. This treatment is very popular in the best-appointed houses, and lends the room a comfortable appearance and a general atmosphere of luxury, comfort and extreme homeliness, which is not so easily achieved by other means.'[16] The high-panelled dado, the top of which was marked by a plate rail, was used in fashionable interiors by the 1900s. Panelling and plate rails filtered down into smaller speculative housing in a modified form after 1905; for example, in Hornsey, houses built by Collins on the Rookfield estate contained these features, a dramatic contrast with other houses in the area built by the same firm in the Queen Anne revival style a decade earlier.

TILED SURFACES

One of the permanent floor and wall coverings most characteristic of late-Victorian and Edwardian houses is decorative ceramic tiles on hearths, walls and floors. The housing boom of the late nineteenth century led to a vast increase in the demand for tiles. Builders bought in bulk, choosing from ranges in the trade catalogues of specialist tile producers such as Maw and Co. or general builders' merchants like Young and Marten. The appeal of ceramic lay in the fact that it was decorative, hygienic and flexible, providing a cheap, up-to-date, colourful and easy-to-clean surface of any size. Inside the house, ceramic wall and floor tiling was popular in kitchen quarters, the often newly acquired bathrooms, and in conservatories and hallways. For example, at the Ideal Home Exhibition of 1908, T. and R. Boote's patent tile factory in Burslem displayed their mosaic and unglazed tiles for hallways and their artistic tiling for bathrooms and lavatories. Floor tiling was not used for most other rooms in the house, such as sitting-rooms, as it was considered too hard and cold for comfort. Tiled hearths and grates, though, were very important in these types of rooms as they helped define room character; for example, W. Furnival reported an enormous demand for 'crimson enamelled tiles, especially in the 6-inch by 6-inch briquette pattern' which had 'proved particularly suitable for dining-room and hall hearths'.[17] Tiles were frost-proof and so could also be used in outdoor locations; again, on account of their decorative and hygienic properties, they were used extensively in well-trodden areas, such as the forecourt and doorstep, and for porch walls, where they might provide 'such permanent decoration which may "make or mar" the first glimpse of the home'.[18] Cardiff is particularly well endowed with elaborate doorways of plain and picture tiles, even for small houses (see plate 19).

The employment of ceramic surfaces in the home increased and diversified, particularly from the last decade of the nineteenth century until the First World War. It was noted in 1904, in relation to fireplace and range hearths, interiors and surrounds, that 'during the last twenty years this particular branch has received considerable attention from designers, artists, and manufacturers. Hardly a mansion, or even a dwelling-house, is now built without being fitted with glazed-tile hearths of one kind or another.'[19] The demand for other, more expensive

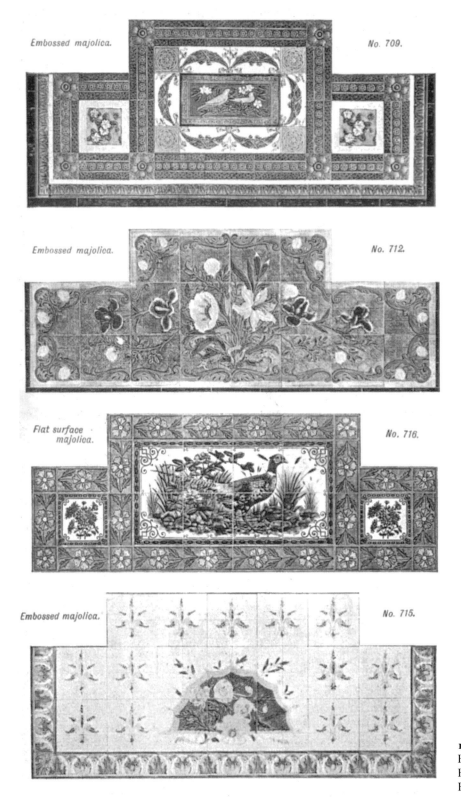

Embossed majolica.   No. 709.

Embossed majolica.   No. 712.

Flat surface majolica.   No. 716.

Embossed majolica.   No. 715.

11.3
Hearth tiles by Gibbons,
Hinton and Co., Brierley
Hill, about 1900

ceramic products, also widened: 'for better-class work, such as vestibules, large conservatories, hotel entrances, shop doorways, and the like, there is now a steady demand for ceramic mosaic'.[20] With expansion of the tile business and the setting up of many new tile firms in this period, the job of fixing tiles and mosaic, which traditionally had been undertaken by plasterers or bricklayers, evolved into a specialised trade. At the same time, the quality of ceramic products became more varied as demand grew at the lower end of the market. As one writer complained, 'unfortunately, there is also a demand for inferior qualities, and there are makers manufacturing accordingly'.[21]

The constant shifting of fashions and the demand for individuality and novelty in architecture and design generally was also reflected in the design, size, colour and finish of tiles. Speaking of tile design, it was noted that 'changing taste … has played an important part in creating demand for different combinations and adaptations … hence continual change is going on in this direction'.[22] Ceramic came to be used, for example, not simply for hearths and the cheeks of fireplaces (see fig. 11.3), but for entire fire surrounds, which were composed of specially curved or moulded glazed fireclay briquette and faience available in 'a large variety of designs, and glazed or enamelled in equally profuse variety'[23] (see fig. 2.10). Technical innovations, for example the development of lead-free glazes, also contributed to visual changes. The range of possible body and surface treatments for tiles expanded to include hand-painting and transfer-printing, relief-moulded Majolica glazing, and tube lining, which were used to reproduce styles from Aesthetic Movement to art nouveau, Adam or plain colour tiles.

In terms of ceramic flooring, the most expensive and desirable type, to be found in hallways of some first-rate houses, was the mosaic pavement, which was available from firms like Doulton and Co. of Lambeth. Ceramic mosaic was generally highly regarded by writers; Mrs Humphry's description of it as 'a cheap, yet novel and beautiful, artistic flooring'[24] was typical of writers' comments. This type of floor was composed of small square or irregular tesserae which were usually dust-pressed, many at a time, in a mould-box which was divided into sections. Less often, the mosaic was first made in long strips which were then chipped or cut up to form tesserae. The increasing scale of demand for marble tesserae prompted changes in manufacturing techniques, as the following passage from 1904 shows: 'some ten thousand tons of marble tesserae are annually imported into England, and this increased demand has caused the introduction of cutting machinery and various labour-saving apparatus, which has so reduced the cost that it can now be laid down for but a few shillings per square yard'.[25] The appeal of mosaic lay in the way it allowed 'elaborate centre-pieces, graceful and foliated borders, pleasing ornamental scrolls at angles'[26] to be incorporated into a floor design where desired, regardless of size of floor. The small size of the mosaic tesserae meant that, in order to aid the fixer's task, the pattern was drawn in reverse on tough paper at the tile works, cut into manageable sections for laying, and the tesserae then placed face down onto the paper and glued, ready for transport and use on site.

If mosaic floors were used in some expensive houses, the more usual type of ceramic flooring for all sizes of middle-class house was tessellated flooring (see plate 22). The design of a tessellated floor was composed from ceramic pieces, standardised in shape and size – square, triangular, octagonal and hexagonal pieces up to $1^1/_{16}$ inches square – so that the parts fitted together easily to form a geometrical pattern to suit almost any space requirement. The complexity of even the simplest of tessellated floors reveals the skills required of the designer. Contemporaries conceded that 'on examination of a floor-tile design, it will be seen that the diversity of colour and size of its component parts is very considerable, and it is at works where the floor-tile department is a large one that the greatest demands are made upon the drawing-office'.[27] The prominent location, extensive area and permanent nature of floor tiling also placed special emphasis on the colours used. As a general rule, it was felt that 'brilliant gem-like tints are not to be expected among coloured earthenware bodies; nevertheless for decorative flooring something more than nondescript hues are needed'.[28] Furnival even suggested a 'system and classification of colours' in order that

> those who possess no intuitive genius in the direction of colour harmony may yet be enabled to manufacture and apply their products intelligently, and so as to give satisfaction to their clients. This is of vastly more importance in the case of ceramic works than of wall-papers, wall-paints, frescoes, carpets, linoleums, oil-cloths and the like, because of the greater permanence of the former.[29]

A tessellated floor could be made up from a combination of two or three types of dust-pressed tile, plain colours, vitreous and encaustic. Plain tiles were made from natural clay colours, which produced red and buff tiles; a metallic oxide, for example, manganese, could be added to produce black, chocolate, greys or drab, salmon and fawn. Vitreous tiles were formed from a mixture of Felspar, ball clay, china clay, Cornish china stone, and flint, which produced a white body. Stains were added to form blue or green tiles; pale pink and silver grey tiles could also be produced by this process but are less often found as they were more expensive to produce. Encaustic tiles involved a pattern being inlaid, by first dust-pressing the pattern, and then pressing a different coloured background on to it in a mould. Cheaper floors, particularly in the kitchen area, tended to use only plain colours, but most hall floors, even in smaller houses, were usually a combination of plain and vitreous or all three types.

The procedure for laying the floor was different from that for mosaic; the tiles were first laid out on a prepared cement surface to check their accuracy compared with the plan. Then two guide strips were laid, eighteen to thirty inches apart, in the centre of one end of the room; mortar was spread between them and levelled with a screed which was notched to allow for tile thickness. When the mortar was stiff, tiles were placed on it and tapped down until they were at level height with the guide strips. When the space between the strips was finished, one strip was moved out another eighteen to thirty inches in order to do the adjoining section of floor. When the completed floor was set, the joints were grouted with pure cement, and the excess rubbed off with sawdust. Wall-tiling was done in a similar way, either laying tiles onto a mortar base between guide strips, or 'buttering' (as it was known) the mortar on the back of each tile before setting it.

The more frequent use of this type of flooring meant that manufacturers offered many more designs than for mosaic, for example, a turn-of-the-century trade catalogue of Gibbons, Hinton and Co. of Brierley Hill, a firm who supplied builders in Cardiff, contained twenty-five designs in multi-colour plain tiles, nine designs in just red and black, nine in black and white, and twenty-six in multi-colour plain and encaustic mixed, compared to only six designs in ceramic mosaic.

Great use was made of tiled floors in Cardiff houses, where the variety of floor designs was remarkable. The tiled floor was not restricted to any particular class of house; by the early twentieth century, even small houses might be built with a tiled hallway. Plain tile floors were cheaper than plain and encaustic tiles mixed and thus were generally used in smaller houses; however, the proportion of elaborate floors found in fairly small houses as well as in large houses is significantly large. Patterns with the more expensive encaustic tiles incorporated were used in medium-sized houses in Cardiff by the early Edwardian period. Distinctions were also often made within the house, as well as between classes of house. Generally, a more expensive pattern would be used for the hallway; it was sometimes continued into the breakfast room and kitchen, but more often a cheaper pattern was chosen for these less important rooms. Contemporaries noted that preferences for colours of flooring varied regionally; 'there is a special leaning in particular localities for tile designs of varied colourings'. In Cardiff, for instance, multi-coloured designs significantly outweighed black and white, although the latter became more commonly used towards the end of the period (see plate 18). In comparison,

> in North Wales light colours consisting of drab, salmon, chocolate, white, and sage, in fairly rich combinations, are often selected. This may be accounted for to some extent by the fact that the roads there are largely of limestone formation; hence, the light-coloured dust and footmarks when wet do not so easily disfigure the pavement... . Again, in London there is a distinct preference shown for black and white tiles; these being used most largely for outside forecourts, porches, and halls, also for scullery floors and underground conveniences.[30]

By the late nineteenth century, fashions were changing in custom-built houses to simpler schemes using plain red tiles. M. H. Baillie Scott advised that 'all patterns which startle or dazzle should be avoided … the elaborate designs so commonly met with should be avoided' and urged instead that 'the use of plain red tiles with a border of green and brown glazed tiles may be suggested. Brick-work on edge laid in herring-bone or other patterns gives warm colouring and homely character to the floor … tesserae with naturally fractured edges used in connection with wide cement joint will give a better result than is gained by the mechanical precision of the average patterns.'[31]

WOODEN FLOORING

As suggested earlier, ceramic tiles were considered inappropriate for living-rooms. Here, parquet was recommended to be used in conjunction with Oriental rugs. C. Jennings of Bristol supplied inlaid parquetry for 'mansions or villas', in greenheart or other woods, such as teak, ash, oak, walnut and plywood, with multi-coloured borders. But its cost limited its use to houses of the upper-middle classes; 'parquetry is the ideal flooring for hall and reception rooms, but its cost is very great, and for this reason it is a luxury to be enjoyed only by the favoured few'.[32] Parquetry surrounds, used with a central carpet, were recommended as a way to avoid the problem of limited means. As with tiling, parquet was advised on grounds of health and convenience, as 'it will never need renewing, nor beating, nor scrubbing, and … it will simplify very much the task of cleaning the room'.[33] Greater attention to health in the home brought a lessening of emphasis on the longevity of furnishings such as carpets, a characteristic of the orthodox approach to housekeeping earlier in the century. Mrs Panton was an example of this new attitude: 'when I consider the dirt and dust … I am only thankful that our pretty cheap carpets do not last as carpets used to do, for I am sure such a possession cannot be healthy'.[34] The movement away from fitted carpets in the 1880s and 1890s also led to the trend in many middle-class houses towards using plain boards, polished or stained to imitate mahogany or oak, with carpet squares or rugs. An alternative for those who did not have a good wooden floor or parquet was to use coloured felt or rush matting with smaller rugs on top.

FLOORCLOTH

Mosaic and tesselated floor tiles, parquet and carpets could all be imitated by cheap, hard-wearing and hygienic floorcloth, in the form either of oilcloth or linoleum, which proved very popular. Oilcloth, first recorded in Britain in 1736, was a canvas composed of a combination of flax and hemp which was then painted. Linoleum was patented by Frederick Walton in 1860 and 1863, following E. Galloway's

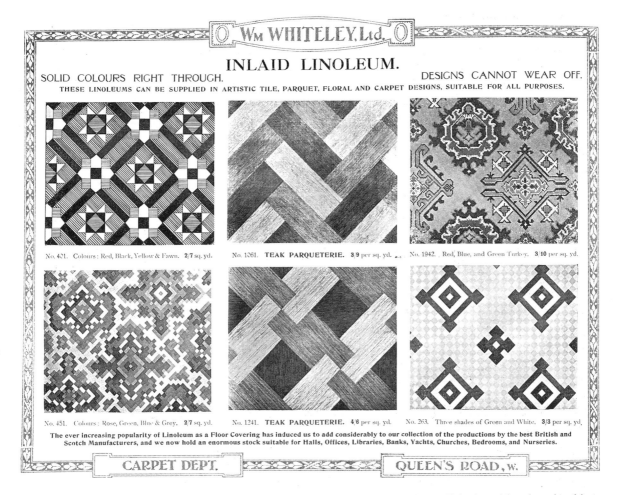

11.4
Wm Whiteley, linoleum
designs, early twentieth
century

'Kamptulicon' of 1844; this was thicker than oilcloth, with a jute backing on which was spread pounded cork and linseed oil, and the pattern was painted on top. Writers of the new century recommended 'inlaid' linoleum, where a durable pattern, often constructed from as many as thirty-five different dyes or punches, was produced from moulds into which was run dyed pounded cork and oil. Frederick Walton's vast inlaying machine produced thirty-five thousand square yards of linoleum a week in 1910 which he claimed was 'as waterproof as indiarubber … almost as durable as the tesselated pavement … much more lasting than the carpet'.[35] While advertised by the manufacturers as suitable for every room in the house, like tiles, it was cold and hard and so tended to be mostly used in the hallway, on the stairs, in the bathroom, and as a surround in the bedroom; as R. Redgrave pointed out, 'floor-cloths are not so much used in this country for dwelling rooms as in halls, staircases, lobbies, and other approaches'.[36]

The patterns for oilcloths available in the late nineteenth and early twentieth century followed those used for eighteenth-century floorcloths, which were either plain, or resembled marble floors or woven carpets (see fig. 11.4). In addition, patterns were available which imitated mosaic and tessellated pavements, parquet and even, according to Eastlake (writing in 1868) designs 'intended to represent the spots on a leopard's skin'.[37] At the Ideal Home Exhibition of 1908, Hembry and Co. of London showed their 'Inlaid Tile, Granite, Carpet and Plain Linoleum in various colours, patterns and qualities'. Indeed, the possibilities were endless. J. C. Loudon wrote earlier in the nineteenth century that 'there seems to be no reason why their patterns should not be as various as carpets'.[38] Some writers disagreed, maintaining that materials should not masquerade as more expensive ones, such as Redgrave, for whom floorcloth designs should 'avoid all imitations of carpet patterns'.[39] Certain designs were deemed more appropriate than others; 'floral designs are quite out of place, the most suitable being the simple geometrical patterns in imitation of tiles or parquetry'.[40] Mrs Panton, despite claiming to know better, could not resist recommending Staines Linoleum Co.'s design, which 'resembles tiny squares of black and white marble, which looks very well down. Of course it is a sham, and as such is to be deprecated'; and she went on 'for those who will not allow any shams anywhere in their houses, nothing looks so nice as the darkest self-coloured linoleum put down all over the passages and halls, with some six-foot and even larger rugs about'.[41] Conventions within the home dictated that there was a preference for the traditional rather than the avant-garde when it came to linoleum design, according to one source of 1905, who also offered a practical explanation:

> adaptations of the forms so popular in L'Art Nouveau have found their way into oilcloth design, but have not attained any great popularity in this field. It is probable that this is due to the fact that the character of this style is not yet thoroughly understood by the public, and that the oilcloth designer has not yet been able to reconcile it properly with the limitations of oilcloth manufacture.[42]

The same source instructed students in floorcloth designing for different markets; designs aimed at the upper classes needed 'to suit a public that is educated and knows what a design should be'; those for the middle classes, who apparently recognised that they could not match this taste, should be 'simple, inoffensive patterns', while for others it was a case of 'where elaborate floral devices in bunches or strewn in garlands form a principal theme in loud or contrasting colors, ... a certain number of uneducated people can best get their money's worth in noise and brilliancy'.[43]

PAINTS AND WALLPAPERS

As mentioned at the start of this chapter, throughout the later Victorian period, the fashion was to divide the wall into three sections, the dado, filling and frieze. Eastlake urged the use of a dado and frieze in 1868 thus, 'the most dreary method of decorating the wall of a sitting room is to cover it all over with an unrelieved pattern of monstrous design'.[44] The Edwardian period was labelled 'the frieze period', as dadoes were increasingly discarded in favour of a more prominent frieze area, friezes of 21", 18", 10½", 9", 7" or 5" deep being the most common by 1902. Special wallpapers were manufactured in accordance with these changing fashions. Dado papers were used from 1870 to 1900, and special frieze papers, increasingly decorative and dominant between 1900 and 1920, with the rest of the wallpaper on a wall toned down in contrast. The frieze was, by 1905, a crucial part of any decorator's showroom repertoire: 'the large and increasing demand for high-class friezes also suggests a field for showroom enterprise ... of either stencilled friezes upon one of the many popular decorator's canvas cloths and plain ingrain papers, or of handwork relief friezes in Alabastine'.[45] Frieze papers also revived hand work, for example, Shand Kydd's friezes, encouraged by a revival of stencilling in the 1880s by Haywood and Sons, and aerographing through stencils, undertaken first by Lightbrown, Aspinall and Co.

Under the influence of new ideas about health in the home, rooms became less cluttered by the Edwardian period and colour schemes grew lighter overall, as dark dull colours gave way to strong colours in the 1890s and to pale colours by the early 1900s (see plates 21 and 25).[46] Walter Pearce maintained in 1902 that 'Light papers are conducive to health as opposed to dark ones.'[47] Electric lighting made previous darker colour schemes seem gloomy, and the cleanliness of electric light made it no longer crucial to have dark colours which did not show the dirt. The use of colour also differed in keeping with the various room types; for instance in 1889 Mrs Panton viewed greens, blues, terracottas and old gold as appropriate for the hall; her schemes included one using Pither's red and white berry paper, a matting dado in red and white from Treloar's on Ludgate Hill (London), with red-varnished woodwork; a more expensive scheme comprised high cream dado and woodwork to match with a gold Japanese-leather paper (see pp. 157-8) Mrs Panton's dining scheme was red, comprising a plain gold Japanese leather paper, a dado of red and gold leather, red-varnished paintwork, along with a yellow and white ceiling and a cream coloured cornice. To contrast, her ideal drawing-room was described as 'delicate sparrow's egg blue, furthermore embellished by long designs of rushes or grasses, either stencilled or painted on'.[48]

The period was characterised by the overall growth in the range available of paints and wallpapers, their convenience of use, and their increasing fall in price. Mrs Panton praised 'delightful Mr Aspinall' who 'has made house decoration mere child's play compared to what it used to be'.[49] The wallpaper industry became increasingly mechanised and specialised, with 140 different jobs identified by 1914. While still repre-

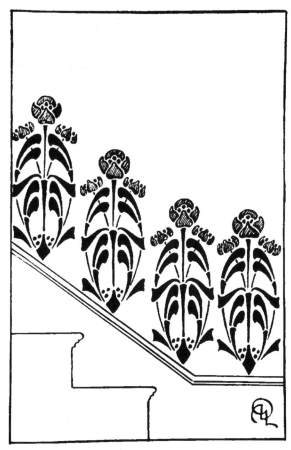

senting a minor part of the overall building costs, the painting and decorating trades increased in importance as standards of living rose. Prices of painting and decorating fell till about 1900, when there was a peak, which was followed by a further fall and then a rise just before 1914.[50] By the 1880s, wallpapers could cost anything from 1s per piece for the cheapest made by machine, where all the colours were printed together on plain paper, up to 70s per piece. For example, Young and Marten's range of wall coverings was highly praised by *The Decorator* in 1905;[51] its range included hand-made paper hangings, from 2s 6d to 24s per piece, silk and velvet surfaces, ingrains, canvas effects, soirettes, leatherettes from 1s 6d to 12s 6d, cheap papers and reliefs, all covering a range of styles including French designs and imitation needlework striped papers. By 1904, W. Shaw Sparrow in *The British Home of Today*, 1904, declared that 'new wallpapers have been so cheap and plentiful. No spring cleaning is considered complete without a change of pattern and colour.'

The cheapest class of wallpapers were pulps where the natural colour of the wallpaper itself as ground or ornament formed part of the final surface. The next cheapest were grounds, where the whole paper was coloured with a ground by machine before a design was printed on

11.5 *left*
T. Parsons, paint manufacturers, designs for friezes, 1908

11.6
Stencilled staircase dado design

156

it. Other types of wallpaper included 'satin' papers, which were polished or glazed before printing using rotary brushes; embossed or stamped papers, where the ground or pattern (or both) was stamped in relief; and grained papers, where papers were given an overall texture in stamping: grained papers in imitation of oak, for example, were very popular. So too were mosaic imitation papers, examples of which can be found in the hallways especially of large and medium-sized houses in London and Cardiff. Imitation marble and tile papers were produced by companies like C. F. Crew and Co. (in 1905). Despite Mrs Panton's hatred of marble paper, 'that monstrosity', it too was commonly used. Varnished papers were also available, ready varnished by machine, recommended for use in bathrooms. Gilded papers, or 'golds', first introduced by Wylie and Lochhead in 1860, were so popular between 1890 and 1900 that they were used as an alternative to floral and period designs; cheaper 'metal' papers used imitation-gold and bronze powder. Flock papers, initiated by S. Scott's patent of 1860, followed by Woollams' patent of 1878, were very commonly used, though they were criticised for looking dusty quickly. They consisted of three types: plain (fine dessicated cloth adhering to tacky printed paper), heavy (three or more flockings producing a raised pattern of $1/16''$ to $1/8''$); and stamped or relief (surface produced using hot dies). There were many variations and combinations of the above wallpapers.

A major trend in this period was the quest for a durable, washable paperhanging. Following the exhibiting of a 'washable' paper at the 1851 Exhibition, attempts were made to perfect such a commodity, notably in 1853 with Stather's patent, Heywood, Higginbottom and Smith's 'sanitary' paper of 1871, followed by many other patents produced by firms such as Potter, Lightbrown, Aspinall and Co., and Walker and Carver. Sanitaries had the printing done in oil colours on a heavily sized ground, giving a glossy look; 'sanitums' and washables, on the other hand, had the ground or pattern or both printed in washable distemper and spirit colour which was insoluble in water to produce a non-glossy appearance. Patterns for early versions of these papers used imitations of Venetian blinds and, particularly popular, a wood-imitation pattern. This category of wallpaper proved very popular, much recommended by writers; indeed, the concern with health led the word sanitary 'on the selling side to contain magic properties, conveying an irresistible impression of excellence'.[52] In 1902, washable and sanitary papers were recommended especially for kitchens, passages, and staircase dadoes. Repair ledgers record that their use was widespread; for example, they were used in houses rented out by the Lower Norwood Cooperative Building Society.

Relief papers, employed largely for dadoes, friezes and ceilings, also saw much experimentation and development. *The Decorator* of 1905 advised showroom organisers that 'ceiling decoration may form a special study, since so much increase of high relief materials is applied to this purpose every year'.[53] The first type on the market were Japanese-leather papers, which, by 1902, were 'legion in their variety'.[54] These were made from paper pulp, beaten into a mould, then dried. Examples of this type are Sanderson's leather paper (1912), Jeffrey's high-relief leather imitations (1885), and Wylie and Lochhead's leather papers (1902). In addition to imitating embossed leather, other materials, such as stucco and panelled and carved woodwork, were copied in relief paper. The pioneer in the market was Lincrusta-Walton, which comprised solidified oil spread on cotton, linen or paper backing and pressed by rollers into relief patterns imitating leather or low-relief plaster. It was very durable, and its flat back made it very hygienic and thus suitable for vestibules, bathrooms and conservatories, though it was heavier than other papers. The most expensive of all relief papers was Tynecastle Tapestry, with a canvas face in low- (leather) or high- (modelled plaster) relief, and its cheaper version, Tynecastle Vellum, which had a vellum-like paper surface. These products were joined by other substitutes, such as Cameoid; Anaglypta, hardened paper pulp pressed in iron moulds, which was extremely durable and the cheapest of all; Cordelova, which was similar, but less sharp and hard, giving a softer but higher relief; Muromana; Salamander, asbestos based; and Lignomur which was wood-fibre embossed. Some of these lighter materials were capable of emulating higher-relief materials than Lincrusta Walton, giving a relief of two to three inches deep. Fibrous plaster, which was plaster on canvas backing, was used greatly for friezes and created the same effect. In 1905, Anaglypta produced styles ranging from 'Adams, Louis XVI, modern English, English Renaissance, Arabian, Chippendale, Old English etc',[55] by key designers of the day including Christoper Dresser. Anaglypta was manufactured also in special strips and fan shapes to make the patterns adaptable to various sized surfaces and to give more freedom to the decorator. In 1905, Lincrusta-Walton had a range of 'Art tints' as well as the standard ones, and introduced a silk design, and Matted Lincrusta-Walton in different colours, to imitate canvas, but with the advantages that it did not shrink and was easily washable. Embossed steel has already been mentioned as a ceiling covering nailed directly to the rafters. Sheet-metal friezes were available in iron, bronze, brass and copper, fixed with cement and copper nails.

Writers of the late nineteenth and early twentieth century condemned earlier designs of mid century. Mrs Panton recalled bedrooms of her youth with 'fearful paper, all blue roses and yellow lilies, or what was worse still, the dreary drab and orange, or green upon green scrolls and foliage, that we used to contemplate with horror, wondering why such frightful papers were made!'[56] Eastlake, like many, argued that the room should determine the choice of wallpaper and that the most important question was whether the decoration should be decoration in itself or just provide a background for the pictures.[57] R. N. Shaw in 1904 stressed that tone was more important than pattern in

wallpaper: 'Let us hope … that a great improvement in English mural ornament, and notably in wallpapers, will be brought about very soon.' The debate about ornamentation led some to argue for plain walls. In 1904, W. Shaw Sparrow in *The British Home of Today* made a plea for plain, stained plaster walls or walls tinted with a 'washable' distemper, which was in practice not entirely washable but was, he thought, tasteful and cheap. He also recommended 'specially prepared canvases in many qualities of texture and tones of colour. They are easily hung, are lasting, and a fairly safe answer to the demand for annual change'.

Until the late nineteenth century, paints were mixed by hand, with white lead and oil. Oil-based paints were difficult to work with and the oil darkened the colour. There were also fears over the safety of certain pigments; in 1911, 'At an inquest held in London a short time ago on the body of a man it was found that his death was due to arsenical poisoning from the cheap green paper on his bedroom wall.'[58] Efforts were made to develop materials which were easy to use, cheap and safe, although some pigments remained a problem. Animal by-products such as glues and casein, and vegetable substances like gums and resins were used to produce semi-soluble vehicles in paints which were the precursors of modern polymer emulsions. Paints such as Hall's Sanitary distemper (see fig. 11.7) and Muraline by Carson's, a washable water paint, which was prepared in dry powder to which water was added, and cost one-third the price of oil paint, 'non-poisonous, washable, and the colours … fast to light and lime',[59] proved very popular. So too did enamel paints, (such as Harland's Flat Enamels, which comprised a pigment base with a varnish medium) on the grounds that 'there is a great demand for flat work which can readily be washed'.[60] *The Decorator* commented in 1905 on the 'enormous strides in public favour made by enamel paints during the last five years or so', explaining it thus: 'the natural swing of the pendulum away from the so-called aesthetic style with its faded greens, bilious yellows, funereal drabs and general murkiness, was favourable to the introduction of a material which made for lightness, cleanness and simplicity'.[61] Thus white paint, associated with contemporary new trends in architecture, replaced the earlier dark paints. In 1905 decorators were urged when considering what to display in their showrooms that 'the popularity of white enamelled work in modern decorations and of "fitments", such as screens to oriel windows, cosy corners, etc., makes it advisable to erect some kind of fitments in a decorator's showroom, and to enamel these ivory white'.[62] Painters' specialities such as marbling, staining, graining and stencilling still remained popular with the force of tradition and the importance attached to ideas of status, even in small houses, with graining examples being a necessary part of any decorator's showroom display in 1910. Such work was the most skilled and thus the most highly paid in the painting trade.

12

STAIRWAYS

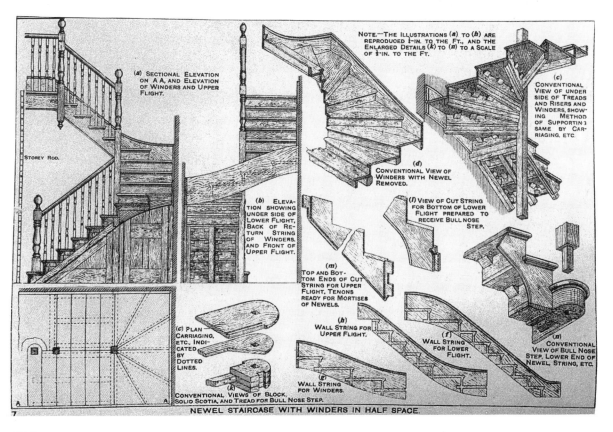

12.1
Staircase design
by Paul Hasluck, 1910

Along with the tiled porch and hallway and the coloured-glass front door, the stairway was the visitor's first view inside the house and, as such, gave the 'keynote' to the house. 'That tiresome man, the builder, appears to consider either that an entrance to a house is not necessary at all, or that the smaller it is, and the more the stairs are in evidence, the better and more appropriate it is to Angelina's lowly station in life' said Mrs Panton.[1] C. Jennings of Bristol's catalogue of about 1914 advertised four designs of staircases; cheap to moderate designs in deal, more expensive pitch-pine, and top-of-the-range designs which had additions such as a special design with fretwork double arch and panelling and fixed seat for a high-class residence, the price of which was available only on application. The most basic staircase design was the straight flight, and many late-Victorian and Edwardian houses had a 'dog-legged' staircase, without a central open well, which 'occupy less space than any other variety with the exception of the spiral, and for this reason are the kind chiefly used in cottages and other small houses'.[2] Many medium and large houses, where space and cost were less of a consideration, in the Edwardian period had an 'open newel' or open-well staircase (a square well-hole at the junction of flights). These were considered 'from a constructive and artistic point of view, the best form of stair there is'.[3] By the Edwardian period, the face of the open string staircase in large to medium houses was frequently decorated with elaborate fretwork brackets, which could be easily manufactured using the new fretworking machines. This latter type of staircase was common in the medieval and Renaissance periods, where the newel post at the foot of the stairs was always an elaborate, dominant and important feature of the staircase. With the introduction of the wider, shorter hall in the Edwardian period and the emulation of such periods of architecture, the stairs and newel post of medium and large houses assumed a more prominent role than hitherto. The newel acquired a new boldness, becoming altogether larger and more ornate, communicating ideas about prestige and status as well as style. Some were even adapted to hold elaborate gas lights.[4] Turning, routing and wood-carving machines combined to produce rich effects, imitating the elaborate hand techniques of the period prior to the Industrial Revolution. Circular recessed work, such as that found commonly on newel posts, was worked by 'elephant', or routing machines, for example. Machines increased the variety of designs, as is evident from Jewson's catalogue of about 1910-19, which offered ten designs for newel posts, with prices to suit all pockets. Square-turned newels were considered superior, and were again available in a range of woods; the hierarchy of woods is apparent from C. Jennings and Co.'s selection of square-cut newels, which listed those in deal as cheapest, followed upwards by pitch pine, canary whitewood, American oak, mahogany, teak, to the most expensive of all, Austrian oak. The irregular-moulding machine made it possible for joinery firms to offer a variety of designs for handrails, also available in a range of woods; for instance, H. Gibbon of Cardiff produced four designs in hardwoods such as pitchpine, mahogany and oak.

The localised nature of joinery firms explains the wide variety of designs along the same general lines. By the Edwardian period, the newel post found in a top-quality house was usually composed of four basic parts: a square base, sometimes with routed decoration; above this, a section either round turned (on cheaper designs), tapered and fluted, angled (each face decorated with 'pressed' wood panels), or round turned with routed or machine-incised panels; above this would be a square block with turned corners, the faces either left plain, routed, or with a carved or concentric circular design applied to the three free faces. The newel cap frequently comprised a ball, a plain or fluted urn, or another fluted shape, to act as a grip for people using the stairs and add height and grandeur comparatively cheaply. Identical or usually plainer newel posts marked the turns on the staircase. In Hornsey, newel posts and ballusters in middle-class houses of the 1890s were of standardised designs, presumably supplied by a local joinery firm such as Bond and White Ltd. Later newel posts were plain and formed the lower part of an arch (see fig. 13.4); in this example, Collins, the builder, arranged plain strips of wood to create an alternative fretted 'Moorish' effect. Sometimes a cheaper wood was used for the newels and handrail above the ground floor, where the staircase would have been out of the sight of anyone but family and friends.

In the seventeenth century, turned ballusters were the most expensive and therefore most prestigious and the work was undertaken by a specialist turner. The cheaper alternative at this time was pierced flat-work which could be made by a joiner. Thus, in the houses of the wealthy, turned ballusters would be used at the foot of the stairs and fret-cut ones at the less visible top end of the staircase. The lathe brought turned ballusters within reach of all and such work was particularly fast and cheap. By 1900, catalogues showed turned ballusters, for instance, once used only on the best staircases, as the cheapest in the range. By 1914, C. Jennings and Co. was selling twenty-five different designs for ballusters, most of them round-turned. As the lathe made turning into a commonplace technique used on ballusters even in cheap houses, architect-designed houses in the Arts and Crafts style began to use pierced fret-cut ballusters along with plain and simple newel posts instead. Ironically, as already mentioned, square and fretwork ones, once used in less visible sections of the staircase, were less cost-effective and therefore became top-of-the range products. For example, Jewson's produced round-turned ballusters, and the more expensive fretsawn ballusters. Some woods such as oak, mahogany and teak, raised the cost further. This style filtered down scale and fretwork or alternating fretwork and plain ballusters became commonly used in medium to small houses in the later Edwardian period.

13

FITTED
FURNITURE

13.1
Screen at G. Candler and
Sons, Brixton, London, 1908

The popularity of built-in furniture, or 'fitments' as they were generally known, which had first come to the general public's attention at the International Health Exhibition of 1884, lay partly in their contribution to health and hygiene in the home, in that they cut down areas where dust and dirt could collect in the house. By the new century, fitted cupboards and dressers in kitchens and living rooms were standard. This chapter looks at a few key fitment types which became very popular in the late-Victorian and Edwardian period, the screen and arch, and the inglenook and cosy corner.

SCREENS AND ARCHES

In the 1890s and early 1900s the pages of *The Cabinet Maker* and other furnishing magazines abounded with examples of, and articles on, screens and arches, or 'grille' and 'Liberty' arch (so-called because they were introduced by Liberty's shop) as they were sometimes known. There appear to have been several reasons for their popularity. Firstly, they provided a cheap, fast way of dividing up space in an interior. This was desirable partly for purely practical reasons; a screen hung with drapery provided a solution to the dilemma facing occupants of either closing the door and suffering the effects of fumes and dirt from what was known generally as the 'raging gasolier', or suffering draughts from having the door open. *Furniture and Decoration* wrote: 'Until our houses are fitted with an effectual system of ventilation by which fresh air is admitted and foul air ejected, I believe screens to be a valuable accessory on this ground alone'.[2] Secondly, the desire to divide up space arose from the growing tendency to consider space in the house as an architectural whole, paying attention in particular to details such as the corners of rooms: 'Screens may be said to be the moveable walls or partitions invented by society for breaking up the hard angular lines of the four square walls that form the boundary line of most dwellings.'[3]

At an affordable cost, the screen and arch also lent an instant architectural style and gave a 'modern' appearance to a room: 'The judicious use of our grilles will give the interior of your home a modern appearance.... We confidently recommend our grilles as a means of beautifying the home at comparatively small expense.'[4] Their easy assembly meant that they could be changed at will and according to changing taste. The eclecticism of the late nineteenth century, which allowed for combinations of styles in the same room, was expedient for the average speculative builder, bound by the merchant's stock and the economic necessity for bulk buying. Moorish and French styles, for instance, were now within reach of the middle middle classes:

> there is no question as to the novel picturesqueness that might be brought about by the introduction of open trellis work, either fret cut in patterns rich or fantastic, or by means similar to the framed and turned spindle work of the Arabian latticed verandahs.

The arch or screen gave the occupant a chance to emulate the 'ideal home'. Manufacturers and writers alike recognised the constraints, imposed by renting, on those wanting to update their homes. *Furniture and Decoration* acknowledged: 'It cannot be expected that a tenant who merely rents a house for seven or fourteen years, as the case may be, will go to any considerable expense in general constructive furniture and decoration, which at the expiral of the lease will be claimed by the landlord as a fixture.'[5]

The arch or screen was especially recommended for use in a reception room or in the hall, where it made it possible for those living in an older house with a long narrow hallway to alter the shape of the hall to a more fashionable squarer shape.

> by the aid of carefully planned woodwork and by using arches on the plan of the Moorish fretwork first introduced by Liberty, a square room can be made quite picturesque, and a long, narrow passage pleasant to contemplate, by simply putting up a series of slight arches, or else curtaining off portions of it by the aid of simple partitions.[6]

Manufacturers devised easy-to-assemble schemes which could be re-moved at the end of a tenancy, and in this way the screen or arch was a cheap substitute for major structural alterations. It is evident from manufacturers' lines that it was aimed at a wide range of middle-class markets. As C. Jennings and Co. of Bristol, emphasised, 'We can adapt our designs to any size.'[7] Similarly, Mrs Panton offered several solutions, one for 'an ordinary, tiresome little hall',[8] comprising a double arch, hung with curtains and screwed to the wall so it could be removed, and a grander one-sided scheme for a six- to seven-foot-wide hall. Jennings' catalogue illustrates the range of screens and arches available, from complex arrangements to a simple arch. Prices varied from the 'ball and spindle' grille up to four feet wide, which was 'a specially cheap line, and should command a ready sale', to the dearest design for a three part screen measuring 9ft x 8ft. Scrolled grilles cost a little more than ball and spindle grilles. Builders were offered price discounts for bulk purchases of the same size and pattern.[9]

Screens and arches were usually supplied ready-painted; for example, Messrs Wallace and Co. of Curtain Road, London, erected arches for clients ready-painted and varnished. They were also frequently painted to match the rest of the room scheme; *The Lady*, 1893, describes,

13.2
Moorish scheme for a half-landing, 1909

13.3
Oetzmann, designs for arches and overdoors

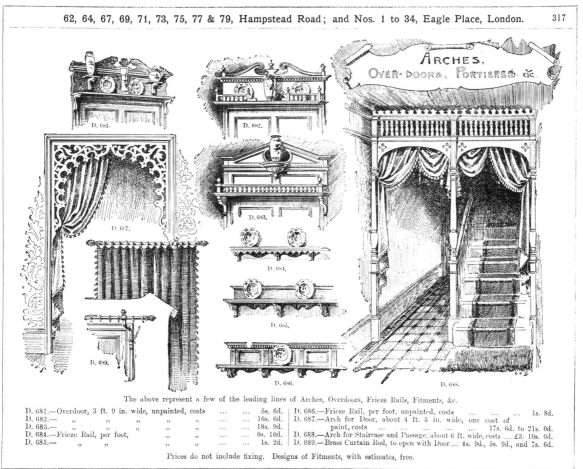

ARCHES, OVER-DOORS, PORTIÈRES, &c.

D. 681.

D. 682.

D. 683.

D. 687.

D. 684.

D. 685.

D. 689.

D. 686.

D. 688.

The above represent a few of the leading lines of Arches, Overdoors, Frieze Rails, Fitments, &c.

D. 681.—Overdoor, 3 ft. 9 in. wide, unpainted, costs ... ... 5s. 6d.
D. 682.— ,, ,, ,, ,, ,, ... 10s. 6d.
D. 683.— ,, ,, ,, ,, ,, ... 18s. 9d.
D. 684.—Frieze Rail, per foot, ,, ,, ... 0s. 10d.
D. 685.— ,, ,, ,, ,, ... 1s. 2d.

D. 686.—Frieze Rail, per foot, unpainted, costs ... ... 1s. 8d.
D. 687.—Arch for Door, about 4 ft. 3 in. wide, one coat of paint, costs ... ... 17s. 6d. to 21s. 0d.
D. 688.—Arch for Staircase and Passage, about 6 ft. wide, costs ... £3. 10s. 0d.
D. 689.—Brass Curtain Rod, to open with Door... 4s. 9d., 5s. 9d., and 7s. 6d.

Prices do not include fixing. Designs of Fitments, with estimates, free.

13.4
Screen in lounge/hall
of a house built in 1907
in Muswell Hill, which
had a rateable value of
£40 in 1914

The Mooresque decoration, the woodwork exhibiting the delicate Arab
arches and tracery which are now so lavishly employed in artistic houses.
This is generally enamelled ivory, as the object in view is to preserve as
dainty an effect as possible; but in the smoking and billiard rooms, which
are often fitted up in a Mooresque style, the woodwork would be painted
Arab red or blue.[10]

Many of the screens and arches destined for the mass market could
cause problems in that, if they were made to fit to ceiling height, the

plaster cornice had to be cut, which was impossible for those in rented houses. One solution to this dilemma was a screen which extended only to three-quarters or two-thirds the height of the room; in 1895, *Furniture and Decoration* advocated, for a hall only four to five feet across, an arch which stopped short ten to fifteen inches from the ceiling, so that a capping moulding could be added without interfering with the plaster cornice.[11]

The arch and screen were used frequently in upper- and middle-middle-class houses from the 1890s to 1910. Examples include those with a fretwork screen with side columns just inside the front door, and on the upstairs landing. Perhaps their popularity was influenced by the increase in home ownership and the willingness to spend more money on the home; they were used by builders as a selling point, as in 1910, when three-bedroomed houses at £295 leasehold and £32 rent on the Hollyfield estate in New Southgate advertised extras which included a fretwork screen to the staircase.[12]

In addition to providing a 'modern look', the screen or arch had another major function which was seemingly in opposition to the new domestic ideal, and, instead, strengthened old values; this was where a fretwork arch was frequently used to reinforce the division between public and private, master and servant, faces of the house and disguise the back part of the house from public view; for example, by placing one in the hall at the foot of the stairs, at the entrance to the kitchen area, or on the landing. Examples can be found which range from large arches made in sections, so that different combinations could be fitted together depending on the complexity required, to small 'all-in-one' grilles which would have simply slotted into place. The designs relied heavily on the fretsaw and lathe for their form and decoration; such stylistic detail and variety of designs at affordable prices would have been impossible without the use of such machines. Cheap versions of these techniques existed, which consisted of straight bars of wood arranged in parallel to give the *appearance* of fretwork. Some arches and screens were more substantial, with a large double arch in the hallway which sprang from the newel post and spanned the width of the hallway at the foot of the stairs. Some schemes were very elaborate and were an integral part of the design of the whole hall.

The rococo style was popular for screens after 1900; in a medium-sized house of 1904 in Muswell Hill, London, three arches spanning a wide hallway enclose a small area at the bottom of the stairs to create a cosy nook, which was raised up and lit by the hall window. The large arch across the width of the hallway was made from two brackets fitted together. Provision for the display of plants or ornaments was built into the design of the ensemble using small round shelves. Plain shallow arches in an Arts and Crafts style were also common. Fig. 13.4 shows an example where one half of the hall, raised and ballustraded off to provide a recess for sitting, was enclosed by a long, shallow fretwork arch, composed of two sections; while at right angles was a smaller arch, composed of a fretwork arch with a straight fretted strip added above to make the arch deeper, spanning the width of the hallway and marking the entrance to the kitchen area and back reception room. Some arches, often in the hallway or on an upstairs landing, were clearly not part of the original design concept, having been added separately.

Manufacturers continued to supply screens and arches well into the 1920s, for example, the 1927 supplement to Jennings' 1914 catalogue noted that 'the demand for this class of work is rapidly increasing'.[13] But in upper-class houses by 1890, the novelty of the Moorish style and screens and arches was beginning to pall:

> we are told that even in the middle class trade, the 'Moresque' is 'played out'. That the shoals of little gimcrack screens and tables which flooded the market a few years since, have completely stifled the popular taste for Oriental furniture and decoration. That the free use of the fret-saw, and the ever-cheapening tendencies of our times, have helped to exhaust in three or four years all that the Moors designed and accomplished in twice as many centuries … the unstudied fret-and-spindle-work that has brought our version of this style into such disrepute.[14]

In fashionable houses they quickly disappeared after 1900, overuse and cheap imitation having contributed greatly to their demise. In 1907, J. H. Elder-Duncan in *The House Beautiful and Useful* condemned 'notorious fretwork fitments' for their flimsiness and absence of real purpose.[15] Many looked back nostalgically to the beginnings of the idea in the examples of the design at the International Health Exhibition, 1884, where the best manufacturers' offerings did not include broken-up recesses with shaped arches and spindles, 'entangled fretwork' or useless pigeon-holes which collected the dust.[16]

INGLENOOKS AND COSY CORNERS

Very closely linked to the screen and arch were the inglenook and cosy corner, which were, in many cases, made up of a series of screens and arches. Like arches and screens, cosy corners and inglenooks were symptomatic of the attempt to consider the design of the whole room. *Furniture and Decoration* declared that for an 'orthodox, uninteresting room without a single nook or cupboard' a recess was 'absolutely indispensable'.[17] Two years later, *The Cabinet Maker* wondered that 'the marvel is that the corner was left in neglect, dust and disgrace for so long'.[18]

The inglenook,[19] which was intended to provide a warm enclosed space for those sitting by the fire, was advocated for any room in the house, in particular for the hall, drawing- and dining-rooms; 'Most modern drawing-rooms will favour the inglenook treatment'.[20] However, inglenooks, usually built-in features, were generally at this date more associated with architect-designed Arts and Crafts houses. While journals advocated the inglenook as indispensable, the occupant of an

13.5
Inglenook in showroom
boudoir at Trapnell and
Gane of Bristol, 1897

average suburban villa could not contemplate such costly structural alterations, even if the landlord allowed it, which 'in nine times out of ten'[21] was not the case. Some builders began to incorporate them into their top-quality houses in the Edwardian period, but they were rare in small houses and most people had to find an alternative solution. The answer for middle-class householders was to install a shop-bought, ready-made inglenook.

Simpler and more convenient even than this was to make do with a 'cosy corner'. Shop-bought or home-made, these were designed to be simply taken away with all other belongings at the end of a tenancy; 'The upholsterer now sells the "cosy corner" as an article of furniture easily removable from one house to another.'[22] 'Portable folding' cosy corners were even advertised for sale by Godfrey Giles, a furniture maker. The practicality of the cosy corner for those in rented houses and its ability to add an instant 'modern' feel to a house in the same way as the screen and arch guaranteed it as 'all the rage'[23] in the 1890s and one of the most frequently recommended furnishings in journals.

As its name suggests, the ideal sought was 'a snug retreat' or 'a sequestered nook',[24] similar to the inglenook, where one could relax in comfort alone or with friends. *Furniture and Decoration* for 1891 defined it thus; 'It smacks of ease and seclusiveness – of soft cushions and draught-excluding curtains – bookshelves within easy reach, and an uninter-rupted nearness to the fire.'[25] The common form for a cosy corner comprised two high-backed settees, fixed at right angles with shelves

above for books and ornaments, which could be placed in the bay of a window, or beside the fireplace or in a corner adjacent to it. The term was thus frequently used to describe what were, in effect, inglenook seats by the fire, and was seen by contemporaries as an inexpensive substitute for a built-in inglenook. The cosy corner could be simply a corner arrangement comprising a chair, a desk, a screen and a potted plant, or even a 'piano cosy corner'[26], a seat fixed back to back against an upright piano. *Furniture and Decoration* summed up the wide variation in scale possible, 'Sometimes it is merely a seat, at other times, it is quite a miniature boudoir. Sometimes it is large enough to contain a whole family, whilst at others it is with equal satisfaction made sufficiently diminutive to only just accommodate two individuals.'[27]

Journals advocated its use for almost every room in the house, namely the drawing-room, library (see fig. 13.7), smoking-room, billiard-room, hall and landing. Cosy corners were also useful in houses where space was limited as a means of doubling up functions in one room, for example, a cosy corner could divide off a space as a study area. They were also useful even in houses with extra rooms such as a morning-room, in that the doubling up of functions saved servant labour and the cost of lighting fires in several rooms. *Furniture and Decoration* of 1894 noted that cosy corners appealed particularly to women and recommended that one should be chosen so as to be 'in keeping with the personality of the mistress of the house. There are, of course, certain colours that harmonize most favourably with one's complexion'.[28]

Not only was the cosy corner a welcome compromise for those who wanted to keep up with the latest fashion but were faced with restrictions of tenancy, it was also expedient from the manufacturers'

13.7
'Library Cosy Corner', from
The Cabinet Maker, 1893

point of view. The depressed state of the furniture trade in the late nineteenth century led to pressure on firms to engage in advertising and offer terms of hire purchase on goods, and also to expand constantly the range of their products, offering the public a stream of 'novelties'. The cosy corner should be seen very much in this context. J. S. Henry for instance, an East End of London wholesaler between 1880 and 1910, who specialised in quality novelties, featured numerous designs for cosy corners in advertisements. Cosy corners were sold at a wide variety of prices by furnishing houses ranging from Oetzmann's of Hampstead, who aimed at a middle-class market with their cosy corners at £5 5s, to Liberty's high-quality designs available only to the well off at £35 each.

Even the cheapest shop-bought cosy corners were too expensive for many middle-class pockets, and advice was frequently offered on how to make your own; for example, a cosy corner could be made from a wooden frame covered with cretonne, two couches arranged at right angles with shelves or a bracket fixed to the wall above, a corner divided off from the rest of the room by a low balustrade, or even a simple corner arrangement of chairs, table, screen and plant. Literature of the period suggests that the home-made corner was quite commonplace, as in the snuggery in the back room of the first floor in Shan Bullock's *R. Thorne, the Story of a London Clerk* (1907).[29]

A range of styles, reflecting the rapidly changing styles in furnishing and decoration, were recommended for the cosy corner. Particularly popular for reception rooms in the early 1890s were white enamel wooden ones in a Queen Anne revival style, with curtains and heavy upholstered seat and shelves, cupboards, decorative mouldings and little ballustrades above. The furniture magazines in the second half of the 1890s showed cosy corners designed in the latest fashionable French taste, in addition to designs in 'national' styles such as early Renaissance. Some of the taste most frequently used for cosy corners particularly in the early 1890s were 'exotic', such as Japanese and Egyptian, possibly because the associations of these styles with luxury, comfort and opulence made them appropriate for a cosy corner. In 1891, *Furniture and Decoration* made the following suggestion: 'A screen, a few cushions and lacquer panels, a kakemono on the wall, and one or two hanging lanterns will suffice to make a very snug little corner which will be quite à la Japonaise.'[30]

While a Japanese cosy corner was thought appropriate for the drawing room, schemes for 'Moresque' or Turkish corners were frequently advised for landings, billiard- and smoking-rooms.[31] Even as late as 1909, Moresque was recommended by Mrs Humphry in her *Book of the Home*, 1909 (see fig. 13.2). Moorish schemes suggested by *Furniture and Decoration*, for 'ordinary people', varied according to personal preference and one's pocket, some more ambitious than others. Recommendations ranged from a simple Moorish fitment in the corner of a room, which was usually the manufacturer's interpretation of the original style rather than one which was authentic in detail, to a backroom fitted out in a Moresque style for use as a study or smoking-room, making it into a cosy retreat where the owner could 'drink his coffee and smoke his chibouk'.[32] In this latter example, aimed at the more ambitious householder, who was not content with simply having a few Oriental knick-knacks and the odd hexagonal table to give an eastern flavour, recommended items of decoration were detailed, such as an eastern lamp, cusped-arched open windows, incense burners and 'ostrich eggs suspended at intervals from a decorated ceiling', covered with one of the many Moorish-style wallpapers available. The style of the ready-made cosy corner began to change under the impact of the Arts and Crafts Movement. Cosy corners became plainer and simpler in design, painted or left plain wood, and ornamented with stained glass heart or tulip motifs.

While the idea of the cosy corner was generally favoured, and considered through to the new century 'a charming and necessary addition to almost every room'[33] and 'one of the favourite spots in the English drawing room',[34] distinctions were increasingly drawn between good and bad versions of the cosy corner. There were rumblings of discontent about the cheap end of the market. Thus the flimsy nature of many shop-bought designs was criticised along with the fact that far too often the 'painted and "tricked out" niches and cosy corners that we see in nearly every drawing room today ... because they happen to be fashionable'[35] were neither functional nor space saving; 'it is a narrow, painted, disappointing imposter, whose looks and title promise much, but whose plentiful drapery and paucity of horse-hair provide anything but cosiness and ease'.[36] Moreover, they were 'squeezed into tiny drawing rooms where there is not half enough space for them'[37] and, even if they fitted in one house, they were such an awkward shape that they seldom fitted anywhere in the next house that tenants moved into. For some, such as designer and theorist Lewis F. Day, the cosy corner became a cliché; in a criticism of the work of female advisers on interior decoration in the early 1890s, he condemned the ready-made cosy corner often recommended for the landing on the stairs, along with a cheap Moorish arch for another room and a stuffed bear to serve as a dumb waiter. Hermann Muthesius, writing in 1904, while not condemning the cosy corner outright, favoured home-made ones as opposed to the ready-made ones available in shops, which lacked 'the desired simplicity and naturalness'.[38] Ultimately, such complaints brought it into disrepute, and this, along with a change in taste towards simpler, uncluttered rooms, caused it, like other fitments, to gradually fade from homes, although catalogues and women's magazines show that it remained a desired item for small and medium homes long after it had gone out of fashion in larger houses.

Such trends in fittings demonstrate the force of the conservatism which underpinned the use of materials and styles in the period. The value system of the middle classes led them to favour styles currently in fashion for, and endorsed by, the upper classes, and in particular recognisable 'period' styles, such as Adam or Jacobean, which carried the status of a traditional country house. With the monopolisation of ornate furnishings hitherto by the wealthy, it was not surprising to find that one of the major tendencies in middle-class housing over the period from 1880 to 1914 should have been a general increase in the complexity of forms, when bandsawing, turning and fretting machinery made this feasible. Variety in the market at any one time also of course included the question of personal taste, although this was generally an issue only at the top end of the market, or in smaller houses if the market was sluggish. The question of 'imitation' versus 'real' materials is important when considering this type of house. Despite the objections of many writers, the use of imitation materials was widespread in all middle-class houses and particularly those at the lower end of the market, where, for example, slate was used to imitate marble and wood, where iron and plaster were intended to look like wood, and where relief papers resembled modelled plaster.

But when the mood changed away from grandeur and public display towards a more homely domestic ideal, prestigious custom-built houses began to follow an Arts and Crafts line, and speculative housing followed suit, with scaled-down versions of the originals, using pebble dashing, leaded lights and inglenooks. Correspondingly, there was a gradual shift in the popularity of certain materials and a growing trend towards simpler style fittings and details. But, while many new product types and materials reflected changing priorities and forward-looking ideas, others associated with morality and rank remained steadfast. Finance may not have allowed an elaborate scheme, and the fashion for an eclectic approach to style may have been a happy coincidence for many builders; nevertheless, ornamental features inside and outside the house played a vital role in establishing the tone of the whole house and the styles intended for each room. There was generally little difference between ideal-home recommendations and actual practice, particularly in the best houses; the lower down the scale, the less accurate or coherent the scheme and the further behind fashionable taste in terms of time. Finally, regional differences caused by local conditions were apparent, but what was as remarkable was the degree of uniformity, with many identical designs for all kinds of detailing appearing in different parts of the country.

Interior of the Linley
Samborne house in Stafford
Terrace, Kensington

PLATE 23

Suggestions for Christmas decorations
arrangement, in Mrs Humphry, 1909

Drawing-room scheme, from Mrs Humphry, 1909

POSTSCRIPT

By the end of the Edwardian period, the basic foundations of the inter-war home had been laid – two storeys, three bedrooms, single-family occupation, inside toilet and bathroom, electric lighting, telephone, and a small garden, with maybe a 'motor house'. The Tudorbethan inter-war house also took its stylistic cue from Edwardian housing with its pebble-dashing, half-timbered gable, and wide bay window with stained-glass upper lights.

For those living in an Edwardian house now, today's comforts such as the fitted kitchen, central heating and radio and television sit happily with memories of another age, bearing witness to the highly satisfactory solution to house form arrived at by Edwardian builders which is as appropriate to today's needs as it was to those of the original inhabitants for whom it was intended. Echoes of the past linger in the present vogue for wallpaper borders and wall stencilling, rugs on wooden floors, and original fireplaces and ceiling roses, although they have of course a different meaning for us as we are part of a different age. Nevertheless, by looking at the forces which informed built form in the Edwardian period – social, technical and economic – we can gain some understanding of the reasons why Edwardian houses looked as they did and the reasons for the use of certain styles and products, which can aid both sensitive restoration and our appreciation of living in such houses.

APPENDIX I
MIDDLE-CLASS
HOUSING CATEGORIES

The values shown are the upper and lower limits for 1914 (except where given as 1909) in selected roads in London and Cardiff case-studies, of rateable values (R.V.) and original building costs (B.C.). Also shown are the level of owner-occupancy and the occupations of residents.

CARDIFF

Parish of Roath

    Albany Rd R.V. £24 10s to £39 10s. B.C. between £550 and £590. Some were owner-occupied. Between 1904 and 1914 occupations of residents listed as musician, accountant, schoolmistress, baker, shipwright, shipowner, master mariner, tailor, explosives expert, boilermaker, commercial traveller, builder, laundry proprietor, cattle dealer, coal exporter, cutter, house agent, timber clerk, carpenter, clerk, manager, shipwright, architect, brewer's agent.

    Amesbury Rd R.V. £16 to £24 10s. B.C.= £440. One quarter owner-occcupied in 1914. Inhabitants included marine engineer, accountant, carpenter, master mariner.

    Arabella St R.V. = £10-15. In 1894, 55 houses in this street were owned by one person, T. H. Fry; in 1904, very few of the 200 houses were owner-occupied. Inhabitants included a traveller, fitter, compositor, drayman, carpenter, postman, clerk.

    Boverton St R.V. = £26-29. B.C. ranged from £595 to £665. Many were rented in 1914 and residents included a captain.

    Diana St R.V. = many £17 10s. B.C. = £355-425. Mostly rented. Inhabitants included clerks, engineer, jeweller, carpenter, cab owner, foreman, commercial traveller, insurance agent, tailor's cutter, plumber, milliner, manager, agent, upholsterer, mate, labourer, grocer, assistant, mariner, brewer, accountant, artist, foreman, carpenter, coal trimmer.

    Ilton Rd R.V. = £20-23. In 1909, over half were owner-occupiers; in 1914, less than one quarter. Inhabitants in 1914 given as boilermaker, pilot, schoolmaster, agent, commercial travellers, master mariner, electrician, joiner, cashier, telegraphist, teacher.

    Kimberley Rd R.V. = £19-£39 10s. B.C. = £420-645, many 610. In 1914, less than half were owner-occupied. Inhabitants listed as accountant, wheelwright, captain, builder, bank accountant, clothier's manager, accountant, master mariner, construction engineer, analyst and bacteriological chemist, fruitier, insurance inspector, grocer, clerk, pastry cook, commercial traveller, decorator, marine engineer, government official.

    Lake Rd East Large houses looking on lake, R.V. and B.C. not available. Residents were listed as F. B. Jotham, of Jotham and Sons Ltd, tailors and outfitters, hosiers and hatters, with three shops in town. W. H. Taylor of W.H. Taylor and Co., steamship owners and brokers.

    Mafeking Rd R.V. = £20 10s and £22. B.C. = £480-510. In 1909, 75% owner-occupied. Occupants included builder, accountant, captain, and inspector between 1909 and 1914.

Ninian Rd R.V. = £32-£59 10s. B. C. = £700-1470. Owner-occupancy fell from about 60% in 1894 to just below a third in 1914. Inhabitants included master mariners, accountants, commercial traveller, schoolmaster, Reverend, chaplain to Seaman's Mission Bute Docks, commission and insurance agent, clerk, potato merchant, construction engineer, marine engineer, tailor, photographer, marine surveyor, auctioneer, ship broker, iron and steel merchant.

Penylan/ Penylan Rd R.V. = £26 to £109. B.C. = £440-7500. Very wide range of houses, including one with a rental of £200 in 1909 costing £7500 to build and another at £150 in 1909 cost £5000 to build and owned by Fideli Primavesi, a China merchant in the docks. Other large detached houses along Penylan Road were inhabited by a barrister, an M.P. and William Geen, one of the big builders in the area.

Shirley Rd R.V. = £27 10s. B.C. = £610-955, many at £610. In 1909 over 60% were rented. Inhabitants included a builder, commercial traveller, foreman carpenter, Reverend.

Parish of Penarth

Marine Parade R.V. (1909) ranged from £61 to £157, with the majority around £96. B.C. = between £1500-4000. Very large houses, some with own ballrooms. Eight out of thirteen owner-occupied in 1909. Occupants given as Krieger of Krieger and Schielmann Ltd., shipbrokers and coal exporters, Jenkins of Jenkins, Sydney, D and Son, Ltd, shipbrokers and chandlers and bonded store merchants, A. W. Travis, colliery agent, The Exchange, E. Gibbs of Gibbs and Co., steamship owners, Moxey of Moxey, Savon and Co., coal exporters. Rents between £150 and £75, costing between £3375 and £1400 to build.

Plymouth Rd R.V. (1909) was between £20 and £65 10s. B.C. = £630-2900, with many up to £1800. 60% were rented in 1909. Inhabitants included a bank cashier, doctor, solicitor, captain, inspector of schools, master mariner, accountant, surgeon.

LONDON

Parish of Camberwell

Beauval Rd. R.V. £24-29
Beckwith Rd. R.V. £24-42.
Burbage Rd. R.V. £42-109, many between £40 and £60.
Danecroft Rd. R.V. £26-32.
Elfindale Rd. R.V. £29-36.
Elmwood Rd. R.V. £31-8.
Half Moon La. R.V. £40-209, many between £60 and £80.
Holmdene Ave. R.V. £34-57.
Kemerton Rd. R.V. £23-31.
Kestrel Ave. R.V. £31-35.
Stradella Rd. R.V. £38-65.
Winterbrook Rd. R.V. £38-60, many at £38.
Woodwarde Rd. R.V. £28-38, many 31.

Parish of Lambeth

Fawnbrake Ave. R.V. £34-42.
Ferndene Rd. R.V. £26-42.
Gubyon Ave. R.V. £31-55.
Herne Hill. R.V. £40-105, many between £60-80.
Poplar Wlk. R.V. £29-42.
Rollscourt Ave. R.V. £42-59.
Woodquest Ave. R.V. £34-55.

Parish of Hornsey

Albert Rd. R.V. £31-40, mostly rented.

The Chine. R.V. £31-42, W. J. Collins owned.

Church Cres. R.V. £46-69, only 2 owner-occupied; rented from W J Collins.

Collingwood Ave. R.V. £35-46, all rented from Collins.

Creighton Ave, R.V. £46-75, owner-occupied.

Crouch Hill. R.V. £40-125, some rented including the most expensive.

Dickenson Rd. R.V. £36-192, most rented including the most expensive.

Donovan Ave. R.V. £30-47, all owner-occupied.

Dukes Ave. R.V. £28-63, many at £42, £46 and £50, some rented.

Elms Ave. R.V. £50-63, owner-occupied.

Firs Ave. R.V. £42-56, all rented from Collins.

Fortismere Ave. R.V. £42-46, all rented from Collins.

Grand Ave. R.V. £38-59, all rented from Collins.

Kings Ave, R.V. £42-50, all owner-occupied.

Lancaster Rd. R.V. £34-42, some rented.

Leaside Ave. R.V. £38-46, all rented from Collins.

Lorne Rd. R.V. £31-35, mostly rented.

Midhurst Ave. R.V. £35-40, 50% were rented.

Muswell Ave. R.V. £42-92, mostly owner-occupied.

Muswell Rd. R.V. £46-52, owner-occupied.

Nelson St. R.V. £24-26, rented. Some were flats.

Onslow Gdns. R.V. £40-53, all rented from Imperial Property Investment Co.

Osbourne Rd. R.V. £31-39, mostly rented.

Park Rd. R.V. £20-46, mostly rented.

Princes Ave. R.V. £59-75, all owner-occupied.

Priory Rd. R.V. £28-109, some rented including the most expensive.

Queens Ave. R.V. £50-84, all owner-occupied.

Rookfield Ave. R.V. £38-46, owned by Herbert Collins.

Southern Rd. R.V. £28-75, some rented.

Tivoli Rd. R.V. £30-31, owner-occupied.

Woodberry Cres. R.V. £38-46, Edmondson owned 18 of them.

Woodland Rise. R.V. £45-60, owner-occupied.

APPENDIX II
THE TRADES

THE TIMBER TRADE

The mid-century free-trade system resulted in a dramatic reduction of duties levied on non-Empire timber, which meant that best Russian yellow deals for joinery from the Baltic and the White Sea, a variety of Swedish woods, and lower-quality woods from Finland and Norway, hitherto subject to prohibitive duties, were imported in huge quantities in the second half of the century, along with wood (also in increasing amounts) from North America. In 1913, a standard of best yellow deal from St Petersburg cost £16-23, compared with £34-44 for the same from Quebec.[1]

Overall, demand was mostly for firs and pines. In 1900, imports of these woods totalled £16,500,000, while about £4,000,000 was spent on hardwoods like oak, teak, mahogany and jarrah, used for higher-class furniture and fittings.[2] Cardiff rose rapidly to supreme position as a timber importing port by 1910.[3]

	Jan-April 1909
Cardiff	309,613 loads
London	192,618
Liverpool	134,830
Newport	100,702
Manchester	72,115
Hull	94,499
Swansea	43,320

Records of shipments into Cardiff in 1904 reveal that 'Spruce deals, red and white deals and floorings go rapidly into the hands of the various contractors for house building, while the joinery works, of which there are several extensive ones, consume large quantities of pine deals and boards, and also red and white deals in the manufacture of their joinery.'[4] Steamships, allowing the faster movement of timber imports, overtook sail imports in the 1880s, and by 1909 steam ships constituted over ninety per cent of the tonnage registered.[5] A good location was crucial to a firm's success; low overheads combined with access to docks and the rapid despatch of goods to consumers meant that wharfs and mills near docks and railway sidings were essential, and ease of access for builders meant locating shop and offices centrally or in a newly established residential area. With a railway siding and wharfs and yards on East Moors in the docks area of Cardiff, the main offices and works of Harry Gibbon were in the heart of a growing residential area.

Timber, graded in three qualities, arrived either rough, to be worked in this country, or, increasingly, as ready-prepared goods. Wood imports such as Canadian and Swedish doors and mouldings, manufactured in their vast planing and moulding mills, along with hewn timber, increased dramatically in annual value between 1854 and 1913, from £8,000,000 in 1854 to £23,000,000 in 1903 and £35,000,000 in 1913.[6] By the 1890s, Swedish and North American goods were undercutting home-produced ones. Home industries fought back: C. J. Jennings of Bristol, 'Manufacturers of doors to compete with foreign doors', exhorted 'Why buy foreign doors? … lend us your aid in building up a branch of the wood-working trade which has been gradually going out of the United Kingdom.'

The pages of the *Timber Trades Journal* around 1900 abounded with new improved designs for machines and reported on the large machinery sections at the big international exhibitions, which displayed numerous designs for band, fret and circular machines, planing and moulding machines, lathes and rounding machines, various classes of mortising, tenoning and boring machines, dovetailing and corner-locking machines, sandpapering and finishing machines, and other specialist machines for preparing or saving labour, such as sawdust-clearing machines. Britain had been the first in the field of manufacturing woodworking machinery. Several firms had emerged who created Britain's position as world leaders in this field by the mid 1870s, such as Thomas Robinson and Son Ltd (f. 1838), and J. Sagar and Co. Ltd (f. 1875) and Kirchner and Co. (London) Ltd (f. 1878). Britain was, however, shortly to face stiff competition from the United States and Germany, who were industrialising fast. By 1900, these three countries between them met nearly all woodworking machinery requirements worldwide.

The circular saw was 'the best all-round tool',[7] but it could not cut curved shapes, so that those forms, in such demand for fire surrounds, overmantel shelves and brackets, for example, had to be made using the bandsaw. The consumer's desire for decorative mouldings led to increased attention to machines for planing and moulding. The need for speed prompted machines with four and five cutters which could work on all sides of the wood simultaneously by 1900. The fastest speed was reached by fixed-knife planers for box wood or venetian blinds which operated at one thousand feet per minute. Late-Victorian and Edwardian houses showed a marked increase in newel posts and fire surrounds that had been worked on 'irregular' moulding machines, characterised by rebates and sunken recesses. One of the most important areas of machinery development was in the field of machines for jointing, such as mortising, tenoning, mitring and dovetailing machines.

These machines may have been within the reach of the bigger firms, but how did the smaller manufacturer, who perhaps could not afford such machines and had limited space in his workshop, cope with fulfilling demand and staying in business? At the same time as the trend towards greater specialisation and diversification in woodworking machines, manufacturers were developing a machine which combined many different functions. This was the combination machine or 'general joiner', costing anything between £20 and £300 in 1902. The great advantage that the general joiner showed in a small shop was that a number of men could do different jobs on the machine at the same time, although it was generally considered better to have separate machines for each type of work if possible. Maximum convenience and efficiency became increasingly the governing factors in the way the factory was laid out. By 1900, electrical drive had begun to supercede the use of steam power in some factories and, free from the shafting systems necessary with steam power, allowed the layout to be arranged so as to gain the maximum efficiency of production.

Machine work was much cheaper and quicker than hand labour; for example, in 1913, a joiner took eleven hours to make a four-panelled 1½" framed door, and seventeen hours for a 2" framed and ledged door; using a machine, this time could be reduced by a half. The cost of a hand-made door was estimated at £1 9s 8d, compared to 12s for a machine-made.[8] In addition, the ratio of labour cost to materials and plant costs was high for joiners, at 60:40. The work of skilled joiners, the 'top hats of the building trade', to use Booth's description, was increasingly threatened by the wood machinist, who earned the same, and the joiner took on the role more of a fitter. The census records show an increase of 24.4 per cent in sawyers and wood-cutting machinists and a fall in numbers of carpenters and joiners from 338,243 in 1901 to 214,366 in 1911. House- and shop-fittings makers experienced a 95.3 per cent increase in numbers in the first decade of the twentieth century. In 1900, some worried that 'the craftsman has, in a very large degree, become merged and obliterated in the machine',[9] though there was still much hand work to be done in the joiners' workshop fitting up staircases, doors and windows.

THE MARBLE TRADE

Marble was mostly supplied from the six hundred quarries in Carrara, Italy, and the fifty-nine quarries in Namur, Belgium. In many ways traditional practice remained unchanged. In Italy in the 1880s, the blocks were cut out of the mountainside, and slid or were rolled down to the nearest road to be worked in the saw mills in Carrara. Oxen then dragged cartloads of marble five miles to the port of Avenza. Rail and steam ships brought some changes, for example, some of the quarries were connected to the pier by rail, and by 1913 a railway had been built to carry the marble all the way from Carrara to Marina, the new main port of export, six miles away. In Belgium, thirty tons of blocks eight to nine feet thick were brought at a time up inclined steam-powered tramways, and quarried blocks which were too large to be cut by frame saw were hand-sawn vertically by four men.

While the use of marble in Britain increased, the quarrying and dressing side of marble working, in particular, failed to develop. *Laxton's Price Book*, 1915, remarked that most marble was sawn abroad rather than in London, which 'modifies the cost very considerably'.[10] A rise of 7.4 per cent in the numbers of all types of stone quarriers, cutters and dressers and dealers between 1881 and 1891 was followed by a sharp decline between 1901 and 1911 of 16.1 per cent.[11] There was some expansion in the business of working the slabs once they had arrived in this country.

Machines were available for all stages of manufacture, but often hand-work was preferred. Marble was sawn into slabs using a frame, consisting of iron or steel sheets which moved backwards and forwards or twisted wire on pulleys. It was then 'smoothed' with fine sand, grit and pumice, using a machine which could comprise a large wooden wheel frame, divided into four or five spoked sections which revolved over a marble bed. The final stage was polishing the sanded marble, often using a block, attached to a rocker-driven shaft, covered with felt and putty powder or rouge and water, which was dragged back and forth over the marble. 'The advantages [of machine] over manual labour are great, the saving on this alone being at least one-third. There is also a large saving of time in production. A machine will do the work of ten men, saving 75 per cent of the cost of working the material... . Machine work is beautifully sharp and absolutely true.'[12] Machinery also played an important role in the manufacture of enamelled slate items, although hand-labour, much of it undertaken by skilled women, was still retained for some tasks. The process of manufacture in one firm in Cardiff, Sessions and Sons Ltd, was described for visitors to the Industrial Exhibition of 1896:

> The slate and marble arrives in the rough material in slabs and blocks, and passes through the processes of sawing, planing, and rubbing down on a circular-revolving table, for all of which machinery of the most modern type has been fitted up, and is driven by a powerful gas engine. After the rubbing down process and the masons have performed their part of the skilled labour of carving into shape, the slate goods are passed on into the enamelling shops, where the decorative part is commenced with imitations of an infinite variety of marbles, with landscapes and gilded and floral designs. These are baked in stoves varying in heat from a temperature of 160 to 300°F. It is then taken in hand by a number of girls who polish the prepared surfaces by hand labour.... The marble is worked in an entirely separate department by a somewhat similar process, minus the stoving.[13]

Good furnaces were vital. 'A large quantity of so-called enamelled slate has been made in poor and imperfect furnaces with cheap enamel, which wears off directly, and this practice has brought discredit on enamelled slate.'[14]

THE PLASTER TRADE

The proportion of the cost of labour to the cost of materials was particularly high in the plastering industry compared to other trades. The price of plaster fell until the 1880s, reaching its lowest point in the mid 1890s, after which it rose until the First World War. Until the late nineteenth century, the division of labour on site comprised skilled master plasterers, hawk boys (to knock up and gauge all materials, keep tools clean, heat up meals, and serve materials when required) and apprentices, although the latter declined in London and the south-east in particular by the end of the century. Specialised branches of the trade developed which included gauge workers and, most notably, the fibrous-plaster workers, and disputes between branches of the plaster trade rose as pressure on employment grew. Employment was insecure, with malpractices undermining casting shops rife, such as Italian casters hawking centre flowers and trusses round building sites and selling to small decorators and 'jerry builders', or carrying old stock moulds with them to cast roses on the spot on a bench set up on site. Problems were compounded by the seasonal restrictions imposed on the trade, which depended on dry, frost-free weather, and time for the plaster to dry out before the house was habitable. New and more convenient wall and ceiling materials and systems, such as Compoboard, which comprised a wooden core between two heavy pressed paper boards nailed to the wall and decorated immediately with paint and distemper or wallpaper or high-relief papers, could be assembled at any time and thus further undermined the traditional plaster trade.

Innovations in manufacture did not generally involve the introduction of machinery, but rather that of new materials and methods of moulding. 'It is a craft entirely independent of machinery, demanding some exercise of brain as well as skill of hand ... there was once an American invention for executing plaster work by replacing the hawk and trowel by a machine'.[15] Gelatine moulding replaced traditional methods where parts, sometimes 'from fifty to sixty casts … to complete a 6-feet centre flower'[16] were cast and undercut individually. By the late 1890s 'Piece moulding, front and back moulds, and undercutting by hand is now obviated by the use of gelatine.'[17]

Some were critical of substitutes for solid plaster; in 1876, Gwilt commented that papier mâché and carton pierre 'have not all the delicacy of plaster cast … but their lightness and [the] security with which they can be fixed with screws renders them preferable to plaster ornaments.'[18] The most successful substitute, which superseded papier mâché by the end of the nineteenth century, was fibrous plaster, developed in 1856, and manufactured in the 1880s and 1890s by specialist firms such as George Jackson, and McGilvray and Ferris, and principal builders and decorators such as Higgs and Hill, Collinson and Lock, and Barker and Co.

> Formerly centre flowers were extensively made in carton-pierre, also in papier-mâché, but these materials are now to a great extent superseded by fibrous plaster. Cast-iron centre flowers have also been used, but owing to their great weight, general flatness, and want of relief, their use is very limited.[19]

One of fibrous plaster's main advantages was its convenience: 'being made in the shop, and dried before being fixed in the building, the work is not delayed by frost or inclement weather. This is a decided advantage where time is a principal consideration.'[20] The Plasterers' Strike of 1896 sealed fibrous plaster's success, providing the opportunity for mechanical fibrous plastering and matchboarding to oust solid plaster, which never really recovered thereafter.[21] But it was criticised for lowering standards of design.

> The reduction in cost brought [fibrous plaster roses] into more general use, and combined with the monotonous employment of stock designs, made their use so common that they soon came to be considered vulgar by one class and superfluous by others. But the extinguishing blow was dealt by the jerry-builder. This gentleman was aided by the piece-worker and the Italian plaster caster, who by their ready-made centres, generally cast in one piece, combined with their poor designing and their coarse workmanship, soon caused them to be an unsought-for decoration. This applies more to a certain class of dwellings in the suburbs of London, and a few large towns.[22]

THE METAL TRADES

The increased demand for and production of cast iron and its falling price led to a growth in labour in this industry over the period 1880 to 1914, and the rise in the numbers of stove, grate, range and fire-iron manufacturers to 6,211 caused them to be classified as a distinct group for the first time in the Census of 1901. Other groups were not so fortunate; gas fitters, locksmiths and bell-hangers scarcely increased in real terms, and contemporaries suggested that 'Possibly this may be accounted for, at any rate in part, by the substitution of electric bells and electric lighting for ordinary bells and gas',[23] an explanation borne out by the rise of figures for electrical-apparatus workers, especially between 1901 and 1911 from 49,518 to 94,021.[24] After a rise in wages from 1896 to a peak of prosperity in 1900, they fell away from 1901.

The structure of the iron trade comprised mainly large firms, such as the Coalbrookdale Company in Shropshire and the Carron Company in

Stirlingshire. Its success was founded on the combination of the use of both power and craft skills. The strong craft base of the labour force was evident at every stage of production and manufacture. The patternmaker was regarded as the elite in the industry and was the highest-paid worker. As the pattern was made from wood and involved joints and complex forms, background skills in cabinet-making and wood-turning were considered essential. The patternmaker owned his own tools, which cost £10-30. Over and above this, grate and range patternmakers required specialist skills:

> These patterns are frequently very intricate, having a large amount of carving on them … stove making differs greatly from ordinary patternmaking and is a peculiar branch by itself … the stove patternmaker has to provide himself with a series of carving tools, which usually consist of 18 to 10 small tools in the form of gouges, paring chisels and gravers … in some cases a stove pattern passes through the hands of three or four men, each doing his own special work. [25]

The quality of the pattern determined the quality of the finished article. New patterns always created the sharpest and best castings, and were always cited in trade catalogues as a selling point for goods. The importance of the pattern in the process of producing the casting was recognised even by the other iron trades; 'a few shillings extra spent in the pattern shop will save pounds in the foundry and fitting shops'.[26] The patternmaker's training in cabinet-making was vital to an understanding of the forms which house detailing took, as it was he who was responsible for inventing new designs. Marks of the woodworking tools can often be seen on cast firegrates.

The ramming of sand into the mould around the pattern was also skilled work and helped determine the outcome of the casting. Patternmaking and moulding were often distinct trades, and thus the moulder might have to return the pattern to the patternmaker because it was impossible to mould. He was lower paid than the patternmaker and had the reputation as 'the wildest, the most grimy, the most independent, and, unfortunately, the most drunken and troublesome of any English workmen who have any claim to the title of "skilled"'.[27] At the final stage of manufacture, the dressing stage, hand skill was also used where dressers smoothed the castings with hand files.

To increase output and meet increasing competition from America and Germany, British foundries were encouraged to introduce labour-saving machinery, for example, the Tabor moulding machine, and Mathewson's Patent Sand Blast Apparatus. Moulding machines were either worked by hand or were powered, usually using compressed air. Moulding machines had been first introduced in the 1850s which had caused a lock-out in 1852, and resistance continued through to 1900, for instance, the Friendly Society of Iron Moulders, whose membership was hand-craft, remained hostile to the machine worker. Machines for stamping and cutting metals such as brass and steel, brought out in the late 1760s and 1770s (John Pickering and Richard Ford) and 1880s respectively, revolutionised traditional craft skills in the industry. Such machine-stamped designs looked indistinguishable from cast products, yet could be produced at a quarter of the cost.[28]

NOTES

ABBREVIATIONS

F. D. = Furniture and Decoration
I. H. E. = The Ideal Home Exhibition Catalogue
I. C. B. = The Illustrated Carpenter and Builder

INTRODUCTION: EDWARDIAN SOCIETY

1 S. Muthesius, *The English Terraced House*, New Haven, 1982, p. xi.
2 See John A. Walker, *Design History and the History of Design*, Pluto Press, 1989.
3 There are very few complete extant interiors. One exceptional example is the Linley Sambourne House, Stafford Terrace, Kensington, London.
4 in D. Read, *Edwardian England*, London, 1972, p. 15.
5 J. Beckett and D. Cherry, *The Edwardian Era*, London, 1988, p. 15.
6 J. B. Priestley, *The Edwardians*, London, 1970, p. 83.
7 ibid, p. 55.
8 Read, *Edwardian England*, p. 32.
9 P. Snowden, *The Living Wage*, 1913, in Read, *Edwardian England*, p. 50.
10 Read, *Edwardian England*, p. 51.
11 ibid, pp. 21-4.
12 P. Thompson, *The Edwardians*, London, 1977, p. 14.
13 Read, *Edwardian England*, p. 48.
14 ibid, p. 152.
15 ibid, p. 27.
16 ibid, p. 29.
17 Thompson, *The Edwardians*, p. 44.
18 *The Builder*, in J. Burnett, *A Social History of Housing 1815-1970*, London, 1983, p. 189.
19 Muthesius, *The English Terraced House*, p. 97.
20 T. W. H. Crossley, *The Suburbans*, 1905, p. 80.
21 Read, *Edwardian England*, p. 40.
22 ibid, p. 39.
23 Priestley, *The Edwardians*, p. 57.
24 'What the Age Looks Like', in *The Nation*, 26 December 1908, in Read, *Edwardian England*.
25 P. Greenhalgh, *Ephemeral Vistas*, Manchester, 1988, p. 123.
26 Priestley, *The Edwardians*, p. 87.
27 Muthesius, *The English Terraced House*, pp. 17-18.
28 J. Burnett, *A Social History of Housing 1815-1970*, London, 1978, p. 95.
29 ibid, p. 185.
30 ibid.
31 4 September, p. 4, in J. Roebuck, *Urban Development in Nineteenth Century London*, London, 1979, p. 147.
32 G. and W. Grossmith, *The Diary of a Nobody*, 1892; reprinted, London, 1983, p. 20.
33 Muthesius, *The English Terraced House*, p. 44.
34 T. Veblen, *The Theory of the Leisure Class*, New York, 1899.
35 in Read, *Edwardian England*, p. 43.
36 A Member of the Aristocracy, *Manners and Tone of Good Society*, London, about 1899, p. 1.
37 G. R. M. Devereux, *Etiquette For Men*, London, pp. 80 and 118.

38 in Burnett, *A Social History*, p. 182.

39 pp. 23-40.

40 G. Routh, *Occupation and Pay in Great Britain*, 1965, p. 20.

41 Mrs J. E. Panton, *From Kitchen to Garrett*, London, 1887, p. 3.

42 in H. J. Dyos, *Victorian Suburb*, Leicester, 1961, p. 191.

43 ibid, p. 186; cf. also M. Hunter, *The Victorian Villas of Hackney*, London, 1981.

44 Mrs S. Macrae, *Cassell's Household Guide*, London, 1911-12, V, p. 1182.

45 V. Woolf, *Roger Fry*, ch. vii and viii, in Read, *Edwardian England*, p. 256.

46 Macrae, *Cassell's Household Guide*, IV, p. 818.

47 Mrs C. E. Humphry, *The Book of the Home*, London, 1909, V, p. 28.

48 Macrae, *Cassell's Household Guide*, IV, p. 818.

49 Macrae, *Cassell's Household Guide*, IV, p. 997.

1 : THE DISSEMINATION OF TASTE

1 S. Lasdun, 'Victorian Magazines and Furnishing Taste', *Country Life*, 9 September 1976, p. 672.

2 Mrs J. E. Panton, *From Kitchen to Garrett*, London, 1887, p. 1.

3 S. Muthesius, *Victorian Architecture*, London, 1978, p. 42.

4 J. Burnett, *A Social History of Housing 1815-1970*, London, 1978, p. 201.

5 The series was edited by the Rev. William J. Loftie (1839-1911). He worked on *The Saturday Review* from 1874 and joined *The National Observer* in 1894.

6 Books on domestic economy were not new. Seventeenth-century titles are recorded in *Peddie's Subject Index*. Early-nineteenth-century examples included Mrs Parkes, *Domestic Duties or Instruction to Married Ladies*, 1825.

7 Women's magazines can be traced back as far as the end of the seventeenth century to examples such as *The Lady's Mercury*. The content tended to be geared towards the upper classes and their needs, with items on fashion, free fiction, embroidery patterns and sheet music. Mass markets were tapped by, among others, Sir George Newnes (1851-1910), the founder of the highly successful *Tit-Bits* in 1881. Other late-nineteenth-century magazines for women included *Sylvia's Home Journal*, 1878-91, *The Household Companion*, 1891-2, and *Home Sweet Home*, 1893-1901.

8 C. L. White, *Women's Magazines 1693-1968*, London, 1970, p. 68.

9 White, *Women's Magazines*, p. 82.

10 Panton, *From Kitchen to Garrett*, pp. vii-viii.

11 ibid. E. Aslin in *The Aesthetic Movement*, London, 1981, p. 35, dates the appearance of the lady amateur decorator to the 1870s and remarks that the concept of home arts originated from the Aesthetic Movement idea of art embracing all the arts.

12 pp. 133-4. Thanks to J. Schwitzer.

13 L. Davidoff, *The Best Circles*, London, 1986, p. 56.

14 F. Jack, *The Woman's Book*, London, 1911, p. 18.

15 *F. D.*, 15 February 1897, XXXIV, no. 764, p. 1.

16 p. 27.

17 P. Greenhalgh, *Ephemeral Vistas*, Manchester, 1988, p. 163.

18 Davidoff, *The Best Circles*, p. 62.

2 : HOMES AND GARDENS

1 p. 147

2 S. Muthesius, *The English Terraced House*, New Haven, 1982, p. 21.

3 *The South London Press*, 15 April 1910.

4 *I. H. E.*, 1912, pp. 9-10.

5 pp. 98-104.

6 See chapter 11 of Muthesius, *The English Terraced House*. Quotation in J. Burnett, *A Social History of Housing, 1815-1970*, 1978, p. 104.

7 Muthesius, *The English Terraced House*, pp. 99-100.

8 Memories of Harriet Smart in *How Things Were: Growing up in Tottenham 1890-1920*, p. 16. See also M. Swenarton, *Homes Fit for Heroes*, London, 1981, p. 22, for the unfavourable reaction of tenants to non-parlour houses.

9 *I. H. E.*, 1908, p. 11.

10 Mrs J. E. Panton, *Nooks and Corners*, London, 1889, pp. 23-4.

11 *I. H. E.*, 1908, p. 11.

12 Muthesius, *The English Terraced House*, pp. 44 and 99.

13 p. 15.

14 Burnett, *A Social History*, p. 204.

15 J. Beckett and B. Cherry, *The Edwardian Era*, Oxford, 1987.

16 Mrs J. E. Panton, *From Kitchen to Garrett*, London, 1887, pp. 5-6.

17 Mrs S. Macrae, *Cassell's Household Guide*, London, 1911-12, VI, p. 1370.

18 F. Jack, *The Woman's Book*, London, 1911, p. 23.

19 Macrae, *Cassell's Household Guide*, II, p. 262.

20 *F. D.*, 1 January 1892, p. 6.

21 Macrae, *Cassell's Household Guide*, VI, p. 1369.

22 Macrae, *Cassell's Household Guide*, IV, p. 963.

23 ibid.

24 Macrae, *Cassell's Household Guide*, VI, p. 1523.

25 V. Sackville-West, *The Edwardians*, pp. 132-3.

26 *F. D.*, 2 January 1893, p. 6.

27 H. J. Jennings, *Our Homes and How to Beautify Them*, London, 1902, p. 73.

28 *I. H. E.*, 1908, p. 63.

29 *I. H. E.*, 1910, p. 14.

30 *The South London Press*, 15 April 1910.

31 *I. H. E.*, 1912, p. 3.

32 G. and W. Grossmith, *The Diary of a Nobody*, 1892, London, 1983.

33 R. Tressell, *The Ragged Trousered Philanthropists*, London, 1983, p. 119.

34 N. Cooper, *The Opulent Eye*, London, 1977, p. 7. Cf. S. Muthesius, 'Why do we buy old furniture: aspects of the authentic antique in Britain 1870-1910', *Art History*, II, no. 2, June 1988, pp. 231-55.

35 F. M. L. Thompson, in Burnett, *A Social History*, unpaginated, and S. Muthesius, *The English Terraced House*, colour plate 15.

36 Muthesius, *The English Terraced House*, p. 200.

37 ibid, pp. 199 et seq. for more information on materials and regional differences.

38 ibid, p. 76.

39 L. Fleming and A. Gore, *The English Garden*, London, 1979, pp. 194-5.

40 Beckett, *The Edwardian Era*, p. 120.

41 J. C. Loudon, *An Encyclopaedia of Cottage, Farm and Villa Architecture and Furniture*, London, 1833, in Fleming and Gore, *The English Garden*, p. 186.

42 H. Havart, *The Back Garden Beautiful*, London, 1909, pp. 1-2.

43 ibid, p. 7.

44 Jack, *The Woman's Book*, p. 580.

45 R. Redgrave, *The Manual of Design*, London, 1876.

46 *Traditional Interior Decoration*, January 1986, p. 10.

47 Havart, *The Back Garden*, p. 14.

48 W. P. Wright, *Beautiful Gardens: how to make them and maintain them*, London, 1907, p. 112.

49 C. H. Rolph, *London Particulars: memories of an Edwardian boyhood*, Oxford, 1980, p. 44.

50 Havart, *The Back Garden*, p. 76.

51 M. J. Daunton, *House and Home in the Victorian City; working-class housing 1850-1914*, London, 1980, pp. 156-8; p. 102 discusses the similar interests of the landlord and tenant in keeping up respectability.

52 ibid, pp. 156-8.
53 A. A. Jackson, *Semi-Detached London*, London, 1973, p. 35.
54 Macrae, *Cassell's Household Guide*, VI, p. 1307.
55 Panton, *From Kitchen to Garrett*, p. 37.
56 ibid, p. 80.
57 Muthesius, *The English Terraced House*, p. 33.

3: MIDDLE-CLASS SUBURBS

1 F. M. L. Thompson, *The Rise of Suburbia*, Leicester, 1982, p. 2
2 ibid, p. 8.
3 C. Treen, in Thompson, *The Rise*, p. 165.
4 M. Girouard, *Cities and People*, New Haven, 1985, p. 266.
5 Thompson, *The Rise*, p. 5.
6 M. Jahn, in Thompson, *The Rise*, p. 94.
7 ibid.
8 J. Burnett, *A Social History of Housing 1815-1970*, London, 1983, p. 161.
9 P. J. Waller, *Town, City and Nation 1850-1914*, Oxford, 1983, p. 137.
10 J. M. Rawcliffe, in Thompson, *The Rise*, p. 78.
11 J. Thorne, *Handbook to the Environs of London*, 1876, reprinted 1970, 2 vols., p. 61, in ibid.
12 Thompson, *The Rise*, p. 18.
13 ibid, p. 20.
14 Burnett, *A Social History*, p. 161.
15 Thompson, *The Rise*, p. 18.
16 S. Muthesius, *The English Terraced House*, New Haven, 1982, p. 21.
17 G. Calvert Holland, *Vital Statistics of Sheffield*, 1843, p. 56, in H. J. Dyos and M. Wolff, *The Victorian City*, 1973, vol. 1, p. 335.
18 Muthesius, *The English Terraced House*, caption to plate 166.
19 M. J. Daunton, *Coal Metropolis: Cardiff 1870-1914*, Leicester, 1977, p. 1.
20 ibid, p. 229.
21 ibid.
22 *The Cardiff Tide Tables Almanack*, Cardiff, 1882, p. 5.
23 ibid, pp. 10-11.
24 H. McLeod, *Class and Religion in the Late Victorian City*, 1974, pp. 6-13, discussed in Daunton, *Coal Metropolis*, p. 143.
25 *Gentlemen's Journal*, 5 October 1907, pp. 484-7.
26 *Souvenir of the Visit of the King and Queen to Cardiff*, 1907, p. 18.
27 The numbers of houses as a whole built in Lambeth rose from 21,547 in 1851 to 40,721 in 1891, the greatest period of development being the decade of the 1860s, which saw a 30.5 per cent increase over the decade.
28 in P. M. Jenkyns, 'A Glance at Herne Hill', *Herne Hill Society*, undated.
29 Its build-up began in 1868 with the Suburban Village and General Dwellings Company's plan to 'provide at the most rapid rate possible, healthy, pleasant and comfortable abodes for the overcrowded population of the metropolis'. The scheme planned to build between 480 and 650 houses to house three thousand people, to be leased or sold outright on what were to become Milkwood, Heron, Poplar and Lowden Roads on the west side of Herne Hill. Each house was to have four to eight rooms and every domestic convenience, including a piece of garden.
30 H. J. Dyos, *Victorian Suburb: a study of the growth of Camberwell*, Leicester, 1977, p. 91.
31 ibid, p. 215, note 68.
32 C. Booth, *Life and Labour of the People of London*, London, 1903, 3rd series, VI, p. 64.
33 *The South London Observer, Camberwell and Peckham Times*, January 1900.

34 p. 1.

35 Booth, *Life and Labour*, 3rd series, VI, pp. 65-6. *Kelly's* shows a few details; Herne Hill had a solicitor, a builder and a dentist. There was an insurance agent and a house decorator living in Gubyon Avenue, a considerably cheaper road, and a solicitor living in Stradella Road.

36 Booth, *Life and Labour*, 3rd series, VI, p. 88.

37 p. 78.

38 'Hornsey and Crouch End', *London*, 19 March 1896, p. 268.

39 See *Catalogue of Sanitary Appliances* at the Museum of the Hornsey Local Board, Highgate, 1892, for 'specimens of the most improved fittings for the guidance of builders and others interested'.

40 in I. Murray, *The Story of a Mossy Well*, undated, p. 16.

41 in D. E. D. Freeman, *Looking at Muswell Hill*, 1984, p. 38. There were a number of other big builders working in the area, each with their own distinctive styles, such as Charles Rook and Charles Tucker.

42 C. Smith, 'The Parliamentary Representation of Hornsey', *Hornsey Historical Society Local History Bulletin*, no. 26, 1985, pp. 4-6.

43 January 13. The life-style can be interpreted also from a study of local newspaper advertisements, which mention Parisian laundries, french polishers, landscape gardeners, caterers for children's parties, and furnishing, for example, Ellis and Co., the piano furnisher and complete house furnisher, who sold pianos on hire for those on low incomes for £14 14s, and offered a complete 'Grovesnor' bedroom for £8.

44 Thanks to Mrs Ross for this information.

45 M. J. Daunton is critical of what he calls a 'refuge in cultural variables' in *House and Home in the Victorian City: working-class housing 1850-1914*, London, 1980, p. 88.

4: LANDOWNERS AND BUILDING TRADES

1   C. Booth, *Life and Labour of the People in London*, London, 1903, 2nd series, I, pp. 51-2.

2   M. J. Daunton, *House and Home in the Victorian City: working-class housing 1850-1914*, London, 1980, p. 76, and S. Muthesius, *The English Terraced House*, New Haven, 1982, p. 21.

3   Booth, *Life and Labour*, 2nd series, I, p. 39. Daunton, *House and Home*, pp. 84-6, examines the impact of bye-laws on housing.

4   D. Cannadine, 'Urban development in England and America in the nineteenth century; some comparisons and contrasts', *Economic History Review*, 2nd series, XXXIII, 1980, pp. 321-2.

5   C. Powell, *An Economic History of the British Building Industry 1815-1979*, London, 1982, p. 48.

6   *Census of England and Wales, 1911, General Report with Appendices*, p. 123.

7   *Census of England and Wales, 1901, General Report with Appendices*, p. 178

8   ibid.

9   *Census of England and Wales, 1911, General Report with Appendices*, p.123.

10 ibid.

11 *Census of England and Wales, 1891, General Report with Summary Tables*, p. 47.

12 Powell, *An Economic History*, p. 77.

13 Muthesius, *The English Terraced House*, p. 28.

14 Powell, *An Economic History*, p. 77.

15 ibid, p. 73.

16 Muthesius, *The English Terraced House*, p. 28, says that the building boom and unionisation brought a reduction in piecework. Such specialisation was, according to Booth, still confined to London in the 1890s, country areas still being characterised by the 'all-round man'.

17 J. Elliot, *Practical House Painting*, 1910, p. 7.

18 *Kelly's Trade Directory*, in Muthesius, *The English Terraced House*, p. 30.

19 *The Builders Merchant*, 1902, p. 113.

20 ibid, April 1898, pp. 81-3.

21 ibid, August 1898, p. 213.

22 ibid, February 1898, pp. 25-6.

23 Thomas O'Brien Catalogue, 1900.

24 Booth, *Life and Labour*, p. 67.

25 *The Builders Merchant*, August 1902, p. 113.

26 *The Timber Trades Journal*, 1 July 1905, pp. 20-1.

27 'Woodworking Machinery and Practice', *The Cabinet Maker*, 30 May 1925, p. 447.

28 A. Lee, *Marble and Marble Workers*, Bristol, 1887, p. 19.

29 *I. C. B.*, 6 April 1900, p. 2.

30 The best-known and most useful was St Ann's, with a dark grey ground with lighter patches and veined with white. There were several varieties, that with the darkest ground and well defined veining being regarded as the best. Red marble was another popular type, called variously, Rouge Royale, Rouge Griotte, Rouge Byzantine, Rouge Fleuri, Malplaquet and Rouge Rose. The best-quality red marble was dark brownish-red ground with veining well defined and white, while the cheapest was light brown in colour with grey and white patches and ill defined veining. Rouge Griotte was considered best quality. There was also a black Belgian marble. *I. C. B.*, 6 April 1900, p. 2.

31 Lee, *Marble*, p. 41.

32 ibid, pp. 20-1.

33 ibid.

34 *I. C. B.*, 13 April 1900, p. 2.

35 Powell, *An Economic History*, p. 83.

36 *Practical House Painting*, p. 5.

37 L. Crane, *Art and the Formation of Taste*, London, 1882, p. 87.

38 Mrs J. E. Panton, *From Kitchen to Garrett*, London, 1887, pp. 58-9.

39 R. Tressell, *The Ragged Trousered Philanthropists*, 1955, London, 1983, pp. 398-9.

40 Booth, *Life and Labour*, 2nd series, I, p. 51.

41 W. Crane, *The Claims of Decorative Art*, London, 1892, pp. 135-6.

42 Heaton, *Beauty and Art*, p. 90.

43 Crane, *The Claims of Decorative Art*, p. 136.

THE HOUSES: INTERIORS AND EXTERIORS

1 Originally, fixtures and fittings were chattels which were automatically part of the property to which they were attached. But by the late nineteenth century, those added by tenants could be taken away with them on termination of the tenancy on the understanding that the original item replaced was put back as found, and were thus known as 'tenant's fixtures'. More structural fixtures were known as 'landlord's fixtures'.

5: EXTERIORS

1 C. Powell, *An Economic History of the British Building Industry 1815-1979*, London, 1980, p. 80.

2 S. Muthesius, *The English Terraced House*, New Haven, 1982, p. 203.

3 ibid, p. 204.

4 Powell, *An Economic History*, p. 79.

5 ibid.

6 ibid, p. 80.

7 ibid.

8 R. Hillier, *Clay That Burns*, London, 1981, p. 38.

9 Muthesius, *The English Terraced House*, colour plate 25.
10 ibid, p. 210.
11 ibid, colour plate 31.
12 Powell, *An Economic History*, p. 80.
13 Muthesius, *The English Terraced House*, p. 210.
14 ibid, p. 215.
15 ibid, p. 219.
16 ibid, p. 220.
17 ibid, p. 215.
18 ibid, p. 217.
19 ibid.
20 ibid, p. 219.
21 p. 2.
22 Muthesius, *The English Terraced House*, p. 229.
23 J. G. Allen, *The Cheap Cottage and Small House*, Letchworth, 1912, p. 84.
24 Muthesius, *The English Terraced House*, p. 50.
25 Powell, *An Economic History*, p. 83.
26 Muthesius, *The English Terraced House*, p. 174.
27 ibid, p. 225.
28 see J. Burnett, *A Social History of Housing 1815-1970*, London, 1983, p. 202.
29 Powell, *An Economic History*, p. 80.

6: LIGHTING, HEATING AND PLUMBING

1 Mrs D. C. Peel, *How to Keep House*, London, 1902, p. 150.
2 ibid, p. 156.
3 See A. Forty, *Objects of Desire*, London, 1986.
4 S. Muthesius, *The English Terraced House*, New Haven, 1982, p. 51.
5 L. Hannah, *Electricity Before Nationalisation: a study of the development of the electricity supply industry in Britain to 1948*, London, 1979, p. 186.
6 Muthesius, *The English Terraced House*, pp. 51-2.
7 G. Allen, *The Cheap Cottage and the Small House: a manual of economic building*, Letchworth, 1913, p. 127.
8 H. Muthesius, *Das Englische Haus*, Berlin, 1904-5, as *The English House*, London, 1979, p. 199.
9 Mrs Haweis, *The Art of Decoration*, London, 1881, p. 353.
10 Mrs J. E. Panton, *From Kitchen to Garrett*, London, 1887, p. 98.
11 Allen, *The Cheap Cottage*, p. 126.
12 Peel, *How to Keep House*, p. 184.
13 Haweis, *The Art of Decoration*, p. 355.
14 Mrs C. E. Humphry, *The Book of the Home*, London, 1909, II, p. 59.
15 J. Marsden, *Lamps and Lighting*, Guinness, 1990, p. 98.
16 R. Hammond, *The Electric Light in Our Homes*, London, 1884, p. 76.
17 C. Powell, *An Economic History of the British Building Industry 1815-1979*, London, 1982, p. 82.
18 Muthesius, *The English House*, p. 199.
19 Muthesius, *The English Terraced House*, pp. 51-2.
21 D. Gledhill, *Gas Lighting*, Shire, 1981, p. 20.
22 This and all the information in the following paragraph is extracted from Borough of Hornsey, *Electricity Supply Committee Minute Book 1*, December 1903-September 1910.
23 Borough of Hornsey, *Minute Book 1*.
24 *Healthy Hornsey*, 1905.
25 Borough of Hornsey, *Minute Book 1*.
26 C. H. Rolph, *London Particulars: memories of an Edwardian boyhood*, Oxford, 1980, p. 42.

27 Marsden, *Lamps and Lighting*, p.71.
28 P. Rose, 'W. A. S. Benson: a pioneer designer of light fittings', *The Journal of the Decorative Arts Society*, no. 9, p. 55.
29 F. W. Thorpe, 'Development and design of lighting fixtures in relation to architecture, interior decoration and illumination', *Illuminating Engineer*, March 1915, pp. 116-18.
30 ibid.
31 Humphry, *The Book of the Home*, II, p. 59.
32 Thorpe, 'Development and design', pp. 114-16.
33 H. J. Jennings, *Our Homes and How to Beautify Them*, London, 1902, p. 236.
34 S. Stevens Hellyer, *The Plumber and Sanitary Houses*, 1877, pp. 234-5.
35 L. Wright, *Deep Fresh*, London, 1980, p. 152.
36 Muthesius, *The English House*, p. 235.
37 ibid.
38 ibid, p. 236.
39 Wright, *Deep Fresh*, p. 157.
40 Muthesius, *The English House*, p. 236.
41 G. and W. Grossmith, *The Diary of a Nobody*, London, 1983, pp. 5-6.
42 Wright, *Deep Fresh*, p. 161.
43 Humphry, *The Book of the Home*, I, p. 174.
44 Muthesius, *The English House*, p. 236.
45 Allen, *The Cheap Cottage*, p. 124.
46 Muthesius, *The English House*, p. 236.
47 *Hints on Houses and House Furnishing*, about 1855, p. 3.
48 Haweis, *The Art of Decoration*, p. 341.
49 ibid, p. 342.
50 p. 145, in D. Rubenstein, *Victorian Homes*, Newton Abbot, 1974, p. 98.
51 H. C. Long, 'The Fireplace 1875-1900', M. A. Thesis, University of East Anglia, 1981.
52 Haweis, *The Art of Decoration*, p. 341.
53 An Engineer and his wife, *The Ideal Servant-Saving House*, London, 1918, p. 123.
54 ibid.
55 Hannah, *Electricity Before Nationalisation*, p. 194.
56 An Engineer and his wife, *The Ideal*, p. 51.
57 ibid, p. 23.

7: FIREPLACES

1 *F. D.*, V, no. 12, December 1894, p. 194.
2 Thomas O'Brien Catalogue, 1900, no. 128a, drawing-room chimneypiece.
3 Young and Marten Catalogue, 1898, p. 29.
4 Mrs J. E. Panton, *From Kitchen to Garrett*, London, 1887, p. 5.
5 *F. D.*, 1894.
6 Mrs C. E. Humphry, *The Book of the Home*, London, 1909, I, pp. 88-9.
7 Panton, *From Kitchen to Garrett*, p. 65.
8 A. Lee, *Marble and Marble Workers*, London, 1888, p. 41. The machine had a hopper that was filled with sand and a vacuum caused by steam pressure then drew the sand into the blast.
9 W. Millar, *Plastering Plain and Decorative*, London, 1897, endpaper.
10 *I. C. B.*, 6 April 1900, p. 5.
11 ibid, p. 4.
12 Patent Marezzo Marble Co. Catalogue, preface, not dated.
13 ibid, preface.
14 ibid.
15 M. H. Baillie Scott, 'The Fireplace in the Suburban House', *The Studio*, VI, 1896, pp. 101-8.

16   *I. C. B.*, 6 April 1900.

17   Mrs S. Macrae, *Cassell's Household Guide*, London, 1911-12, VI, p. 1371.

18   *F. D.*, 1890.

19   *F. D.*, 1 January 1892.

20   Baillie Scott, 'The Fireplace', p. 101.

21   *F. D.*, 1892.

22   *F. D.*, I, no. 2, 1 November 1890, p. 164.

23   L. Crane, *Art and the Formation of Taste*, London, 1882, p. 52.

24   *F. D.*, 1892.

25   *I. C. B.*, 1900, p. 5.

26   *F. D.*, 1 January 1891, p. 4.

27   *F. D.*, 2 January 1893, p. 6.

28   ibid.

29   *F. D.*, XXXII, no. 743, 15 May 1895, pp. 69-70.

30   *F. D.*, I, no. 1, 1 November 1890, p. 163.

31   ibid, p. 164.

32   *I. C. B.*, 29 June 1900, p. 4.

33   C. Eastlake, *Hints on Household Taste in Furniture, Upholdstery and Other Details*, London, 1878, p. 93.

34   Baillie Scott, 'The Fireplace', p. 105.

35   See also Carron Company catalogues. Fashions in materials for fenders followed a similar route, from cast iron to Berlin black and bronze, from steel to steel and ormolu, through black and brass, to all brass; at the end of the century, under the impact of the Arts and Crafts Movement, fenders were also available in black and copper, all copper, or wrought iron, in a 'hand-beaten' style produced by machine, and finally in ceramic by the early twentieth century.

36   W. Shaw Sparrow, *The British Home of Today*, London, 1904, unpaginated.

8: DOORS AND DOORWAYS

1   *F. D.*, 1 October 1891, p. 132.

2   ibid, p. 131.

3   R. W. Edis, *The Decoration and Furniture of Town Houses*, London, 1881, p. 141.

4   L. Crane, *Art and the Formation of Taste*, London, 1882, p. 52.

5   G. Allen, *The Cheap Cottage and Small House: a manual of economic building*, Letchworth, 1913, p. 86.

6   H. Muthesius, *Das Englische Haus*, Berlin, 1904-5, as *The English House*, London, 1979, p. 189.

7   *F. D.*, 1 December 1891, p. 163.

8   Mrs J. E. Panton, *Nooks and Corners*, London, 1889, p. 42.

9   *F. D.*, 1 December 1891, p. 163.

10   ibid.

11   *F. D.*, 1 December 1891, p. 163.

12   *F. D.*, 1 October 1891, p. 132.

13   Mrs J. E. Panton, *From Kitchen to Garrett*, London, 1887, pp. 47-8.

14   Muthesius, *The English House*, p. 189.

9: WINDOWS

1   L. Crane, *Art and the Formation of Taste*, London, 1882, p. 88.

2   Mrs C. E. Humphry, *The Book of the Home*, London, 1909, I, p. 226.

3   Mrs J. E. Panton, *From Kitchen to Garrett*, London, 1887, p. 96.

4   *Kelly's Post Office Directory*, p. 1946.

5 *The House*, IX, April 1897.

6 Humphry, *The Book of the Home*, I, p. 230.

7 *The Women's Encyclopaedia*, III, 1912, p. 2024.

8 Humphry, *The Book of the Home*, I, p. 226.

9 *Hornsey Journal*, 6 October 1905, p. 7, and C. H. Rolph, *London Particulars: memories of an Edwardian boyhood*, Oxford, 1980, p. 71.

10 Rolph, *London Particulars*, p. 44.

11 Ledger, 1875; 1877.

12 Repairs book, IV/115/7, 1904-6.

13 Committee minutes, 1881.

14 Panton, *From Kitchen to Garrett*, p. 91.

15 A. Heaton, *Beauty and Art*, London, 1897, p. 122.

16 H. J. Jennings, *Our Homes and How to Beautify Them*, London, 1902, p. 121.

17 Humphry, *The Book of the Home*, I, p. 228.

18 Jennings, *Our Homes*, p. 121.

19 Mrs Macrae, *Cassell's Household Guide*, London, 1912, II, p. 290.

20 Mrs Haweis, *The Art of Decoration*, London, 1881, p. 242.

21 *Sears Roebuck and Co. Home Builders' Catalogue: the complete illustrated 1910 edition*, New York, 1990, p. 44.

22 Pittsburg Glass Co., *Glass - Paints*, USA, 1923, p. 125.

23 M. H. Baillie Scott, 'The Decoration of the Suburban House', *The Studio*, V, p. 19.

24 ibid.

25 p. 109.

10: CEILINGS AND CORNICES

1 p. 60.

2 p. 41.

3 p. 89.

4 A. Heaton, *Beauty and Art*, London, 1897, pp. 104-7.

5 Heaton, *Beauty and Art*, p. 105.

6 C. G. Rothery, *Ceilings and their Decoration*, London, about 1910, p. 249.

7 G. Allen, *The Cheap Cottage and Small House: a manual of economic building*, Letchworth, 1913.

8 Rothery, *Ceilings*, p. 251.

9 Heaton, *Beauty and Art*, p. 103.

10 Rothery, *Ceilings*, p. 264.

11 ibid, p. 252.

12 W. Millar, *Plastering Plain and Decorative*, London, 1897, p. 302.

13 G. L. Sutcliffe, *Principles and Practices of Modern House Construction*, London, 1898, pp. 166-7.

14 'Architects' Craftsmen No. 1', *Architectural Review*, 1908, unpaginated.

15 *Beauty and Art*, p. 99.

16 Millar, *Plastering*, p. 344.

17 Young and Marten, *General Illustrated Catalogue*, 1898.

18 Reverse moulding was invented in the 1870s by J. M'Donald, who worked for L. A. Desachy, the inventor of fibrous plaster, and later for G. Jackson and Sons. Reverse moulding involved producing a reverse piece mould from the inner profile of a design, rather than working from the outer profile to produce a model from which a mould would be made. This process thus cut down the number of stages required for production.

19 Millar, *Plastering*, p. 344.

20 ibid, p. 302.

21 Sutcliffe, *Principles and Practices*, pp. 166-7.

22 Millar, *Plastering*, p. 303.

23 R. W. Edis, *The Decoration and Furniture of Town Houses*, London, 1881, p. 151.
24 Rothery, *Ceilings*, p. 252.
25 Heaton, *Beauty and Art*, p. 104.
26 Cast-iron roses tended to be used in large public buildings, where the design often incorporated ventilating apparatus for removing gas fumes from the room.
27 Rothery, *Ceilings*, p. 257.
28 J. H. Elder-Duncan, *The Home Beautiful and Useful*, 1912, p. 68.
29 *I. C. B.*, 15 June 1900, p. 3.
30 Millar, *Plastering*, pp. 35-6.

11: WALLS AND FLOORS

1 H. Muthesius, *Das Englische House*, Berlin, 1904-5, as *The English House*, London, 1979, p. 166.
2 H. J. Jennings, *Our Homes and How to Beautify Them*, London, 1902, p. 55.
3 Muthesius, *The English House*, p. 201.
4 The dado was sometimes covered with wooden panelling. Vertical tongue-and-groove matchboarding was widely used in Cardiff in bathrooms and in the living-kitchen area of houses throughout the period 1899-1909; sometimes these were decorated with panel mouldings or fretwork. Panelled bay windows were used in some front ground- and first-floor rooms of better houses. Cheaper versions of this feature existed where a plain panel was added below the window, with decorative angle brackets joining it to the skirting or window frame.
5 Mrs J. E. Panton, *From Kitchen to Garrett*, London, 1887, p. 78.
6 A. Ransome, *Modern Woodworking Machinery*, London, 1902, p. 169.
7 G. Ellis, *Modern Practical Joinery*, London, 1921, p. 405.
8 H. Gibbon and Sons, *Catalogue of Mouldings*, 1909.
9 Ellis, *Modern Practical Joinery*, p. 412.
10 Jennings, *Our Homes*, p. 56.
11 ibid.
12 Muthesius, *The English House*, p. 166.
13 G. Allen, *The Cheap Cottage and Small House; a manual of economic building*, Letchworth, 1913, p. 87.
14 R. Phillips, *The Servantless House*, London, 1920, p. 30.
15 A. Heaton, *Beauty and Art*, London, 1897, p. 117.
16 Muthesius, *The English House*, p. 166.
17 W. J. Furnival, *Leadless Decorative Tiles, Faience and Mosaic*, Stone, 1904, p. 806.
18 ibid, p. 812.
19 ibid, p. 805.
20 ibid, p. 804.
21 ibid, p. 801.
22 ibid, p. 805.
23 ibid, p. 807.
24 Mrs C. E. Humphry, *The Book of the Home*, London, 1909, I, p. 93.
25 Furnival, *Leadless Decorative Tiles*, p. 539.
26 ibid, p. 804.
27 ibid, p. 814.
28 ibid, p. 445.
29 ibid, p. 784.
30 ibid, p. 802.
31 M. H. Baillie Scott, 'The Decoration of the Suburban House', *The Studio*, V, p. 19.
32 F. Jack, *The Woman's Book*, London, 1911, p. 18.
33 Humphry, *The Book of the Home*, I, p. 96.
34 Mrs Panton, *From Kitchen to Garrett*, London, 1889, p. 104.
35 *The Furniture Record, the Furnisher and Hire Trade Review*, 8 April 1910, pp. 324-5.

36 R. Redgrave, *Manual of Design*, London, 1884, p. 106.

37 C. L. Eastlake, *Hints on Household Taste in Furniture, Upholstery and Other Details*, London, 1878, p. 51.

38 in J. Ayres, 'Oilcloths', *Traditional Homes*, July 1985, pp. 55-7.

39 Redgrave, *Manual of Design*, p. 106.

40 Jack, *The Woman's Book*, p. 21.

41 Mrs J. E. Panton, *Nooks and Corners*, London, 1889, pp. 28-9.

42 I. C. S. Reference Library, *Carpet, Wallpaper, Linoleum etc.*, USA, 1905, p. 23.

43 I. C. S., *Carpet*, Part 9, §10.

44 Eastlake, *Hints*, p. 123.

45 *The Decorator*, 29 March 1905, p. 273.

46 See bibliography under N. Cooper, A. Service, M. Turner and others for further reading on colour schemes and furnishings.

47 W. Pearce, *Painting and Decorating*, London, 1902, p. 91.

48 Panton, *From Kitchen to Garrett*, p. 46.

49 Panton, *Nooks and Corners*, p. 93.

50 C. Powell, *An Economic History of the British Building Industry 1815-1979*, 1982, p. 83.

51 *The Decorator*, 29 March 1905, p. 282.

52 J. L. Sudgen and A. V. Edmondson, *A History of English Wallpaper 1509-1914*, 1925, p. 179.

53 *The Decorator*, 29 March 1905, p. 273.

54 Pearce, *Painting*, p. 90.

55 *The Decorator*, 29 March 1905, p. 301.

56 Panton, *From Kitchen to Garrett*, p. 103.

57 Eastlake, *Hints*, p. 119.

58 Jack, *The Woman's Book*, p. 21

59 *The Decorator*, 29 March 1905, p. 273.

60 ibid, p. 303.

61 ibid, p. 311.

62 ibid, p. 272.

12: STAIRWAYS

1 Mrs J. E. Panton, *From Kitchen to Garrett*, London, 1887, p. 40.

2 G. Ellis, *Modern Practical Joinery*, 4th ed. London, 1921, p. 379

3 ibid.

4 F. T. Hodgson, *Stair-building Made Easy*, The Industrial Publishing Co., New York, 1884, p. 90.

13: FITTED FURNITURE

1 *F. D.*, 1 April 1890, no. 4, I, p. 49. The popularity of 'fitments' grew rapidly from the 1880s. According to Hermann Muthesius, the widespread dissemination of the idea of fitted furniture can be attributed largely to one person, Robert W. Edis, whose designs were shown at the International Health Exhibition of 1884. 'The employment of fitments in the ordinary home cannot be too highly recommended, both on account of their convenience aswell as their appearance', said *F. D.*

2 *Furnisher and Decorator*, 2 February 1891, p. 94.

3 ibid, p. 88.

4 C. Jennings and Co., Bristol, Catalogue, about 1914.

5 *F. D.*, 1 April 1890, p. 50.

6 Mrs J. E. Panton, *Nooks and Corners*, London, 1889, p. 24.

7 Jennings, Catalogue, p. 135.

8 Panton, *Nooks and Corners*, pp. 24-6.

9 Jennings, Catalogue, p. 130.

10 p. 18.

11 *F. D.*, 15 October 1895, p. 167.

12 A. A. Jackson, *Semi-detached London*, London, 1973, p. 37.

13 Jennings, Catalogue, p. 130.

14 *F. D.*, 1 February 1890, no. 2, I.

15 p. 29.

16 *F. D.*, June 1893, p. 82.

17 *F. D.*, 1 February 1890, p. 18.

18 *The Cabinet Maker*, August 1892, p. 32.

19 Inglenooks made a reappearance during the 1860s and 1870s in the work of the vernacular revival architects who placed a special emphasis on details of the interior such as recesses, staircases and inglenooks. One of the earliest examples of the use of the inglenook, for instance, was in the hall at 'Willesley', built by Norman Shaw in 1864; most of Shaw or Nesfield's subsequent houses built in the Old English style had at least one inglenook. Baillie Scott also advocated the use of the inglenook and Ernest Gimson put inglenooks in Stoneywell and window seats in The White House. The cottage ideal was particularly appropriate for small houses, and Parker and Unwin included inglenooks in even their smallest garden-city houses.

20 *F. D.*, 15 February 1897, p. 24.

21 *F. D.*, 1 February 1890, p. 18.

22 *F. D.*, 1 January 1894, p. 10. The cosy corner, J. Gloag suggests in *Victorian Comfort: a social history of design from 1830-1900*, London, 1961, may have derived from the fashion for ottomans around 1850. The term was in common use by the 1870s and lent its name to a whole range of novels and women's magazines in the late Victorian and Edwardian period.

23 *F. D.*, 2 March 1891, II, no. 15, p. 34.

24 ibid.

25 *F. D.*, 15 August 1895, p. 136.

26 ibid.

27 *F. D.*, 2 March 1891, p. 34.

28 *F. D.*, 1894.

29 p. 147. See also F. Thompson, *Lark Rise to Candleford*.

30 *F. D.*, 2 March 1891, p. 35.

31 The Turkish corner, as it was sometimes also called, and cosy corners in general were also very popular in America, and many contemporary photographs show corners festooned with drapery, tassels and Turkish couches, which were even available by mail order from companies such as Sears Roebuck in the late 1890s and early 1900s.

32 *F. D.*, 1 February 1890, I, no 2, pp. 18-20.

33 *F. D.*, 2 March 1891, p. 34.

34 H. Muthesius, *Das Englische Haus*, Berlin, 1904-5, as *The English House*, London, 1979.

35 *F. D.*, 1 April 1890, p. 52. Edwin Foley in *F. D.*, 1895, recommended an extension of the cosy corner idea, the centrement, which was a free-standing piece of furniture based on the same principle.

36 *F. D.*, 2 March 1891, p. 34.

37 *F. D.*, 1 April 1890, p. 52.

38 Muthesius, *The English House*, p. 214.

APPENDIX 2

1 J. T. Rea, *How to Estimate: being the analysis of builders' prices*, London, 1913, p. 351.

2 'The Ideal Machine Shop', *I. C. B.*, 2 March 1900, p. 6.

3 *Timber Trade Journal*, 21 May 1910, p. 783.

4 F. W. Hybart, 'The Timber Trade in Cardiff' in J. Ballinger, *Cardiff: an illustrated handbook*, Cardiff, 1896, p. 185.

5 P. Mathias, *The First Industrial Nation*, London, 1969, p. 288.

6 G. T. Jones, *Increasing Return*, 1933, pp. 66, 83 and 94, in C. G. Powell, *An Economic History of the British Building Industry 1815-1979*, London, 1982, p. 81.

7 S. Ransome, *Modern Woodworking Machinery*, London, 1902, p. 106.

8 Rea, *How to Estimate*, pp. 314 and 321.

9 J. Horner, 'The Modern Machine Shop', Supplement to *I.C.B.*, 30 March 1900, p. 6.

10 p. 118.

11 *Census of England and Wales, 1891, IV, General Report with Summary Tables*, pp. 55-6; *Census of England and Wales, 1911, General Report with Appendices*, p. 119.

12 Rea, *How to Estimate*, p. 208.

13 J. Ballinger, *Cardiff: an illustrated handbook*, Cardiff, 1896, appendix, unpaginated. At the top of the hierarchy within the marble and slate trades were the marble and slate masons; polishers required little skill and were a branch totally distinct from the masons (C. Booth, *Life and Labour of the People in London*, London, 1903, 2nd series, I, p. 65).

14 *The Builders' Merchant*, December 1898, p. 339.

15 W. Millar, *Plastering, Plain and Decorative*, London, 1897, p. 548.

16 ibid.

17 Millar, *Plastering*, p. 318. Gelatine moulding was first introduced by a Frenchman, M. H. Vincent, in 1850, and it caused a sensation at the Great Exhibition of 1851.

18 J. Gwilt, *Encyclopaedia of Architecture*, 1876, p. 679, §2251, in J. Ayres, *The Shell Book of the Home in Britain*, London, 1981, p. 144.

19 Millar, *Plastering*, p. 344.

20 ibid, p. 346.

21 J. T. Rea, *How to Estimate*, p. 47.

22 Millar, *Plastering*, p. 302.

23 *Census of England and Wales, 1891, IV, General Report with Summary Tables*.

24 *Census of England and Wales, 1911, General Report with Appendices*, p. 121.

25 I. C. S. Reference Library, *Woodworking, Patternmaking , Moulding etc.*, 1905, §48, p. 13.

26 *The Foundry Trade Journal*, 1902, p. 70.

27 *Recollections of English Engineers*, p. 218, in R. Samuel, 'Workshop of the World', *History Workshop Journal*, Spring 1977, p. 39.

28 Mathias, *The First Industrial Nation*, p. 248.

SELECT BIBLIOGRAPHY

RECENT SOURCES

Adburgham, A., *Shopping in Style*, Thames and Hudson, London, 1979.

Agius, P., *British Furniture 1880-1915*, Antique Collectors Club, Woodbridge, 1978.

Aslin, E., *The Aesthetic Movement*, 1961; Ferndale Editions, London, 1981.

Austwick, B. and J., *The Decorated Tile*, Pitman House, London, 1980.

Ayres, J., *The Shell Book of the Home in Britain*, Faber and Faber, London, 1981.

Beard, G., *Craftsmen and Interior Decoration in England 1660-1820*, Bartholomew, 1981; Bloomsbury Books, London, 1986.

Bowley, M., *Innovations in Building Materials: an economic study*, Duckworth, 1960.

Briggs, A., *Victorian Things*, Batsford, 1988; Penguin, London, 1990.

Burnett, J., *A Social History of Housing 1815-1970*, Methuen, London, 1980.

Burnett, J., ed., *Useful Toil*, Allen Lane, 1974; Penguin, London, 1984.

Calder, J., *The Victorian Home*, Book Club Associates, London, 1977.

Calloway, S., *Twentieth Century Decoration*, Weidenfeld and Nicholson, London, 1988.

Campbell, C., *The Romantic Ethic and the Spirit of Modern Consumerism*, Basil Blackwell, 1989.

Carter, T., *The Victorian Garden*, Bell and Hyman, 1984; Bracken Books, 1988.

Cherry, D., and J. Beckett, eds., *The Edwardian Era*, Phaidon, Oxford, and Barbican Art Gallery, 1987.

Cooper, N., *The Opulent Eye: late Victorian and Edwardian taste in interior design*, The Architectural Press, London, 1977.

Daunton, M. J., *Coal Metropolis: Cardiff 1870-1914*, Leicester University Press, 1977.

Daunton, M. J., *House and Home in the Victorian City: working-class housing 1850-1914*, Edward Arnold, London, 1980.

Davey, P., *Arts and Crafts Architecture: the search for earthly paradise*, The Architectural Press, London, 1980.

Davidoff, L., *The Best Circles: society etiquette and the Season*, The Cresset Library, London, 1986.

Denvir, B., *The Late Victorians 1852-1910*, Longman, London, 1986.

Dyos, H. J., *Victorian Suburb: a study of the growth of Camberwell*, 1961; Leicester University Press, 1977.

Edmondson, J. L., and A. V. Sugden, *A History of English Wallpaper 1509-1914*, Batsford, London, 1925.

Forty, A., *Objects of Desire*, Thames and Hudson, London, 1986.

Franklin, J., *The Gentleman's Country House and its Plan 1835-1914*, Routledge and Kegan Paul, 1981.

Girouard, M., *Sweetness and Light: the Queen Anne movement 1860-1900*, Yale University Press, New Haven, 1977.

Girouard, M., *The Victorian Country House*, Yale University Press, New Haven, 1979.

Gloag, J., *Victorian Comfort: a social history of design from 1830-1900*, A. and C. Black, London, 1961.

Greenhalgh, P., *Ephemeral Vistas: the expositions universelles, great exhibitions and world fairs, 1851-1939*, Manchester University Press, 1988.

Grier, K. C., *Culture and Comfort: people, parlors and upholdstery 1850-1930*, The Strong Museum, New York, 1988.

Hall, C., L. Davidoff and, *Family Fortunes: men and women of the English middle class 1780-1850*, Hutchinson, London, 1987.

Hills, N., *The English Fireplace: its architecture and the working fire*, Quiller, London, 1983.

Hobsbawm, E. J., *Industry and Empire*, Weidenfeld and Nicolson, 1968; Penguin, London, 1976.

Hunter, M., *Victorian Villas of Hackney*, Hackney Society, 1981.

Jackson, A. A., *Semi Detached London*, Allen and Unwin, London, 1973.

Kirkham, P., R. Mace and J. Porter, *Furnishing the World: the East London furniture trade 1830-1980*, Journeyman Press, 1987.

Long, H. C., 'The British Domestic Interior 1880-1914: a study of fixed decoration in middle-class housing', PhD Thesis, CNAA, Brighton Polytechnic, 1990.

Mathias, P., *The First Industrial Nation*, Methuen, London, 1969.

Muthesius, S., and R. Dixon, *Victorian Architecture*, Thames and Hudson, London, 1978.

Muthesius, S., *The English Terraced House*, Yale University Press, New Haven, 1982.

Naylor, G., *The Arts and Crafts Movement*, Studio Vista, London, 1980.

Otterwill, D., *The Edwardian Garden*, Yale University Press, New Haven, 1989.

Phillips, J., and H. Barrett, *The Suburban Style: the British Home 1840-1960*, Macdonald, London, 1987.

Powell, C. G., *An Economic History of the British Building Industry 1815-1979*, Methuen, London, 1982.

Priestley, J. B., *The Edwardians*, London, 1970.

Read, D., *Edwardian England*, Harrap, London, 1972.

Rolph, C. H., *London Particulars: memories of an Edwardian Boyhood*, Oxford University Press, 1980.

Schwartz-Cowan, R., *More Work for Mother*, Basic Books, USA, 1986.

Service, A., *Edwardian Architecture*, Thames and Hudson, London, 1977.

Service, A., *Edwardian Interiors: inside the homes of the wealthy, the average and the poor*, Barrie and Jenkins, London, 1982.

Stevenson, J., *British Society 1914-45*, Penguin, London, 1984.

Swenarton, M., *Homes Fit for Heroes*, Heineman, London, 1981.

Thompson, P., *The Edwardians*, 1975, Weidenfeld and Nicholson, London, 1984.

Thompson, T., *Edwardian Childhoods*, Routledge and Kegan Paul, London, 1981.

Thornton, P., *Authentic Decor: the domestic interior 1620-1920*, Weidenfeld and Nicholson, London, 1984.

Turner, M. A., *London Design Studio 1880-1963; The Silver Studio Collection*, Lund Humphries, London, 1980.

Waller, P. J., *Town, City and Nation*, Oxford University Press, 1983.

White, J., *Rothschild Buildings: life in an East End tenement block 1887-1920*, Routledge and Kegan Paul, London, 1980.

Woodham, J. M., *Twentieth Century Ornament*, Studio Vista, London, 1990.

Wright, G., *Moralism and the Model Home: domestic architecture and cultural conflict in Chicago 1873-1913*, University of Chicago Press, 1980.

CONTEMPORARY SOURCES

A Member of the Aristocracy, *Manners and Tone of Good Society*, Warne, London, 1898.

Bankart, G. P., *The Art of the Plasterer*, Batsford, London, 1908.

Barnett, Mrs S. A., *The Making of the Home: a reading book of domestic economy etc.*, Cassell, London, 1885.

Blair, W., *House Taking and House Holding for Small Incomes*, C. Arthur Pearson, 1906.

Booth, C., *Life and Labour of the People in London*, 16 volumes, Macmillan, London, 1903.

Consult Me, W. Nicholson, London, about 1898.

Crouch, J., and E. Butler, *The Apartments of the House*, Unicorn Press, London, 1900.

Davidson, E. A., *A Practical Manual of House-Painting, Graining, Marbling and Sign Writing etc.*, Crosby, Lockwood, London, 1876.

Day, L. F., *Ornamental Design*, Batsford, London, 1897.

De Salis, Mrs, *Household Wrinkles*, Longmans Green, London, 1892.

De Wolfe, E., *The House in Good Taste*, New York, 1913.

The Decorator's Assistant, Crosby, Lockwood, London, 11th ed., 1920.

Downing, A. J., *The Architecture of Country Houses*, 1850 (reprinted Dover Publications, New York, 1969).

Duthrie, A. L., *Stencils and Stencilling*, The Decorator's Series of Practical Books, No. 10, The Trade Papers Publishing Co., London, 1914.

Eastlake, C. L., *Hints on Household Taste in Furniture, Upholdstery and Other Details*, 4th ed., Longmans, London, 1878 (reprinted Dover Publications, New York, 1969).

Edis, R. W., *The Decoration and Furniture of Town Houses*, C. Kegan Paul, London, 1881.

Elder-Duncan, J. H., *The House Beautiful*, Cassell, London, 1911.

Ellis, G., *Modern Practical Carpentry*, The Library Press, London, 1914.

Furnival, W., *Leadless Decorative Tiles, Faience and Mosaic*, W. J. Furnival, Stone, Staffordshire, 1904.

Gissing, G., *In the Year of Jubilee*, 1894 (reprinted Watergate Classics, London 1947).

Gissing, G., *Will Warburton*, 1905 (reprinted The Hogarth Press, London, 1985).

Grossmith, G. and W., *Diary of a Nobody*, 1892 (reprinted Penguin, London, 1983).

Harrods Ltd., *Victorian Shopping: Harrods catalogue, 1895*, David and Charles, Newton Abbot, 1972.

Hasluck, P. N., *House Decoration*, Cassell, London, 1894.

Hasluck, P. N., ed., *Cassell's Carpentry and Joinery*, Cassell, London, 1910.

Haweis, Mrs, *The Art of Decoration*, Chatto and Windus, London, 1881.

Heal and Son, *Heals' Catalogues 1853-1934: middle-class furnishing*, Newton Abbot (reprinted David and Charles, Newton Abbot, 1972).

The House and its Furniture, Ward Lock, London, 1879.

Humphry, Mrs C. E., *The Book of the Home*, 6 volumes, The Gresham Publishing Co., London, 1909.

Kerr, R., *The Gentleman's House: or how to plan residences from the parsonage to the palace*, London, 1864.

Kirton, J. W., *Cheerful Homes*, Ward, London, 1882.

Jennings, H. J., *Our Homes and How to Beautify Them*, Harrison and Sons, London, 1902.

Laxton's Builders' Price Books, 1875-1920, Kelly's Directories, London.

Leaning, J., *Building Specifications*, Batsford, London, 1901.

Lee, A., *Marble and Marble Workers*, Crosby, Lockwood, London, 1888.

Leland, C. G., *The Adornment of the Home*, Useful Arts Series, Dawbarn and Ward, London, 1900.

M. C., *Everybody's Book of Correct Conduct*, Saxon, London, 1893.

Millar, W., *Plastering, Plain and Decorative*, Batsford, London, 1897.

Murphy, Sir S. F., ed., *Our Homes and How to Make Them Healthy*, Cassell, London, 1883.

Muthesius, H., *Das Englische Haus*, Berlin, 1904-5 (*The English House*, B. S. P. Professional Books, Oxford, 1987).

Newbold, H. B., *House and Cottage Construction*, Caxton Publishing Co., London, about 1910.

Norman, H., *How to Build or Buy a Country Cottage and Fit it Up*, Heineman, London, 1905.

Oliver, C. E., *The Painters' Business Book*, The Trade Papers Publishing Co., London, 1914.

Panton, Mrs J. E., *From Kitchen to Garrett*, Ward and Downey, London, 1887.

Panton, Mrs J. E., *Homes of Taste*, Sampson Low, London, 1890.

Peel, Mrs D. C., *The New Home*, Constable, London, 1902.

Ransome, S., *Modern Woodworking Machinery*, W. Rider and Son, London, 3rd ed. 1902, Rider's Technical Series No. 6.

Rea, J. T., *How to Estimate*, Batsford, London, 1902.

Rothery, G. C., *Chimneypieces and Inglenooks*, T. Wernie Laurie, London, 1912.

Sackville-West, V., *The Edwardians*, 1930 (reprinted Virago, 1983).

Scott, M. E., and A. Newsholme, *Domestic Economy*, Swan Sonnenschein, London, 1892.

Scott-Mitchell, F., *Practical Stencil Work*, The Trade Papers Publishing Co., London, 1906, The Decorator Series of Practical Handbooks No. 2.

Seddon, H. C., *Builders Work and the Building Trades*, Rivington's, London, 1889.

Sparrow, W. Shaw, ed., *The British Home of Today*, Hodder and Stoughton, London, 1904.

Sparrow, W. Shaw, *Our Homes and How to Make the Best of Them*, Hodder and Stoughton, London, 1909.

Spon's Architects' and Builders' Price Book, 1900-1.

Stevenson, J. J., *House Architecture*, Macmillan, London, 1880.

The Studio Yearbook of Decorative Art, London, 1907 and 1909.

Sutcliffe, G. L., *Principles and Practices of Modern House Construction*, Blackie and Son, London, 1898.

Sylvia's Home Help Series, *Artistic Homes or How to Furnish Them with Taste*, Ward Lock, London, 1881.

Taylor, F., *Private House Electric Lighting*, Percival Marshall, London, 5th ed. 1913, Marshall's Practical Manuals No. 2.

Teale, T. P., *Economy of Coal in House Fires*, J. and A. Churchill, London, 1883.

Tomson (afterwards Marriott Watson), R., *The Art of the House*, Bell and Sons, London, 1897, Connoisseur series.

Tressell, R., *The Ragged Trousered Philanthropists*, 1955; Granada, London,1983.

Veblen, T. B., *The Theory of the Leisure Class*, New York 1899.

Weaver, L., *The 'Country Life' Book of Cottages*, Country Life, London, 1919.

Wells, H. G., *The History of Mr Polly*, 1910 (reprinted Pan, 1982).

SELECTED JOURNALS

The Building News, *The Cabinet Maker and Complete House Furnisher*, *The Construction History Journal*, *The Furnisher and Decorator*, *Furniture and Decoration*, *The Hornsey and Finsbury Park Journal*, *The House*, becomes *The House Beautiful and the Home*, *The Illustrated Carpenter and Builder*, *The Journal of the Decorative Arts Society 1850 - present*, *The Journal of Design History*, *The Plumber and Decorator and the Journal of Heating, Ventilation, Gas and Sanitary Engineering*, *The Queen*, *South London Press*, *The Studio*.

STREET DIRECTORIES

Butcher's Post Office Directory, *Cardiff and District Trades Directory*, *Finchley and Palmers Green Directory*, *Kelly's Hornsey and Crouch End Directory*, *Kelly's London Post Office Directory*, *Kelly's Post Office Suburban Directory*, *Kelly's Wood Green, Muswell Hill, Bounds Green, Fortis Green Directories*, *Slater's Post Office Directory of Cardiff and its Suburbs*.

FIRMS' ARCHIVES AND TRADE CATALOGUES

A. E. G., Army and Navy Stores, Artisans, Labourers and General Dwellings Co., Barnard, Bishop and Barnards Ltd, Berger Manufacturing Co. (Ohio), Best and Lloyd Electric Fittings, Bond and White Ltd, Borough of Hornsey Electricity Supply Co., British Land Company, Carron Co., The Coalbrookdale Iron Co., Commercial Gas Co., C. Churchill and Co. Ltd, Denny Mott and Dickson Ltd, William Dibben and Co., Doulton and Co., Edison and Swan Electric Light Co., Hobbies Ltd, H. Gibbon and Sons, Gibbons, Hinton and Co., J. and F. Grover, Incandescent Gas Light Co. Ltd, The Industrial Dwellings Society (1885) Ltd, C. Jennings and Co., Jewson and Sons, Liberty's and Co., The Lower Norwood Cooperative Building Society, MacDowall, Steven and Co., Macfarlane's Castings, Maples and Co., Elkin Mathews, Meggitt and Jones Ltd, R. Melhuish and Sons, Messenger and Co., Nicholls and Clarke Ltd, T. O'Brien and Co., Pittsburg Plate Glass Co., D. Platt and Sons, W. Pryor and Co., T. Robinson and Son Ltd, T. Parsons and Sons, J. Shoolbred and Co. Ltd, South Metropolitan Gas Light and Coke Co., Swan Sonnenschein, Tidmarsh and Sons, Tynecastle Ltd, William Wallace and Co., Waring and Gillow Ltd, Wm Whiteley, Wylie and Lochhead, Young and Marten Ltd.

OTHER RECORDS

Abridgements of Specifications, Cardiff, Newport and Swansea Timber Importers Association, The Building Trades Exhibition, Census of England and Wales, Hornsey Urban District Council Sessions, house and block plans (London and Cardiff), The Ideal Home Exhibition, The International Health Exhibition, Lloyd George Doomsday Land Valuations (1909), rate books for Camberwell, Cardiff, Hornsey and Lambeth, and bills, contracts and inventories for specific properties,

INDEX